John Lennon's Secret

The front cover pictures John Lennon on his last day in the life.

'They're going to crucify me'
The Ballad of John and Yoko 1969

John Lennon's Secret

by
David Stuart Ryan

Kozmik Press Ltd
London   Cincinnati   Sydney   Vancouver

John Lennon's Secret. First published by Kozmik Press Centre
1982. © David Stuart Ryan 1982. 1990.
Reprinted 1982, 1983 (twice), 1984.
This new revised edition, 1990.
ISBN 0–905116–20–8

Library of Congress Catalog Card No. 82-82571

Kozmik Press Ltd, 134 Elsenham Street, London SW18 5NP, UK
49 Central Avenue, Cincinnati, Ohio, USA
1000 Parker St, Vancouver, Canada
162-8 Parramatta Road, Sydney, NSW 2048,
Australia

Library of Congress Cataloging in Publication Data
Ryan, David Stuart
  John Lennon's secret.

  Bibliography: p.
  1. Lennon, John, 1940–.   2. Singers – England –
  Biography. I. Title.
ML420.L38R9   1982   784.5′4′00924   [B]   82-82571
ISBN 0–905116–07–0
ISBN 0–905116–08–9 (pbk.)

Printed in Great Britain by
Whitstable Litho Printers Ltd., Whitstable, Kent.

Thank you to . . .

Anna Maria from Brazilian TV who gave me the first leads in my research.

Bob Wooler for a marvellous night out. Bob Eaton for letting me see his play.

Eddie Bishop, Pat and Monica for their insights.

Allen Williams for a memorable lunchtime session.

Brian Southell for getting me inside Abbey Road studios.

Brian Brooks of Brooks, Davies and Nicholas Ltd, Hove, for the genealogical research aided by that of Achievements Ltd.

Pauline Lennon for her help and consultation of Freddy Lennon's manuscript.

Aunt Mimi for her patience.

Paul McCartney, Peter Brown, Clive Epstein and Eric Clapton for their good wishes.

Captain Botting of Strawberry Field children's home for an inspirational visit.

Jeff Marsden and Peter Jacobsen for the design help.

Pam Ayscough for the word processing.

The Time Inc librarians in London and New York for the daily clipping of the newspapers all those years ago.

Arthur Ballard and Mr Pobjoy, Lennon's teachers, who still give encouragement today.

Acknowledgements

The author and publisher would like to gratefully thank all those whose copyright photographs are reproduced in this volume. Every effort has been made to acknowledge all those whose photographs appear, any omissions we will be pleased to acknowledge in any future edition.

Photograph with Chapter 1 Hunter Davies Chapter 2 Hunter Davies Chapter 4 Hunter Davies Chapter 5 Sunday People Chapter 6 Hunter Davies Chapter 7 Jurgen Vollmer Chapter 12 Bob Gomel/Life Mag © Time Inc Chapter 13 John Launois/Camera Press Chapter 18 Keystone Chapter 20 Daily Sketch Chapter 22 Rex Features Chapter 23 Associated Press. Front cover illustration drawn from an original Annie Leibowitz photo Chapter 24 Rex Features.

The music lyrics quoted in the text are the copyright of Northern Songs Ltd. Except for the lines from 'Hey Joe' and 'Mother's Little Helper' which are the copyright of the songs' music publishers.

Contents

John Lennon's background

Opposite and overleaf are five pictures which have become part of a Beatle tour of the city.
They are as follows:
1. The City of Liverpool. A port with cramped crumbling buildings, more dream than reality. Wherever you are, you are here.
2. Aunt Mimi's house in the respectable suburb of Woolton. When his parents broke up, she was the one who could afford to raise him.
3. Paul McCartney's house in his teens lay across Allerton golf course, not much more than a mile from John Lennon. It was owned by the town corporation.
4. Liverpool Art School where John Lennon sporadically studied art and more often studied playing the guitar with Paul McCartney, a pupil of Liverpool Institute, part of the same building as the Art School.
5. The old gates of Strawberry Field Salvation Army home for children. The home has been rebuilt since John Lennon was a child, and four acres of its woods have been sold off.

Introduction

Ladies and Gentlemen, direct from Pepperland . . . John Lennon!

I arranged to meet the young Dutch poet, Christian Konstadt, in an old church in London's East End which had been converted into a community theatre. There was going to be a Beatles Revival Evening I told him, it would be an interesting side of English life – a little different from the Institute of Contemporary Art where we were sitting waiting for the performance of his play about Nazi occupation and the function of the artist in totalitarian regimes. And yet the artist is always the needed voice in any modern landscape. Articulating the dreams, fears, hopes, lives of an increasingly inarticulate public. A public which has become used to being entertained and manipulated, whose ideas are inevitably drawn from its few information systems. It is surprising that the voice of the artist is allowed to percolate through – but more exactly the public search out the expression for themselves.

Just such an expression was the voice of John Lennon. By the time the Dutch poet arrived in the murky streets of Hackney, the party had been in full swing for some time. The large hall was packed to overflowing, a stage at the far end was surrounded by a mural of the four Beatles in white suits just as they had appeared in *Magical Mystery Tour.* In flight from the increasingly gloomy job prospects and drop in living standards outside, the crowd in their 60s' geometric patterned dresses, their swirling coloured shirts and beads, seethed with excitement.

The songs were all known, even by those who could only have been babes in arm when they were written. 'Yesterday', 'Do You Want To Know A Secret?', 'Lucy In The Sky With Diamonds', 'Hey Jude', 'A Day In The Life'. Songs that were a part of the lives of everyone there, the new folk songs. Seeing the show live, with a Beatles lookalike band, the magic of the group was there to be felt and sensed, the inexplicable phenomenon that had entranced the world. It was the Edwardian music hall reincarnated, an expression of a people with belief in the future, it was the backslapping bonhomie of a predominantly working-class Liverpool where the four lads had grown up.

The music of Paul McCartney and the poetry of John Lennon captured the optimistic mood of that town and then the whole country as Britain emerged from the long austerities of war. Such was its infectiousness that it spread round the world and became part of the fabric of a whole generation.

That magic has not entirely faded. As midnight came and went I felt the initial reluctance to plunge back into a 'golden age' drop away, the rhythms and the songs overwhelmed and forced exuberance upon you. The whole hall joined in singing 'Hey Jude' while the only song that drew even more applause and participation was 'Imagine', Lennon's hymn to the future. Now as the night advanced and the dream once again took over, it was the music that fascinated. I found myself fulfilling the dream of being a drummer in the Beatles band, the power of the music was flowing through me, it was so natural, so full of life. Reflection reminds how ruthlessly the real Beatles' drummer was dropped on the brink of stardom. John Lennon claimed that to succeed you had to be a bastard. That is too simple. The demons that drove him – and his prolific partner, Paul McCartney – were the demons of genius. This book is an exploration of how that genius manifested itself in the life of one man, John Lennon. In searching his soul, you are also searching your own. But what he found there was both revealed and exceptionally well hidden behind the persona of a pop star. Now has come the time to fully draw back the curtain . . . Ladies and Gentlemen, direct from Pepperland, John Lennon in person!

David Stuart Ryan. Summer 1982.

John Lennon's Family Tree

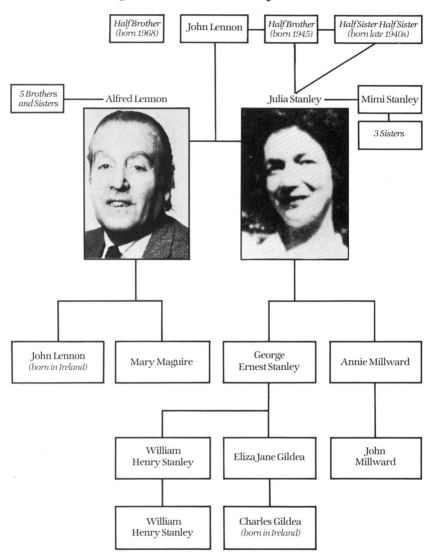

Half Brother (born 1968) — John Lennon — *Half Brother (born 1945)* — *Half Sister Half Sister (born late 1940s)*

5 Brothers and Sisters — Alfred Lennon

Julia Stanley — Mimi Stanley

3 Sisters

John Lennon *(born in Ireland)*

Mary Maguire

George Ernest Stanley

Annie Millward

William Henry Stanley

Eliza Jane Gildea

John Millward

William Henry Stanley

Charles Gildea *(born in Ireland)*

◄ The Lennon family tree. He spent a considerable amount of money researching his mother's side of the family.

1 'I've Married Him'

As we all tend to forget, John Lennon's life story begins well before he was born. With the verbal fluency of this singer, song-writer and mystic, with his unfailing capacity for audacious imagery, with his natural reverence for the world of nature, it should come as no surprise to learn that he was, by ancestry, more than half Irish.

Jack Lennon, born in Dublin in the 1850s, had emigrated to America where he sang professionally most of his life with an early group of Kentucky Minstrels. However, in the early 1900s, he came to Liverpool and in 1912 was working as a freight clerk when, in his mid-50s, he had a son Alfred by Mary Maguire on December 14. There is no record of a marriage. Jack Lennon, professional American singer, passed his name to John Lennon, and an exquisite singing voice. There were six children in the household which played and sang as happy as the day is long.

At the age of 9, in 1921, Alfred Lennon became an orphan when his father died of liver disease. He and another brother were 'farmed out' to a Blue-coat school in Liverpool, until the age of 15.

Lennon is the anglicised version of O' Leannain, a clan to be found in the Cork, Fermanagh and Galway area of southern Ireland.

John's mother, Julia, was born on March 12, 1914, in Liverpool, youngest of five daughters to George Ernest Stanley and Annie (née Millward). George worked for the Liverpool Salvage Company as a deep sea pilot and was often away on salvage work. Curiously, though, his father had been a musician and was called William Henry Stanley, though at the time of George's birth he was working as a book-keeper. William Henry was also the son of a clerk, in Victorian times a far more respected occupation than now. The Stanleys, in fact, did not like to think of themselves as 'wackers' – working-class Liverpudlians – and as is the way with the lower middle-classes there was a strong consciousness of their elevated (slightly) status. Julia's mother, Annie Millward, was the daughter of a solicitor's clerk, John Millward, further reinforcing the claims of the family to middle-class respectability – a very important attribute in the unemployment-racked Liverpool of the 1930s. What Julia's father, George Ernest, was less keenly aware of was that his mother, Eliza Jane, was the daughter of Charles Gildea, an Irish immigrant fleeing from the terrible famines that swept Ireland in the 1840s. However, the gene pool, with its tendency of like attracting like, was sufficiently Irish in Julia's blood for an instant attraction to develop when she met John Lennon's father in the heady days of 1927 – the Jazz era. She was just 14. Alfred, clad in the new suit his prestigious school had thoughtfully provided him to find his way in the world, had also acquired a bowler hat and his first job in an office. To go with his newly-found status, he wanted a girlfriend. His friend urging him on, Alfred paraded importantly past the daughter of a long line of clerks – the errant musician decently buried in family memory. 'You look silly,' said Julia, too young not to reveal her attractions. The scent in the air was of fun. The terrible war of 9 years before and its ghosts, all one million of them from England's green and pleasant land, were being laid to rest. The realisation was dawning that there was an alternative to a Victorian sense of duty now that its accompanying wealth had disappeared in 4 years of mad dissipation. The ethos, felt by the young most of all, was to live out the today and follow whatever whim came along. And in the late 1920s, the whims were becoming wilder, along with the hopes. The war to end all wars had been fought and had been won. Now the victory celebration! 'You look lovely', said Alfred, boldly joining the girl, who was at least a year younger, on the bench.

'If you want to sit down with me, you'll have to take that stupid hat off.'

Alfred did. His status as a proud clerk whizzed out across a shining lake, and sank into the waters. He was never to wear a hat again, the waters and their irresistible lure were to claim him as their own.

By the age of 16 he had signed on as a ship's waiter. Over the next 10 years, during his spells on *terra firma* he larked about with the fun-loving Julia. A lot of their best fun came from singing together, in fact the musical Alfred taught Julia to play the banjo almost as well as himself. He had risen to head waiter and was much in demand on the luxurious, dream-filled cruises as a singer during the non-stop celebrations that rocked the sumptuous ocean liners and dazzled their privileged passengers.

One day in 1938, the 24-year-old Julia suggested in her joking way that she and Freddy get married. It is a rare woman of 24 who does not feel the urge to marry and produce one of her kind, especially if the year is 1938. The storm clouds of war – a distant German dictator called Hitler, a piece of paper signed in Munich – have begun to move into the corner of vision.

Much to her family's disgust, Julia married the orphan Irishman and after a honeymoon in the back row of the Trocadero Picture Palace she triumphantly returned home to tell her parents. Her mother had a soft spot for the cheery, handsome Alfred. Her father thought his youngest had thrown herself away. Her older sister, Mimi, thought he would be no good for her. But a marriage was a marriage in 1938. Mimi, in any case, married an older, more prosperous man – George Smith. He had his own farm and small dairy business in the smart village of Woolton on the outskirts of Liverpool. It was a step up in the world.

Alfred was allowed to stay at the Stanley home on his return from each voyage. George Stanley could not see how Alfred, on his wages as a head waiter, would be able to find accommodation for Julia, at least for some time. Even places to rent were not easy to find; Liverpool had been steadily decaying from its Victorian prosperity when the slave trade, then the cotton mills and commerce had brought a rush of fine public buildings and a certain pride to the town. The port was still very busy, but it was not the centre of a vast trade as it had been at the time he was married in 1906 at the age of 21.

Then the unthinkable happened. War, which they had all believed would never be allowed to take place again, was declared. At first little happened, now that England had called Germany's bluff, the invaders of Poland would have to be content with that remote gain. In January 1940, Alfred was home on leave at the Stanley house. His partner from the fun days of the 1920s clung to each hour of their time together before Freddy set out across a very dangerous sea. By the time she found out she was pregnant he was far away. He was still at sea as the time drew near for his birth. Early in October there was a total eclipse of the sun. In the ancient sayings of astrology it is recognised that those born at or near an eclipse will enter a very changing world which will also provide exceptional opportunities.

◀ John Lennon at five. The age when he lost his parents, note the suspicious eyes belieing the forced smile.

2 'Do You Want To Stay With Mummy Or Daddy?'

The evening John Lennon was born on October 9, 1940, at 6.30 p.m. in Liverpool's Oxford Street Hospital, there were not – as he liked to imply – any bombs falling. There had been an unexpected interruption which was quickly shattered by the following evening when the docks were again hammered by German bombs around Pier Head – from where the ferry across the Mersey departs.

At the Stanley household, George Stanley was informed by Mimi, who quickly visited her younger sister, that 'it's a boy, and he's beautiful.' 'He would be,' replied George, still very doubtful of laying full claim to this half-Irish child as one of his own. The Republican war was of recent memory.

Julia duly brought the baby back home where all four of her sisters took a hand in looking after him, Mimi most of all. It was as if she knew her husband George Smith would not father any children.

The subject of Freddy was not brought up too often in the Stanley household. At least his steamship company regularly paid Julia the housekeeping money he sent. But they were never sure with the blackout of news on all ships' movements where Alfred was, or when he should be expected back. Julia, like many of the women of England, had lost her man to the Government, there was an unprecedented amount of regulation in everyday life with instructions on what should be done in each eventuality – from a gas attack, to a mass evacuation. In fact, all the young children were being evacuated from the prime target of the Merseyside docks area, but Julia decided to stay in the bosom of the family.

The young John Winston Lennon was the centre of attention. His first name honouring the legendary singing grandfather Jack, who Alfred had eulogised to Julia on many an evening during their long courtship, the middle name in honour of the only obstacle there appeared to be in the all-conquering path of Adolf Hitler.

There was little to distract the family during these dark hours. France and the Low Countries had fallen. The previous month the Royal Air Force had lost hundreds of men and machines trying to push back the Luftwaffe. Fresh attacks were expected daily, and the pummelling of the docks, stunning in its ferocity, was an indication that a new phase of warfare existed – total war. As was inevitable, it was people's houses which were hit and with the Oxford Street maternity hospital little more than a mile from the docks, Julia was glad to be back in the apparent safety of the family home, Newcastle Road, Wavertree, with faces she knew.

Further out still from the city in what was then the village of Woolton, Mimi lived in a spacious new semi-detached house with a large garden and plenty of greenery all about. Just down from Menlove Avenue was a turning which led even further into the undisturbed countryside – called Beaconsfield Road. In this road was a fine country house with several acres of tree-covered grounds – the owner had left the property in the 1930s to the Salvation Army. They had turned this magnificent bequest into a childrens' home called Strawberry Field. Sometime previously it was said it had been a field where strawberries were grown. At this time, its name seemed merely picturesque, but then most of the houses in prosperous Woolton – soon to become a suburb of Liverpool – had picturesque names. Indeed, George and Mimi named their house 'Mendips' after a mountain range in Wales.

Early on Mimi decided that John would be far better off living with her and George. But it was not until Julia went to collect the money that the shipping line office passed on to her from Alfred, and found there was none, that it ever seemed possible.

Alfred, caught up in a world war, had been told in New York to report for duty on a Liberty Boat bringing in much-needed supplies to a beleaguered Britain through the submarine infested waters of the Atlantic. To his dismay he was told that instead of being a head waiter, as on the passenger ship he had sailed with to New York, he would be an assistant steward. Alfred rebelled at the loss of rank; his captain came up with a solution, 'miss the Liberty Boat'. Freddy – who needed little encouragement duly did so. In a war there is no room for such acts of defiance. Freddy was duly despatched on the next Liberty Boat out after being interned. When his boat reached North Africa he was jailed for three months on a charge of stealing a bottle of vodka from the stores – it was a put-up job. Freddy, ever the outsider, had been singled out to be made an example of after the ship's crew had broken open the cargo. So Freddy's money to Julia stopped. He had none. Magnanimously, he wrote to Julia from his cell advising her to get out and enjoy herself. As he had previously discovered, there was a war on. Julia – in her turn – needed no encouragement. She had been used to living life as a lark, it was what she and Freddy had always done, and in the early months of 1942, she went out when she could. It was, for Britain, the darkest days of the war. Nothing was going right anywhere. Russia was crumbling under the mechanised might of the Nazi war machine. America had just come into the war, but few troops had arrived. In North Africa the British armies were being relentlessly pushed back by Rommel. Crete had been lost, along with Greece; Singapore had fallen, symbol of all Britain's empire in the East. There was, in reality, very little to celebrate. Food was rationed, money – even if you had it – could buy precious little. All resources were being channeled into the war effort. Fashion for women, glamorous places of entertainment, stockings, make-up, all had ceased to exist. Liverpool, grey and grimy at the best of times, now appeared in unrelieved monotones. The 'Prince Charming' Julia found was deficient in the qualities Walt Disney would have given to a hero. He was a Welsh soldier.

Julia continued to live at home, and eventually Freddy re-appeared, only to go off to sea again. He sent back happy sounding letters to cheer up the family on the grim, monotonous home front, including ship's concert lists where Alfred Lennon would be announced as singing 'Begin the Beguine'. In a war, it was the closest you could get to glamour, and all through the 30s he and Julia – like so many millions of others – had lived out their lives vicariously in the Hollywood dream of rich, indulgent living.

John Lennon's earliest memory was of a song from one of the dream merchants – Walt Disney – as his mother sang

'Do you want to know a secret?
Promise not to tell.
You are standing by a wishing well.'

Significantly – as we will find out – this treasured memory

turned into a song was given by Lennon to George Harrison to sing as his first 'B' side on a Beatles single. It is an early example of how precious any association with his mother's memory was to become.

At the age of 4, John Lennon remembered walking with his grandfather, George Stanley, by the Pier Head. In 1944 the signs of victory were palpably in the air. The devastation and bleakness could be viewed with some hope. American servicemen, several million of them, were preparing to launch the invasion of Europe, and a flourishing black market had developed in anything American. It had become synonymous with quality. For war weary Britain, a new low water mark had been reached when one of the many ministeries which ordered every detail of the people's lives had invented the 'utility' mark as a sign of quality. It really meant that the cheapest possible materials had been used in the most mean way. Any concept of elegance or beauty of line had been buried under the debris of the bomb sites, the air raid shelters where miserable nights were spent in the company of a jostling crowd, the ration books, the drab clothing, the unchanging fashions year after year, the chronic housing shortage. . .

John complained to his grandfather that his new shoes hurt. The lifelong sailor drew out his penknife and slit the heels. That was one instant cure for shoddy goods. He wondered what sort of chances the fatherless 4-year-old would have in the entirely new post-war world, with his mother involved with another man, and now – worse – a baby on the way. American money flooding in had undermined all morals he thought bitterly to himself. The Yanks only had to produce a pair of silk stockings and promise a girl a good time, they were that deprived. His own children and their generation were undoubtedly the casualties of war. It would be up to the little mite and his generation to try to put some order back into the world when all the killing and butchery had stopped, and when the country woke up from the frenzy of the moment to find that there was nothing – absolutely nothing – left in the coffers. Yet 40 short years ago when he had married, Britain was the unchallenged ruler of the world; with a vast amount of the exports Britain sent out to the dependent colonies and the former colonies of the Americas being channeled through the Liverpool docks. He looked about him, all that was left were blackened bomb sites. It was going to be a ruinously expensive victory.

John spent more and more time at Aunt Mimi's. As far as she was concerned, Julia's marriage had come to an end when Freddy had stopped sending money at the time John was 18-months-old. Certainly, the outward forms had been preserved for another year or so, but she could see that Alfred Lennon would never be any good for Julia, who in any case had given birth to a boy in the spring of '45.

The war had taught people a new ruthlessness. The baby was adopted by a Norwegian sea captain and his wife, money was very very tight. It was a good home.

Then at last the war was over. John spent as much time with Mimi as he did at his grandparents' house with Julia. He liked the big garden at Mimi's. Once or twice, his Uncle George had taken him to the dairy farm very early in the morning where he milked his cows before selling their produce at his dairy. One benefit of the war had been to put a premium on home-produced food with the shipping lanes in so much danger. George Smith – and his wife Mimi – had been one of the war's winners. Alfred Lennon was one of its many losers. Now, after his three-month stint in jail on a technicality, he had learnt the ways of the black market in stockings and at war's end found himself for perhaps the first time in his life with some ready money.

He was told by his son's grandfather that John was at Mimi's. Julia seemed unwilling to try to make a go of it. A plan formed in his mind. He went round to the forthright Mimi, who he knew as one of his keenest critics, and asked if he could take John off to Blackpool for the day. Reluctantly, she said yes.

John, now 5, was thrilled at the prospect of making sandcastles, paddling in the sea, eating candyfloss, all the trappings of a British day out at the seaside. He found out when he got to Blackpool, 45 miles to the north, that Freddy – on the profits of his trade in black market stockings – was planning to emigrate to New Zealand with a friend. They stayed at his friend's flat for several weeks making the final preparations.

Julia arrived unannounced at the flat. She said very firmly that she wanted John back now she and a waiter friend had a nice home (accommodation at this time was almost impossible to obtain).

Freddy tried turning on the Irish-inherited charm.

'I can tell you still love me Julia. This is our chance to start all over again. The war's gone, that was the villain. This man, he's only to fill in time, one of the civilians, doing very nicely while we were fighting the war.'

'You'll never get to New Zealand,' Julia replied flatly, so unlike her usual musical voice. 'No, I want John.'

A 5-year-old boy came into the room. The parents stopped arguing briefly.

'John,' Freddy said, a flash of hope breaking through the sudden gloom in his mind.

John bounded up to the father he had become used to having around in the last few weeks. He, at least, had never given up waiting for Freddy to return when the war was finished.

'Is she coming back with us?' he asked his father, looking short-sightedly at the beautiful auburn-haired Julia across the room. She radiated in his sight.

'No. You have to decide if you want to stay with me or with Mummy,' Freddy said, as brightly as he could make the dread words sound. It was an awful but logical decision. He would stay with his father.

'Now John, are you sure about that? You have to choose. Do you want to go to another country with Freddy? or stay here with me?' Julia asked.

'With Daddy,' said John, beginning a deluge of tears.

'That's enough Julia, you've had your answer, leave him alone, can't you see you're upsetting him, haven't you upset him enough while I was away at sea, giving away his brother?'

Julia turned with her usual grace, and walked out the door. John heard the door shut, the person he had spent all his life with was leaving him. The thud of the door had a deadly echo to it. He ran, as though possessed. Down the street he ran crying out 'Mummy, mummy, mummy, don't go.' But Daddy couldn't come home to live with the waiter Julia had now moved in with.

◀ The bedroom where John cried for his parents, and wrote the Beatles'
first big hit, 'Please Please Me'.

3 'This Boy's As Sharp As A Needle'

Something had cried out to follow Julia when she quietly and with finality walked out of the Blackpool 'digs' of the would-be emigrant to New Zealand. As the servicemen came home, many thousands, hundreds of thousands in fact, decided that they would start all over again in a new place; South Africa, Rhodesia, New Zealand, Australia, America. If nothing else, the war had opened people's eyes to what was possible, the dreary war-scarred landscape they returned to in Britain was not, they were determined, to be the end of the dream.

However, inexplicably to the young boy who was 5½, it was not with Julia that he spent his days, instead he was taken to Aunt Mimi's. He became even more confused. He tried calling Mimi mummy.

'You can't have two mummies', she explained. Thereafter she was Mimi.

Julia, intent on consolidating her relationship with waiter 'Twitchy', found that all she could manage were occasional visits to her son, reminder of a failed wartime marriage which she hoped to put behind her in the new Socialist Britain. It was a time of enormous hope, in spite of the evidence of desolation all around. The austerities of the war persisted, the same ration books for food, the niggardly allowance of half a dozen eggs per week, the rare treat of more than a dubious mince or stew for meat. A Labour Government had been returned by a landslide with talk of a wholesale nationalisation of key industries so that the people could share in the country's wealth. The only problem was that the country had no wealth. By 1947, the situation was grim in the extreme. A savage winter coincided with a huge shortage of coal, the country's foreign currency reserves were finished, thousands were starving to death in occupied Germany, France looked as though it would become Communist, Russia continued to annex and retain the Eastern block countries it had 'liberated'. At this critical juncture an American launched what became known as *The Marshall Plan*. The pound was devalued, in exchange American money propped up the British and European economies, it was a shoreing up of the status quo. America had done very well out of the war as manufacturer of the West's armaments and – with payment for these arms – the world's banker. The war had solved that vast country's problem of over capacity in industry and unused natural resources. Now a ravaged world cried out for its products from the wartime factories. And America – its treasury loaded with money – could afford to supply on credit. Indeed, with *The Marshall Plan* it freely gave to build up Europe from the ruins. It was a wholly generous and enlighted move by the young American nation – but it did provide assured markets for American goods for a decade and more. The framework was being built for the consumer goods boom that was to propel the democracies to an undreamt of height of prosperity by the year 1960.

The grand plan was less obvious in war-ravaged Liverpool. Julia had her first child by Twitchy (as John Lennon immortally named the very nervous man) followed by a second. She had problems coping on Twitchy's waiter's wage, life was extremely hard, especially if you would rather dream and live in a world of make-believe as her Piscean nature dictated.

John appeared to be settling down with Mimi, he had in any case spent a great deal of time at the house in Menlove Avenue even before permanently moving in. He had started to go to Dovedale Primary School and with the help of his 'Uncle George' – Mimi's dairy farmer husband – he could read and write after five months. At Mimi's house he was on his best behaviour: quiet and sensitive, distrusting of all adults, aware that he depended on his aunt and uncle now that his parents could not look after him. Mimi, strangely, never mentioned this, it was just that he felt obligated, expected to be grateful.

After his third day at school, he insisted that Mimi let him go there by himself. She resorted to the subterfuge of following him at a discreet distance. The first school medical revealed that John had weak eyesight and his first glasses soon sat on his nose. In those days the wire-frame model of spectacles was the only one available – it was to take 20 years before they had become quaint. John hated the glasses and would only use them as a final resort. The last thing he wanted to be thought of as was a 'cissy'. From day one at school, he fought for dominance. Woolton, being more village-like than tough city school, was not prepared for the explosion of energy and devilment that the 'orphan' boy unleashed upon them.

Unbeknown to Mimi, the sensitive child who at home liked nothing more than to disappear into his own world of drawing, crayoning and reading, turned into another character at school.

He had a super-abundance of energy which led him to always seek to be in charge of his peer groups. He quickly formed his own gang and struggled for supremacy. At the same time his headmaster was particularly impressed by his versatility.

'He can do anything he chooses to do, that boy's as sharp as a needle', Mr Evans, the headmaster, told Mimi, 'but he won't do anything stereotyped'.

It was in those days called 'high spirits' – today a child psychologist might call the behaviour disturbed. But in post-war Britain it was still considered quite normal for children to be allowed to get on with their own games – just as long as they did not disturb the adults who had plenty of problems of their own. So John Lennon quickly teamed up with two other boys who lived near Menlove Avenue – Peter Shotton and Nigel Whalley. Nigel knew John from the Sunday school and church choir at St. Peter's, Woolton. In fact, John, as he later admitted, was always religious in his own impish way.

And it was at a St. Peter's church fête that he was to meet another friend, but that was later. . .

At this time, the ease within the church community showed itself in an irreverent awareness of the vicar's idiosyncrasies. At one fête organised by nuns, he was even found dressed as a monk talking in an unintelligible language to other monks seated on a bench.

The addition of another boy, Ivan Vaughan, formed – significantly – a foursome of miscreants. And from then on, egged on by Lennon, they roamed with an enviable freedom around and about Woolton. Hurling clods of earth at the passing train at the tunnel in Garston, riding on the back of trams in towards the big city – that scared Lennon, but he wanted to prove how tough he was to the world, it hadn't paid, he had found, to be too trusting in the world of adults, they would pick you up and drop you down at the call of some unexplainable whim.

His aunt only realised what a handful she had taken on when one day near Penny Lane (the road Menlove Avenue led into on the way towards the Liverpool city centre), she came upon a group of boys urging on two others engaged in a ding-dong fight. Mimi was relieved to see the boys were not from Dovedale when suddenly the ruck parted and out came Lennon, his smart blazer askew.

For some reason, even then the young Lennon lived a charmed life. The plot to derail a tram was not discovered, since luckily it failed. The day the police chased them off the golf course for hitting balls across Menlove Avenue, no names were taken. The girl who lived nearby and taught John lots of dirty jokes, never let on. The woman whose shop they visited to surreptitiously remove dinky toys while asking her for the hardest-to-reach sweets, came up with the answer – she put a glass screen in front of the toys. The old wartime spirit of 'we're all in the same boat' was, she realised, not something the children shared. They viewed the adults as lost in a grim world, peopled by harsh memories. The pig swill dustbins disappeared, as the worst economy measures of the war years eased. By the end of the 1940s everyone wanted to take part in mass entertainment. The football matches were always filled. The dogs. The speedway.

Mimi did not restrict John's movements in the Woolton area. Not much harm would come to him there among the garden parties, the parks and golf courses, the rubbish tips and quarries. She did not, fortunately, know about his gang's essays into pulling girls' knickers down, the dangling of their legs from a tree above Menlove Avenue to see who could actually knock the top of the big new double-decker buses.

Mimi restricted the visits to Liverpool itself to twice a year. Once to the Christmas Pantomime at the Empire, and once in the summer holidays to a suitable children's film. These visits proved an inspiration to the already active pen and crayons of J. W. Lennon as he described himself. He filled books with characters and cartoons based on what he had experienced. But his greatest inspiration was a small boy called William who, in the early 1920s had – good-naturedly – terrified his genteel neighbourhood with a gang of boys. The 'Just William' stories of Rachmael Compton found fanatical devotees in a latter-day gang.

But the high spot of the school holidays for the gang was when the childrens' home round the corner from Menlove

Avenue held its garden party. As soon as the Salvation Army band struck up, John whooped for joy. He and the gang would sell bottles of pop for a penny a piece, help in the good cause of supporting the abandoned children, and in the seven or eight acres of grounds, thickly grown with trees, it was possible to entirely lose oneself in play – in another, altogether better world. The young John dimly remembered he was himself abandoned.

The freedom of childhood began to fade, John passed his '11 plus' examination with no trouble and he was selected as one of the top 20% of pupils who the 1944 Education Act in Britain had ordained were to be the high flyers. The bright ordinary boys who would be given the very best education, and in return would regenerate the country from its sorry state.

In his first year at Quarry Bank Grammar School, just a mile from 251 Menlove Avenue, through winding lanes, John Lennon in his specially tailored blazer came near the top of his year. He had been joined by Peter Shotton at Quarry Bank and the two friends were soon inseparable.

However, in John's second year tragedy struck. Uncle George died from cirrhosis of the liver. The quiet kindly dairy farmer, John's secret ally in his battles with the stern discipline of Mimi, had suddenly gone. Mimi did not believe in physical punishment, but in ignoring the offender, or sending him to his room to solitary. Uncle George would then smuggle a bun to him, or in some way show the boy he was not entirely out of disfavour.

It was like the time Julia had come round after some accident with blood on her face and John had retreated to the garden rather than see the evidence of pain. Now on hearing the news of George's death he retired to his bedroom, sharing the strange 'hee hee' sardonicism he felt with his cousin from Scotland who was visiting. Even well-ordered lives came to a scrappy, unpredictable end the two conspirators in glee hysterically realised.

◀ The Quarreymen perform before the addition of the 15 year old Paul McCartney.

4 'He Only Failed By One Grade In 8 'O' Levels'

At about the time George Smith, John Lennon's closest male relative, passed out of his life, Julia re-entered it.

He suddenly realised that she was living no more than a short bus ride away from Woolton. Soon John took to visiting her, sometimes cutting school to see her – and taking along his trusted friends, Ivan Vaughan and Pete Shotton. Julia – in sharp contrast to her older sister – liked nothing better than a good laugh. The pangs of guilt she felt at not being a better mother were transformed into a jocular elder sister–younger brother relationship. Her 'live for today' attitude, which had never completely left Julia from her formative years in the twenties, was passed on to John and his friends. She bought him his first coloured shirt – in 1954 white along with grey were the only colours for shirts – she told him not to worry about increasingly bad school reports. By his second year at Quarry Bank, John together with Peter Shotton had decided to take the rebel's road, they were in constant trouble for minor acts of insubordination – such as throwing a blackboard rubber out of the window, going AWOL, gambling on the school playing field. First the school and then Mimi discovered John's penchant for obscene verses and drawings. The rows between Mimi and John became more frequent and with both being indomitable characters, the rows were bitter while they lasted but would end with both erupting into laughter.

Julia, in contrast, did not consider it part of her function to castigate, but rather to encourage. Mimi one day threw out a lot of John's poems. He realised that she – like the schoolmasters – was totally unable to see that he was different; in his own estimation he was an isolated genius, he would see what no one else could see, look at himself in a mirror and see his face turn from a sensitive, withdrawn, frightened person into a figure flowing with all the energies of the universe. He would walk through the woods in Strawberry Field, climb the trees and be in his own created world, a world at once lyrical and utterly removed from the constraints civilisation tried to place upon it. It was unfettered, how he wished to be. On visiting his cousins up in Scotland he would walk on the hills surrounded by the deep tang of the heather and feel himself fully alive in this natural world which cared nothing for regulations. By winning Julia over gradually, John established a bolt hole for himself when the relationship grew too tense with Mimi. On one occasion he returned to find Mimi had got rid of the dog – Sally. She said it was because there was no one to take it for walks. John recognised the cruelty and broke down in tears. Something he previously only did in the privacy of his room when he fell into thinking about his lost parents.

He was proud of the way his friends took to Julia, who like him had a macabre sense of humour. She would walk along the street with a pair of woolly knickers on her head pretending to be unaware of the source of merriment as people stared and stared on the semi-detached streets. Another favourite trick was to wear a pair of glasses without lenses. She would fix someone with her gaze in conversation and then nonchalently push her finger through the frame to rub her eye.

John could relate to her his larks at school. He had quickly decided he would have to fight his way through, but the boy who felt the need to protect himself with a show of toughness lost his first fight at secondary school. He sharpened his tongue, so that any sign of weakness would be immediately seized upon – a characteristic he was never to lose. The famous Lennon caustic 'wit' had been born.

Somehow, he survived at the school. Expulsion would have been a case for the Liverpool Education Authority, Lennon needed to go just as far as the cliff edge and look down. He did receive a week's suspension, and innumerable canings, but this helped to confirm him in his tough guy persona.

Year by year, he descended from the top form, until he was twentieth in the C stream, bottom of the school, by his fourth year. At this point a way of escape filtered through to the confused angry man. He would go off to sea just like his dad had at 16. Mimi received a 'phone call from the shipping line's employment office. She advised them strongly against taking the young Lennon.

Mimi had never thought John had the discipline for learning the piano, so she was hardly aware of the ease with which he had won his first musical instrument. She took in student lodgers to help with the house-keeping, and one had bet John that if he could learn a tune on it by the following morning, he could have a harmonica. John learnt two tunes.

On another occasion, he had travelled to Scotland by bus – as he did each Christmastime – to stay with his cousins and aunt in Scotland's Highlands. On the way he had been playing with his harmonica. The bus conductor had been sufficiently impressed to say that if John met him at the bus garage the following morning, he would give the boy a really good harmonica.

But music was not John Lennon's first love, nor was writing. He liked nothing better than to go fishing, here he could tune in to the peace all about, but that was a private side which would have shocked his masters at school; Lennon in league with Peter Shotton was considered the school's leading trouble-maker, although it was his wicked humour that troubled them most. Lennon in his turn considered all but one or two masters as stupid – for not recognising his talents.

In 1955, with the war 10 years behind, Britain was learning of the good life – mostly through American films which were even glossier and more dreamlike than they had been in the 1930s. There was the big daddy of them all with Bing Crosby and Frank Sinatra and Louis Armstrong in *High Society* – it represented the ultimate dream of the rich life – even if it was a life utterly lacking in taste. Frankie Lane and Johnny Ray provided more of the heart throb that women appeared to be demanding – indeed Johnny Ray was sensitive enough to even cry on stage. In the late 1940s there had been bee bop, but by the early 50s the crooners had taken over. The British radio, still an important institution with its monolithic coverage of the country and many households still not possessing television, concentrated more on singalongs of popular tunes. *Music While You Work* was still played – as it had been in the war to keep the production wheels humming. There were diary programmes, the most famous being *Mrs Dale's Diary* – a doctor's wife who every afternoon could be heard wondering and worrying about Jim – her husband, we hasten to add. The BBC took its task of providing moral uplift for the nation seriously. The only time it dropped its guard of earnestness was in comedy – and this was one area where Liverpool had provided a rich source of talent – Arthur Askey and Ken Dodd hailed from the port. All the great comics came to the Liverpool Empire, for the old splendid Edwardian theatre days of variety were an unconscionably long time dying. By the mid fifties in more risqué places than Liverpool, the reviews had turned blue with nude women who by some quirk of the Lord Chamberlain's office were deemed not obscene if they stayed stationary. In retrospect, entertainment had reached a dead end, something new would have to come in its place. Television, with the introduction of a commercial channel in 1955, was about to mop up all the old devotees of the theatre. It happened, naturally enough, in America first: the discovery of a new customer called a teenager who wanted to go out and be entertained, who had money to spend – but it was the film industry which responded immediately. In 1954, in America, *Rock Around the Clock* starring Bill Haley and the Comets was premiered. It caused riots. The theme song found its way over to the 51st State by 1955. *Rock Around the Clock* was like nothing the young had heard before. It had the raw jungle rhythm that stirred the senses and set the feet tapping, it was an explosion of fresh energy in a world stuck in inertia where the young went off to be conscripts in armies preparing for Armageddon – indeed it later transpired that the world had come the closest ever to all-out nuclear war in 1955, though typically the news-managed masses knew next to nothing about it. The cinema newsreels simply appeared to be showing an awful lot of hydrogen bomb explosions in the atmosphere. Radioactive pollution was barely understood in its enormity – and there was little organised resistance.

Teenagers instinctively recognised the clarion call of rebellion against the old conformity. The young Lennon went to see the film; ready, not to say eager, for the destruction of cinema seats the film inevitably, he had read, provoked in its audience. He saw a chubby middle-aged white American with a kiss curl hanging down over his forehead and was baffled that such a man could produce such music. What he did not know was that Haley – an old pro of 20 years – had indeed learnt a new syncopated beat. It was natural rhythm, descendant via the American blacks and their slave forebears of the sensual, rich, free music of Africa. The wheel had come full circle, a port which had

grown rich on the profits of the slaving ships, was redis-
covering a naturalness altogether foreign to the regimen-
ted life. Rebels like Lennon had never fully taken on board
the stiffness and alienation of the post-war world, and he
along with many thousands of others was about to embark
upon an odyssey which would let the western civilisations
rediscover their own bodies, instead of the awkward shells
they presently inhabited. Such freedom of the body would
demand its accompanying freedom of the mind . . . but that
was all much later.

After Bill Haley, 'If a Body Digs a Body Rocking Through
the Rye', came early the following year of 1956 a skiffle
craze, of which one of the leading proponents was an Irish-
Glaswegian called Lonnie Donnegan.

> 'Does your chewing gum lose its flavour on the bed post
> overnight? If your mother says don't chew it, do you
> swallow it in spite?'

He showed that anyone could make music, all you
needed was a washboard, and a tea chest and a broom
handle with a piece of string. Skiffle groups were formed
up and down the long narrow shape of the British Isle by
the thousand. Including a group called the Quarrymen.

John badgered his mother into buying him a guitar 'on
the drip' – weekly instalments paid through the post by
mail. It cost £10, and was a Spanish guitar guaranteed not
to split. One of the happy results of Julia and Freddy's relationship was her ability to accompany him on the banjo –
an instrument used to great effect by another worthy Lan-
cashire comedian/singer, George Formby.

> 'I'm leaning on a lamp-post at the corner of the street
> watching all the pretty ladies go by . . .'

Sung with a perpetually beaming, impish face. It could
almost have been an early version of the Beatle public persona. Indeed on one Beatle song, 'Hey Bulldog', John Lennon went into a Formby impersonation – too late to get it
on record.

Although Julia could, she claimed, play any stringed
instrument, she taught John banjo chords. It made no difference – the public was not musically discerning, and
thought skiffle a passing fad like pogo sticks, hula hoops, and
yo yos. The young wanted to play again.

But the first Quarryman group – comprising John Lennon on guitar, Peter Shotton on washboard and four

others: Len Garry, Colin Hanson on drums, Eric Griffiths on guitar, Rod Davis on banjo – were influenced by the moody, sullen tones of a white American from the South who sang with a sultry sex appeal. 'Heartbreak Hotel' by Elvis Presley grabbed hold of the young 15-year-old Lennon who had been drifting for over a year and gave him a purpose in life. He modelled himself on Elvis' version of young manhood, his hair sprouted a quiff, the sides of hair were swept back and hung down low at the back. Elvis, for Lennon as for countless other teenagers, was the King. The Idol.

But the first song Lennon learnt to play right through was by the high-voiced leader of The Crickets, a bespectacled slight young man called Buddy Holly, whose music was both catchy and easy to play. On Empire Day, 1956, the Quarrymen gave their first concert in Rose Street from the back of a lorry. No fee was paid, but a good time was had by all.

John's friend, Nigel Whalley, set about trying to get the group gigs, at fêtes and parties. The personnel, under the pressure of approaching 'O' levels changed frequently but the standard was sufficient for them to get the odd gig and even on occasion actual payment. Lennon had begun to experiment turning his shoulder towards the audience and leering at the young girls, already some of the palpable psychic magnetism of his stage persona was starting to emanate from the moody 16-year-old.

'O' levels were finished, it was the summer of '57. John entered for 8 'O' levels, he failed them all, though he had, noted his new headmaster Mr Pobjoy, only failed each subject by one grade. Mr Pobjoy, a young 35-year-old in his first headmastership, spoke to both Lennon and Mimi. To Lennon he was forthright. 'You'll either be an artist or a labourer,' he bluntly told him, recognising that the boy's only real interest seemed to lie in art. (He had failed 'Art' 'O' level too, illustrating the subject of 'travel' for instance with an inspired picture of a hunchback covered in warts.)

Mr Pobjoy now called in Mimi. Was she prepared to finance John through his first year of art college until he was eligible for a grant? Mimi agreed, she wanted her nephew to have some career, all too aware of how his father had drifted, superstitious of the effect of the inherited genes.

Mr Pobjoy wrote as good a reference as he could in the circumstances. The school, founded in 1922 by a grandson of the aristocracy who was educated at Eton, had modelled itself on the house system of public schools with masters in gowns, prefects and canings. Even with an apparent 'ne'er do well' like Lennon, Pobjoy felt a headmaster's duty to do something for the chap. On the strength of Pobjoy's claim that Lennon had lately changed for the better, and on the basis of a striking portfolio of work, John Winston Lennon was accepted by the Liverpool School of Art for an Intermediate Course of General Study followed by two more years of specialisation. Aunt Mimi, who accompanied the suit-clad rebel to the interview, was relieved. The normal minimum requirement was 5 'O' Levels. The right background, the right school, even Uncle George's old suit had done the trick. John at home with Mimi had always spoken properly, without much trace of the 'Scouse' accent he was later to adopt in public.

THE BEATNIK HORROR

—For though they don't know it they are on the road to hell

...ees them. He admitted quite openly that he scrounges most of his meals from relatives in the Liverpool area.

Take another pair of beatniks—of the more "refined" sort.

John Stevens, aged 22, and his wife, Janice, live in a basement in Hyde Park Terrace, Leeds.

They have not gone in for scruffy living, but in their way are also in revolt against society.

Uncombed

John is an artist. He goes about with uncombed hair, shaggy beard and weird clothes.

Janice has just given up a job as a teacher of fashion...

She wore baggy black jeans and a sweater reaching half-way down to her knees. No make-up, of course.

Their object in life, they told me, is to seek happiness through meditation. So they are taking lessons in Buddhism.

John is one of those who...

his way out of National Service by posing as a psychiatric case.

"I was in for one year and 126 days before they finally decided I was 'permanently unfit' and let me go," he said.

Both John and his wife appear to enjoy shocking...

quite happy this way, thank you."

Artists and students are not the only youngsters who have fallen for the beatnik cult. In London hundreds of boys and girls from all walks of life copy at least one part of the "beat" way

They revel in filth

were really orgies—but they get very naughty. Quite a lot of beatniks believe in free love, you know."

Brian Dovey, a singer...

Most beatniks like dirt. They dress in filthy clothes. Their "homes" are strewn with muck. This, for example, is the...

◀ In the summer of 1960 John Lennon made his first bid for notoriety in this national newspaper exposé – 'This is the Beatnik Horror'. It was his and Stuart Sutcliffe's flat in Gambier Terrace.

5 'I'm Afraid Your Mother's Dead, Son'

In the summer of '57, things were beginning to look up for John Lennon. Entrance to Art School meant he would not have to work for a living, and although Mimi had tried to encourage John to do chores about the garden, if he wanted more than his strictly regulated pocket money, he resolutely refused any such deal.

The great summer occasion in Woolton was at the social centre of the village, St. Peter's Church, when the Annual Fête was held. In 1957, the date set was July 7. On the rising slopes above Menlove Avenue, marquees were erected in the church grounds, the procession that would wind through the streets to the church was prepared. The Quarrymen – being well-connected through John – had naturally been booked for the young people, not as a star turn, more as a side show. The main spectacular came from the band of the Cheshire Yeomanry.

Ivan Vaughan, a friend of John's from their days at Dovedale Primary, used the occasion of Woolton's big day to invite along a fellow student at the Liverpool Institute, a prestigious grammer school in the city centre, which was literally alongside the Art School, to which John had – by some beneficient guiding hand – just obtained entry.

Two years previously Ivan's friend, Paul McCartney, had moved to Allerton from the more industrial area of Speke. Allerton had plenty of open space – it was where Quarry Bank School was situated. McCartney had just turned 15 and felt curious about neighbouring Woolton's big day. As far as he was concerned Woolton people were snobs and very well off. His recently widowed father had been very lucky to obtain their Corporation-owned small terrace house with a few yards of garden. It was definitely a step-up. Since his mother had died the year before he had begun to play guitar more and more seriously and felt – with one parent dead – very old for his years. Ivan had mentioned this great band; Paul McCartney felt good enough to become part of them – first he would check them out.

John was in full cry – never one to be able to take his drink, he had drowned his frayed nerves after Mimi had seen him for the first time in full 'Teddy Boy' regalia – more exactly, a heavily padded jacket across the shoulders, long and cut lean at the hips, with extremely tight, suggestive trousers – it was the uniform of the 'King'. And just like Elvis, Lennon had greased his hair back at the sides.

McCartney got in close to the stage so that he could study John's technique on lead guitar – although the sound was raunchy, there was something strange about the way he played his chords, it didn't matter, this guy couldn't even remember the words, so he made up dirtier ones. Thus 'Come Go With Me' had become –

'Come little darling, come and go with me'

Nevertheless, the band seemed unpretentious enough even if they were all Woolton people. Paul was taken to meet them backstage in the church hall by the prescient Ivan Vaughan. Lennon was not over friendly to McCartney but they were introduced and talked.

They quickly discoved they shared an admiration for Eddie Cochran – still one of the most under-rated of the early rockers –whose driving energy and power was something different again from Elvis' sultriness. McCartney offered to write down all the words of Cochran's new number 'Twenty Flight Rock' after he had played the song on a borrowed guitar. John was impressed, even though well under the weather after having begun drinking early in the morning. The young auditionee – for they both understood it to be that – launched into Gene Vincent's, 'Be-Bop-A-Lula' and again he knew all the words. Lennon remained silent, McCartney played a couple more standards from his repertoire. The audition came to an unannounced end. John showed his appreciation by thanking Paul for the words of the song.

'Yeah, Cochran, now that guy's something else Paul.'

A week later after Lennon had carefully weighed up if he wanted someone as good as McCartney in the group, the word was passed on to Paul by Pete Shotton that 'the band would quite like to have him in the group, if he'd like to join.' Paul McCartney, sure that he would keep one or two stages ahead of John Lennon musically, agreed.

The unchallenged leader of the group had noticed a

potential rival, but he was nearly two years younger, and Lennon had told himself that the band had to be as good as possible. Which meant taking in equals – equals musically at least – Lennon was confident enough of his power to dominate the group as he sought to dominate everybody.

The first gig with the new guitarist was at a Conservative Club. The nervous McCartney on lead guitar went into his solo on the nod from John on rhythm and immediately blew it. The leader recognising his chance, demoted Paul to playing rhythm along with himself. McCartney was never again to play lead. First round to John Lennon.

The Art School was a relative liberation after Quarry Bank, John Lennon quickly took to arriving as an Elvis lookalike with a suitably tough expression. The Art School on Hope Street is not too far from present-day riot-scarred Toxteth, and in the late 50s the area was known for its mixture of big city characters – the occasional girl on the game, the professionally idle, the small time crooks, the slightly dubious characters who need the shelter of a city if they are not to stand out. He calculated that the best defence against running into a crowd of real 'Teds' was to not look an easy target – for in reality he had spent very little time up to this point in the city, it was like moving to another town, even though at night he returned to Menlove Avenue. Mimi's protests about his dress had increasingly less effect upon him. He was on far better terms with his mother, who sympathised with his outlandish clothes, who shared his pleasure at the exposure of human frailty. They were united in their sense of the ridiculousness of life. In fact, Julia positively encouraged him to find his own way. It was what she had done in going out with Alfred and she recognised the similarities – not least the scotched attempt by him to go to sea.

John Lennon got to know his mother, to appreciate that she was an innocent in the world who preferred her dreams to the toiling reality of a Liverpool living from week to week. Her beauty was of that unostentatious ethereal kind that does not immediately attract notice but instead gradually percolates and takes over its audience without them realising what has happened.

John was at her house with 'Twitchy' and his two half-sisters when she went round to see Mimi – just a short bus ride from Spring Wood. He had had another bust-up with Mimi and had extended his weekend stay through to this moonless Tuesday night.

Nigel Whalley went round to Mimi's to ask for John, just in time to catch Julia taking leave of her sister. She had a joke for Nigel as they walked 200 yards down Menlove Avenue, then Julia walked across the dual carriageway to her bus stop on the other side of the road. She emerged from the centre of the carriageway, where some old tram tracks are hidden, into the fast lane – in the dim night a car appeared from nowhere. The speeding vehicle struck her as its brakes squealed, Nigel Whalley turned around at the gut-wrenching sound to see her tossed into the air.

The car was driven by an off-duty policeman. Nigel Whalley noted in the corner of his numbed mind the smell of drink as they ran to the inert body lying in the road, gently picked her up out of the route of on-coming cars. She made no sound, was perhaps still breathing. By the time the ambulance got her to Sefton Hospital she was dead, aged 43.

A policeman arrived at the door of Twitchy's house. To Lennon it was a scene played out as melodramatically as at the cinema. The upright policeman asks if he is Julia's son; factually announces that he's afraid to say she's dead, killed in a road accident.

'Where is she?' asked the always nervy Twitchy. 'Sefton General,' comes the reply. John playing his part on the worst day of his life talks incessantly to the driver, trying not to let his feelings come through, swearing to himself as he listens to the distraught character chattering madly, realising that he is now completely on his own, with no obligations to anyone, bitterly thinking that the mother he had lost at 5, has again been taken from him at 17 and just when he had won his way into her house, alarming the increasingly sharp Mimi who realised that the mother's call was proving stronger than her own care of him.

As the taxi stopped outside the hospital, Lennon refuses to see the shattered body. It is not how he wishes to treasure her memory, that will take 10 years to work out. Twitchy goes in and comes out hysterical. The finality of death is only apparent when the body without its life is viewed – it always produces the shock of recognition, the stir of forgotten, shut-away knowledge. John allows Twitchy to cry his tears of grief, remaining dry-eyed himself.

◄ Lennon and McCartney take it away for the big London impresario, Larry Parnes, but recognition was slow to come.

6 'Larry Parne's Coming Up From London'

Julia's house in Spring Wood retained its magic for John Lennon. Knowing the times that Twitchy was out, John would get in through the back and the fledgling group would practise. Paul McCartney had introduced a boy from the form below his at school, George Harrison. At this time (the turn of year from '57 to '58) George was precisely 14 years old. Lennon affected to wish to have nothing to do with such a child apart from asking him to play 'Raunchy' – a dig at the sexually innocent George from the worldly 17-year-old who did not find it too difficult to get girlfriends – however, his total unreliability and off-hand treatment of girls meant they did not stay long. No place was found in the band for George for a long time. Paul was his only supporter. But he was allowed to fill in when one of the other members of The Quarrymen failed to show – a not infrequent occurrence. And it was George who was sent round to try to get John out of the house when he moped solitarily for weeks over Julia's death. Mimi was quite literally shocked by the broad Liverpool scouse accent of George. She accused John of always being attracted to low types.

Accent is one of the many subtle signposts of the English class system – and Mimi was determined that her John was not going to speak like the working class, none of the family did, she insisted. Paul too, coming from a council house, she found a bad influence. Both were banned from the house. Mrs Harrison's realisation of the need to shake the bereft Lennon out of his slough of despair was timely. George, on her side of the family, had Irish antecedents. Both Paul's parents were wholly Irish by blood. John was slightly more than 50% Irish. The link between the three was of an elemental, tribal nature, that for many years   as to form them into a tightly knit group which the outside world was unable to penetrate. And so it was that the dutiful George practised relentlessly learning the intricacies of his instrument – bought approvingly by his bus driver father; it was a cutaway job, infinitely more stylish than either John's or Paul's. George by virtue of application and persistence became the unappointed lead guitarist for the frequent jam sessions held at Twitchy's house. To John, it was the nearest he felt to being at home – Mimi would banish him to the front porch if he wanted to play – telling him that he would never make his living with the guitar, what he needed was to get some qualifications behind him. She was vaguely aware that one of the Stanleys had turned into a musician, but her affinities lay more with the long line of respectable and respected clerical workers, and her own 'white collar' deep-sea pilot father. The family house in Newcastle Road, Wavertree, was a solidly respectable terraced house, but in the sliding fortunes of Liverpool on the decline it was vital to keep up appearances. Mimi's battle to prevent her errant nephew going off the rails was an heroically fought one – being as strong-willed as him, Mimi's all-pervasive watch over his progress had to be evaded by elaborate subterfuge, especially while she financed him through the first part of the course until he qualified for a grant.

Practice by the nucleus of three musicians meant that just occasionally they would emerge from the hard labour of searching for the right chord to that magical moment when the music takes off into a dimension all its own. Theirs was a long and arduous apprenticeship only broken up when they performed the occasional gig at a friend's party. But already a partnership in writing new material had grown up between Paul and John, who agreed over a handshake that all compositions would be jointly credited to Lennon and McCartney.

To this day, Yoko Ono and Paul McCartney are involved in a gigantic financial game to win back the copyright material that was produced on the basis of that handshake. The price of £21 million ($39 million) is, it appears, too low.

During the spectacularly unsuccessful first two years of the partnership more than fifty original compositions were produced – the only recorded ones being 'Love me Do' and 'The One After 909' – a reference to a local bus route.

The beginning of 1959 found John beginning to emerge from the ashes of his mother's death. A girl, who had shared the same lettering class as him ever since he joined the college 18 months before, had – completely against her better judgment – become infatuated. Most of the time he

terrified her, but his strange personal magnetism over-
came even her strongest feelings of reticence. John's tutor,
like everyone else, was astounded at the match, finding it a
most unlikely, and unsuitable, combination. John Lennon
for two long years after his mother's death kept separate
from the other students, only minimally altering his tough
Elvis image to accommodate the shaggy jumper and jeans
bohemian image of the art students. Together with two
cronies, Jeff Mohammed and Bill Harry, he preferred to
entertain (and keep at a respectful distance) the rest of the
students with a now finely honed wicked sense of humour
that relentlessly searched out the unfortunate recipient's
weak spot. Cynthia — who came from the Wirral on the
classier side of the River Mersey, was a perfect foil.
Whenever she walked into class he would draw attention
to the painfully shy, dutiful and rather mousey bespectacled woman.

'Please, no dirty jokes, Cynthia's come in.'

On the surface she smiled, inwardly she writhed yet continued to supply him with all the rubbers and instruments
for lettering he never seemed to have. But they discovered
during one self-examination in a student group that they
shared nearly the same chronic weakness of sight. The
wounds of a lost parent — in Cynthia's case her father —
were also there. He had died when she was 16. She was a
year older than John, a prudish Virgo, in contrast to his
hedonistic Libran inclinations. Cynthia was a younger version of Aunt Mimi. When, after 18 months, John at a dance
enquired as to her availability, she apologised profusely
saying she was engaged.

'I didn't ask you to marry me, did I?' he returned.

Cynthia found herself (in spite of the white lie) in the Ye
Cracke pub with the object of her long-suffering desire. A
whole group were celebrating the end of the term, which
she attempted to keep as unnoticeable as possible so that
she could slip out the door. The loud mouthed jester at the
bar would catch her out.

'Did you know Miss Powell used to be a nun?' he loudly
asked the assembled students.

Cynthia had to grin and bear it, had to drink and go
along with the celebration. Before the night was out, she
was his lover. He was 18, she 19.

It was at this point too that another far-reaching
influence came into Lennon's life — an intensely serious
and acknowledged brilliant student called Stuart Sutcliffe.

He created a moody atmosphere of avant-garde progres-
sivism, wore black and appeared to only live for his art. As
in fact he did. Stuart Sutcliffe rang a bell somewhere in
John Lennon – a bell of recognition and understanding.
The friendship quickly developed, Sutcliffe's paintings
were surreal, they revealed almost as idiosyncratic a view
of the world as Lennon's. Sutcliffe was obsessed by people's cruelty, Lennon by their deformities, recognising in
the physical a manifestation of his own crippled inside.
The ingénue Cynthia frequently died the death of embar-
rassment as Lennon would get off a bus and perform a
grotesque routine in the worst possible taste, jaw hanging
open, face twitching, legs wobbling along in a crazy, grav-
ity-defying hunchback gait. All-night discussions between
John and Stuart and whoever else was in Stuart's flat, gave
Lennon the first hint that someone else saw the world in his
own hallucinatory way. His deepest secret could be let out,
the inner visions and voices mocking the whole pretence of
everyday life. The pair hid their ultra-sensitiveness behind
a cloak of amused indifference and indulged in an existential spree of sensual exploration. As the new art school year
opened in the Autumn of '59, Lennon moved in with Stuart
Sutcliffe, sharing a vast room of a flat overlooking the
Anglican Cathedral. Good fortune in the shape of his tutor,
Arthur Ballard, had seen to it that John was allowed to continue his course and start a National Diploma course that
carried a scholarship grant with it. He still had no qualifications, having failed his lettering examination. But the
association with Sutcliffe produced an explosion of paintings from John in whatever material came to hand. Ballard
pleaded the case that there had to be room for 'characters'
in an art school if anywhere. The exploits of Sutcliffe and
Lennon soon gained a notoriety beyond the college . . .
The 'Sunday People' national newspaper did a fearless
exposé of the 'Beatnik crazies'. The flat of John Lennon
and Stuart Sutcliffe was featured in a photograph in the
first article, plus the beatniks themselves. A legend was
already being born.

   With John's grant miraculously preserved – tutor Arthur
Ballard was convinced of Sutcliffe's brilliance and the
two's fortunes had become inextricably linked – John
refused Mimi's implorations to return home. John Lennon
had cut loose and shipped out into an unknown future.

   Believing – in spite of all the evidence – that he would
somehow become very rich, he spent even less time at col-

lege than previously. He and Stuart passed their days in a Liverpool 8 coffee bar club called 'The Jacaranda' which was run by Welsh-descended Allan Williams, a thirtyish sometime singer with a chequered history of wandering around Europe. The Jacaranda had become a venue to be seen at and was used by the top groups in Liverpool, like Cass and the Casanovas and Derry and the Seniors.

Lennon thrived just being on the scene, with Paul McCartney still attending school and George now working as an apprentice electrician, he and Stuart Sutcliffe were happy to spend all their days there, bumming the odd cigarette or running up a coffee on 'the slate'. The waitresses, in spite of themselves, obliged. Lennon had the power to charm the birds off the trees, while Allan Williams was appaled to see how little food they were prepared to survive on. Their money, such as it was, was blasted on drink and on exploration that was to earn Lennon the title 'Marco Polo' of the senses. Lennon's gargantuan appetite began to show itself, as with the mutually reinforcing bravado of Sutcliffe, the pair went to the very edge, pushing the slightly understanding Art School into throwing out Lennon. Again, Sutcliffe's brillance pulled him through. Lennon insisted that Sutcliffe join his band, which in an unconscious tribute to Buddy Holly, model for the first song he played all through, he called 'The Beetles' after 'The Crickets'. Under the influence of the drink the pun on 'beat' if Beatles was spelt with an 'a' sounded brilliantly clever and to the point. 'Beat' was the music people wanted, but the old Quarrymen had no one to supply the beat. They needed a bass guitarist. So Sutcliffe willingly agreed to oblige. He bought a new guitar on the time-honoured weekly payment basis, putting himself into debt and painfully plucked away with his sensitive artist's fingers which were soon in shreds. John wanted his confidant to learn in weeks what had taken him years, also – unfortunately – Sutcliffe had no great inborn musical ability. It was the style and the pose he liked. The visual language.

John, by pestering Allan Williams, eventually persuaded him to let The Beatles play downstairs when the regular groups failed to show. Williams was only too aware how raw the band was, of how inept Stuart Sutcliffe was on bass but the Lennon persuasiveness cut through his reservations. Eventually, he found the group a gig at the very rough Grosvenor Ballroom in Seacombe. Fights and bloody battles between gangs were at this time part and parcel of the ambience of such pop group's sessions – hence the loathing in which the older generation held them. The bands – usually in pubs or 'ballrooms' such as the Grosvenor – were there to arouse tribal passions in groups of teenagers who went there not to woo women but to look for action and excitement and if that included a fight, all well and good. This underground world was the very opposite of the old ballroom dancing where men were expected to sedately foxtrot demure young women around the room and make polite conversation while their bellies touched 'so that they would be able to guide each other around the floor' intimated the hard-bitten instructors and instructresses, survivors from the pre-war world of an ordered, class-stratified Britain. Such was the reputation for violence associated with live rock bands that black-leather clad males far outnumbered women at the dances – a potent mixture for male territorial aggression. The Bea-tles' mentor, Cass of the Casanovas, persuaded them to call themselves 'The Silver Beatles' for the gig but they soon dropped the name. The years of practice paid off, their roadie – lent by Williams – stayed to hear them play, then reported back 'they were fucking marvellous'. The promo-ter asked for them again for a place in Neston with an even tougher reputation. At their first professional show, fee £10, it had been Paul who attracted the women while the men were hypnotised more by the scornfully superior, heavily macho John Lennon. It was a phenomenon he was conscious of all his life. Years later when he had retired and was living in New York a stunning blonde came up to him in a restaurant and asked for his autograph. He pulled the girl to him, nibbled her ear, and signed shouting out 'Hey Paul, got you in the end, I pulled a chick!' But in these early days, John was so macho that the girls were fright-ened of the gyrating figure who tore into his wild rock numbers. It was the men's frustration he released in manic bursts of energy. Indeed, the girls before Cynthia had tired of Lennon taking his tantrums out on them violently, he was bitter, the chip on his shoulder had indeed become bigger than his feet. Cynthia, for reasons only she could understand, stayed in spite of the savage beatings. One took place at the college in front of a charlady. Shocked by the way Lennon tore into his girlfriend, she advised Cynthia 'to have nothing to do with that sort'. But the girl who had lost her father hung on, convinced that if she could show him one person in the world believed in him then the terrible past would start to heal. Nevertheless, 75% of the time she was terrified of him, he was a man deliberately going out of control, who couldn't take his drink without becoming violent, possessive and jealous. Although Cynthia was the epitome of Virgoan faithfulness, Lennon checked on her, did not allow her to get into conversation with strange men, aware through his own untrustworthiness that she too could be like that.

The second gig at Neston was to prove to the super sensitive John that he needed the protecting front of a super tough warrior if he was going to survive. As they played the most violent rockers in their repertoire, a 16-year-old was kicked to death on the dance floor in front of them. None of the group even thought to intervene. It was the cruel streak noted in Lennon by early Beatle drummer Tommy Moore, who died in Liverpool in 1981 a forgotten man. The shadow of violent death crossed the path of Lennon very early on and was never to entirely leave him. Yet he exulted in being able to witness the barbarity that the raw music could unleash: later in the year they were to tour Scotland at small venues. Tommy Moore remembered the way Lennon had recounted every detail of another bloody fight where the boot went in. He was revolted by the way the hungry wolf of a man scoffed his food, as though there was an unfillable gap somewhere inside him – as in fact there was. Tommy Moore, the best drummer the Beatles ever had, left them after the 2 week tour giving Lennon as the reason. 'He got a sadistic delight out of guys putting the boot in' he disgustedly told Allan Williams. He found him a nasty piece of work. The sensitive artistic soul who dwelt within was not apparent to him, in fact was hardly apparent to Lennon himself. The part of him which sat back, compared, evaluated and composed was at more than one remove from the everyday character, the genius was however always there as some early contacts realised. One of these people was the man who had inherited a national trait of second sight – Allan Williams, ex-singer, presently pop promoter.

Williams could sense the magic in rock music, but for him it was coloured with money, lots of it. He had seen it at his first major pop promotion backing Gene Vincent with all the big local beat groups. The crowd had gone wild with a sexual/moneyed pulse throbbing through them. In essence it was naked, mass power. Williams, without realising it, sought to control what in actual fact controlled him.

He again contacted the big London promoter, Larry Parnes, after he had successfully supplied Parnes with the local talent for the Gene Vincent show. The biggest name in Parnes' stable was a lean, lanky blond-haired former sailor called Billy Fury – he hailed from Liverpool.

Parnes announced that he and Bill would come up to audition some budding groups for Fury's next tour. The auditions were fixed to be held at Allan Williams' new club, the Blue Angel, which was still being rebuilt. Business was booming at the Jac, and he was expanding. John, George, Paul and Stuart were in with a chance, they bullied Williams mercilessly until he agreed to put them into the audition with three other groups, Cass and the Casanovas, Derry and the Seniors and Rory Storm's Hurricanes.

Cass and the Casanovas were allowed the privilege of accompanying Duffy Power on a tour of Scotland. Fee £18 each a week. It caused a lot of bad feeling with the band, they complained they couldn't live on such a pittance, Parnes was really after cheap musical fodder backing his big names out in the sticks – that was how anywhere outside of London looked to a Cockney impresario. He was right. London dominated the country in every way.

The disappointed Beatles badgered Williams to find them new work. In desperation, after some very lean weeks, Williams offered them the opportunity of earning ten shillings each a performance if they played music at a new venture, the basement of a house where he was daringly producing striptease. Williams impressed by the marvellous perpendicular appendages of a real trouper called Shirley, had agreed to provide her with a live band. Even Lennon protested, this was a bit much. But they dutifully supplied some of their standards – including 'Ain't she Sweet', which reappeared on a 1971 Beatles release looking back at the early days. Most people associate a record with the time and place it first came to mean something. 'Ain't She Sweet' was ineradicably linked with the moment when Shirley, just in front of them on the seven foot square stage, got down to nothing and the silent, hands-in-pocket audience came with an audible gasp. The engagement lasted a week.

But their audition in front of Parnes had created more of an impression than they realised. He wanted to send his least-known singer, Johnny Gentle, on a tour of Scotland.

Williams suggested the Beatles as the backing group – they were least likely to complain about the all-in pay of £18 a week (£70/$130 today). Williams received an irate 'phone call from Parnes who had been contacted by the promoter of the first event in Scotland.

'What were these scruffs called Beatles doing on the tour?'

Williams handled the complaint tactfully. The promoter hadn't heard the group play yet. Let him hear the music. The storm blew over.

Lennon, away from Liverpool, went from bad to worse. Insulting waitresses, grabbing the best room at the cheap hotels they stayed, dragging Tommy Moore out of a hospital bed (where an unfortunate accident with the Beatles' van had put him) in order to fulfil a concert. The first tour had all the chaos and confusion of the later ones, only the scale was smaller, the instigator of the travelling cirus was still the same. Travelling circus with one difference. A group which had preceded them had slept in the beds they were to use. Lennon – who had a fixation about cripples and the handicapped – learnt that there was a dwarf in the group. He checked to find which bed the dwarf had slept in, then arranged that Stuart Sutcliffe should sleep in it. However, his fortune was about to be changed by a circus clown.

◀ John Lennon on stage in Hamburg, now in black leather thanks to the influence of Stuart Sutcliffe's girlfriend, Astrid Kircheer.

7 'We Became A Power House In Hamburg'

Allan Williams, manager of the Jacaranda, the Blue Angel and now the Beatles, had the most time for Stuart Sutcliffe. It was his help in preparing some floats for Williams first big promotion – an Arts Ball that turned into a Peter Sellers riot with flour and fire extinguishers – that had started the relationship. Then his Caribbean band wrote to him from Hamburg – to where they had moonlighted – telling him of the great openings for English groups. The overnight departure of the group had left him with a hole he filled with the Beatles in the Jacaranda basement. Business was going from strength to strength, and the energetic Welsh-Liverpudlian decided to set out for Hamburg to check out the potential. He had a few years previously done the beat generation hitch-hike through the continent – making him, in Liverpool terms, a seasoned traveller.

Chance led him into a small dingy club off Hamburg's Reeperbahn, a wide carriageway of a road separated clubs, bars and sex shows. The post-war economic miracle had rebuilt the city in a styleless imitation of American towns, much neon and functional faceless buildings. The Hamburg people suddenly had money in their pockets, the newly formed Common Market offered a vast outlet for the products of the humming reconstructed factories. Ironically, Germany was the first to shake off the gloomy clouds of the war, the people wanted to celebrate, to enjoy themselves, most of all they wanted to forget themselves and the whole sorry past. The numerous bars, the flashing lights, the strip shows and the dance clubs were just the place. Especially as there were girls in all shapes and sizes who would provide momentary relief – for a consideration.

Allan Williams asked the very tough looking waiters at the seedy, dim Kaiserkeller that was putting on another evening's strip show if he could speak to the manager. He had with him a tape of the Beatles which they had recorded for him. He was ushered into a back office where a tightly coiffeured man of about 50 with a very square face sat behind a desk. The intuitive Williams had noted that when – between the strip shows – a live German band played, the atmosphere remained as desultory and morose as at any other strip club. But when in a *'pause'* the juke box came on, suddenly all the customers were jumping about with their 'escorts'.

The tiny Liverpudlian smilingly talked in English to Koschmider, who looked at him stonily then raised his hand.

'Ein moment, bitte, Herr Williams.'

He went out the room, while Williams wondered what grave offence he had given the tough looking German. Koschmider came back with an even tougher looking waiter.

'Ottho here speaks perfect English. Talk to him about deine deal.'

Williams launched into an inspired sales pitch about the great bands in his native Liverpool, how one which had played at his club was now pulling in great crowds here in Hamburg. The German said nothing, listened intently, their country had become as rich as Britain starting from nothing 15 years before. New ideas were welcome, it had brought about the economic miracle, and the old ways just had to be bad. Williams did not need to carry out the world's hardest selling job. He triumphantly played his tape, the tape prepared for just such an audition. First Derry and the Seniors, a good group Williams knew. Suddenly a man came in speaking in a low tone; the ex-circus clown reached into a drawer, pulled out an ebony stick and muttered 'ein klein Problem' to Williams who went to the office door in time to see a group of waiters separating some fighting customers and then beating them to the ground where they aimed some ruthlessly clinical kicks at them. Koschmider made his way to the front of the crowd and laid into the screaming customers with his ebony stick. Satisfied the unruly customers had learnt their lesson, Koschmider indicated that the groaning bodies could be hauled out into the street.

Williams felt playing the Beatles' music after the incident was not going to combat this excitement – but a wailing banshee noise came out the instrument, John who had been left in charge of the recording had blown it. Koschmider was very polite and Williams promised to send a better recorded tape as soon as he returned to Liverpool. He left having saved whatever face he could. He put it down to being just one of those nights. After hanging around the clubs for a couple of nights with negro friend, Lord Woodbine, they found they had got through all their cash apart from the train fare home. It had been an experience.

At this point in our story a chain of events was set in motion which has led confirmed sceptics like Allan Williams to conclude that there was some guiding force behind an emergent phenomenon. Be that as it may, the story is extraordinary. And it should be emphasised that Allan Williams' ambitions were to be a successful pop promoter.

The Beatles were still the last string to his bow in the summer days of 1960. Derry and the Seniors, Rory Storm and the Hurricanes (drummer 'Ringo' Starkey) and Gerry Marsden and the Pacemakers, were far classier acts. The Beatles, however, were always around at the Jacaranda as his cheap fill-in band and the sensitive side of Williams enjoyed rapport with the serious intelligent Stuart Sutcliffe. Williams could understand the rage of Lennon against the world. He himself had lost his mother at 4 and had no time for his father. But warmth was not an attribute of the 19-year-old Lennon, he was on constant look-out for victims of his acerbic wit, he was the hard man savagely repressing any sign of weakness in himself, so much so that any weakness or sign of deformity in another was a gross insult to him. Outside a small circle of intimates he was against the whole world, living out the dream of the rebel, the beatnik, the rocker. The image changed to whatever was currently the most outrageous. Another side of Lennon found comfort – and some financial support – in Cynthia. She would always oblige with a cigarette, a meal, she was his security. George, meanwhile, would follow the couple around. John was his hero. Even within the group Lennon had to dominate, to shock. Only with Stuart Sutcliffe did he feel some intellectual equality; in the ash-strewn, vast first floor flat in Gambier Terrace he stayed up night after night talking about the miserableness of life and the pain, he confided to Stuart that he thought of his childhood and only remembered the distress and isolation. There were at one time 8 people 'crashing' on the floor of the flat. John intimated he slept in the coffin that along with a Belisha beacon provided some of the minimal decoration in the barn of a room that looked out over the

Anglican cathedral.

Larry Parnes was in touch with Allan Williams, promising summer season work for Derry and the Seniors. On the strength of this promise the group bought new clothes and equipment, gave up their daytime jobs. Then the roof caved in – Parnes cancelled the bookings. Williams, left with 5 very irate musicians about to work him over in Liverpool style, pulled himself up to his full five foot two inches and suggested they go down to a 'contact' of his who ran the 2'I's coffee bar, famous as *the* London place to get exposure. Rock singers Tommy Steele and Cliff Richard were, as legend had it, discovered there.

The threat of dire physical violence drove the desperate Williams down the long road of 200 miles to London where anything he felt could happen. The big city was the place to make money. The 2'I's, in the redlight district of Soho, was a coffee bar on the ground floor, downstairs in a large cavern-like interior the space was given over to the 'jivers' who worked themselves into a frenzy with one of the numerous London beat groups who had some style. It was lack of style and of stage presence that froze out the bands from the North where the audiences were hard-up teenagers. In London the fans had more money, the audiences were in their late teens or early 20s, they demanded a more sophisticated sound than just a battery of guitar noise, preferring a background of hard driving music they could dance to. In the North it was a background to drink and fight to. The 2'I's had as many – if not more – women as men, strict licensing laws meant no drinks; the thrills had to come from the music and the atmosphere the band created – the northern groups were just not into providing the atmosphere rather than blending in with what was there.

The threat of violence in the shape of Derry and the Seniors concentrated Williams' mind wonderfully. He quickly found the owner, Tommy Littlewood, when they arrived at 7 in the evening, and miraculously he agreed to let them play straight away that night. During the course of the evening Williams got into conversation, as he was wont to do and found himself speaking to a customer who thought the band was great. The man intimated that there was a German present who was interested in booking groups for his club in Germany. Williams, quick as a flash, asked who that might be and went over to buttonhole him. Success beckoned. The man drinking his expresso coffee looked vaguely familiar to Williams, even in the gloom of the noise-filled basement. Face to face with him in the dark was the man he had last seen sitting on the other side of a desk in Hamburg. Both men were startled but acted as if it should be quite normal to meet up in the 2'I's.

'Die group ist sehr gut,' Bruno told Williams. 'Ein moment,' he attempted holding up his hand as Williams launched into his spiel. He sent out for a waiter, an Austrian he knew, working at the Heaven and Hell coffee bar opposite. Bruno wanted Derry and the Seniors; on the strength of a handshake they were in Hamburg 3 days later. And proved a sensation compared to the stiff 'oom pah pah' of the German bands aping old American records, the Seniors were raw, exciting, as though from the jungle. Just what the on-the-town Hamburgers wanted after a hard day manning the non-stop production lines of offices and factories.

It transpired the reason Koschmider was visiting London was that he had had a certain Tommy Sheridan – star of early TV rock programmes like 'Oh Boy' and 'Six-Five-Special' – playing to packed crowds at the Kaiserkeller Club. Then a rival club 'The Top Ten' had lured him and Bruno's custom away. He was as desperate for a replacement group as Williams was to get just such a group off his back so he could sleep easy at night. The enterprising Koschmider, who had been in a Panzer division during the war, saw the sensation Derry and the Seniors caused and wrote to Williams asking for another group just as good. The fee, £150 per week, of which Williams, as agent, would get 10%. Williams got on his bike, getting signatures from a local clergyman and policeman for the first ever passport of John Lennon. With no parents who could sign the documentation and difficulty over even finding a birth certificate, it was touch and go, but Williams made it. The big time beckoned. Allowing for inflation, Williams commission would be £100 ($190) per week.

Feeling responsible for a group still in their teens he had to persuade Paul's father, George's parents, John's Aunt Mimi and Stuart Sutcliffe's mother, that it was alright. John told Mimi he would be earning £100 a week (today's money £600/$1,100); that was language Mimi found difficult to argue with, it was success, a real career.

Finding a drummer was the major problem to be solved. They had found their latest recruit Norman Chapman by patiently tracking down the sound of drumming for two nights in the back streets of Liverpool. In an attic, if ever the group could find it, was a brilliant undiscovered drummer. When they eventually found the originator of the sounds above the National Cash Register company, he was willingly recruited into the band.

He stayed three months – his most vivid memory being of a time they played at the notorious Grosvenor Ballroom. For some reason the song 'Hully Gully' – rather like the Stones' 'Sympathy for the Devil' – always ended in pitched battles. While bottles flew and groups battered each other on the dance floor, an enthralled John Lennon hid behind the curtain still playing his guitar. Lennon's wish was to watch the violence, not get involved in it, if he got caught up in a confrontation where he thought he would lose he would switch to the plausible tongue and winning wit in his armoury. The only time anyone can remember him plunging into a fight against the odds was at Litherland Town Hall when – as happened to groups not infrequently – they were waylaid coming out and some local thugs started putting the boot into Stuart Sutcliffe's head. John, like a man possessed, tore in to rescue his beloved Stuart.

But Norman Chapman's memory is of Paul as the leader of the group, a perfectionist trying to improve the sound of the band from day to day – and succeeding. In Hamburg when they arrived, one of the Liverpool bands there noted Lennon could only play chords with three fingers and described him as a pretty poor rhythm guitarist. But the drummer was the problem for Hamburg – they had played gigs at the Casbah, a club in the basement of the house owned by Mrs Best. Her son, Pete, had a drum kit and wacked out a good solid dancing beat. He accepted the invitation to Hamburg and the trip – with a treasure trove of money to be earned – was on. The contract ran for two months from August 18, 1960.

The Beatles – and Lennon in particular – had had too many false starts over a 5 year period to make it possible to describe the Hamburg opportunity as a make or break one. Lennon, even at school and in the face of every scrap of evidence, had decided that what he really wanted to be was a millionaire, and if that meant being a little crooked along the way, that was fine by him. He knew deep down in his gut he had to succeed, for he had experienced the grinding debilitating effect of poverty. He had known it in his early childhood, had seen what it had done to Julia, how the rich aunt had moved in to whisk him away, how his parents couldn't afford a home, how the child born in

1945 had disappeared into the arms of a foreigner. He realised people could be bought – he knew them deep down inside without having to be told about them. Poor, and you were the pawn at the beck and call of those with money. They made the decisions.

The club they played on arrival was called the Indra, a basement that was small and seedy. They were replacing a strip show in order for Bruno Koschmider to see if he could fill this club just as he had the larger Kaiserkeller with Derry and the Seniors. Hardly had the weary group arrived in Allan Williams' van than they were on stage. There were six people in the club. The Beatles let loose – realising that these people were not going to pay their princely wages of £150 per week. Koschmider didn't look like a man given to charity, in fact he looked pretty terrifying with his limp and his boxer's crooked nose. They adopted what was to become their stage positions ever afterwards. On the audience's left were George on lead and Paul on rhythm (though he often turned to the piano). On the right up front, John alone with rhythm guitar. Behind John but back some way, Stuart Sutcliffe on bass, painfully aware that he could only follow where the others led. On the drums at the back, Pete Best – mean, moody, unsmiling and unsociable; a James Dean of a character who inexplicably bowled over the young German women with his brooding handsome looks. Each customer lured into the club by the band was considered a triumph, they searched the faces as they played seeing what music, what style, what vocals got through to an uninterested audience who spoke hardly any English.

Koschmider was a demanding client. He wanted the group to put on a show, to bring some life into the dead eddies of air and the tattered dreams which peopled the place. Yet he then complained of the tremendous volume of noise the band put out night after night as they tried to lure passers-by from the numerous diversions on the street. A woman in her flat above the Indra Club took to ringing the police regularly about the noise. It being necessary for any club owner to keep in with the police, Koschmider decided soon enough that the deafening Beatle band would be put to better use at his much larger Kaiserkeller Club, which was a sea of tables spread out from a stage at the far end of the hall. Here Derry and the Seniors were performing to packed houses. Now Koschmider had a second band which would build on that success. Watching

Williams coaching the band one night into 'making a show', Koschmider in his possessive Germanic way was soon ordering the band to 'mak show', 'mak show'.

It was like an invitation to a reformed alcoholic in another country. All the restraints were off, it was unreal, no-one knew about or cared about the Beatles. John Lennon – who had a horrid fascination with the German mentality – took the boss's words and twisted them into a long repressed character who now burst out of himself. That night he drank and drank, shouted, gyrated, took the mild cavortings he remembered from Gene Vincent's show in Liverpool when the girls had gone wild, and turned them into a heart and soul performance of orgasm on stage. It was precisely what the audience wanted. A barely sublimated sexual passion pounded out to their tables as they drank their beer, shouted out encouragement and eyed the women who were mostly looking for customers.

The meticulously detailed contract stated that they should play from 8 in the evening to 2 in the morning with the odd 15-minute *'pause'*. Appreciative customers sent beer up to the stage all night long, one look at their gangsterish faces convinced the band that it would have been most impolite to refuse it. Besides, this was how stars acted, they did everything bigger and better than in 'real life'. The all-night stints stretched their musical vocabulary to the limit. Soon they had a great repertoire of rock 'n' rollers interspersed with their own compositions. The stronger the beat, the louder the music, the more dramatic the show, the more raw the sexual content, the better the customers liked it. And the more customers arrived night after night, until the hesitant struggling band quickly transformed itself into a power house of energy, in line with a German audience used to such drive and forward thrusting at work and in a town that was being transformed by gangs of building teams working from dawn to dusk. In wild, rip-roaring Hamburg, there was only one way to play it. Hard. 'Hippy Hippy Shake', 'Long Tall Sally', 'Roll Over Beethoven', 'Be-Bop-A-Lula', 'Twist and Shout'. This was the genesis of the Beatles' super dynamic song treatment. After two months Koschmider signed them up to another contract, they had passed the audition.

John Lennon had just turned 20 and he could see the route to riches and success. The demands of playing 6 hours a night were fantastic but a solution was near at hand which only Pete Best declined. Preludin. A slimming pill which worked by stirring the system into hyperactivity and destroyed the urge to eat. It meant for the taker that until the drug wore off after about 12 hours he could hardly be still with so much adrenalin pouring through the system. It also produced mental side-effects, the energy demanded expression, producing a combativeness that was both mental and physical. You felt able to take on the world and saw just how competitive life was and how they were all out to get you. The depressant alcohol eased the rough edges of the drive and diverted it into bizarre behaviour. George bet John £10 he wouldn't go down into the street in his underpants. John spent five minutes reading the Daily Express, causing the passing townspeople hardly to look around. On the Grosse Freiheit there were any number of distractions.

Still wide awake at three in the morning, Lennon was playing cards with some fellow musicians – 'brag,' a variation on poker – when a South African drummer walked in and feeling annoyed at the teasing of the Englishman about 'Boer' groups he solemnly poured a glass of water over Lennon's head. Lennon in a flash reached for a beer bottle and brought it down on the sleepy South African's head. The force of the blow was such that the bottle shattered. They stood staring at each other wordlessly. Eventually the South African spoke, 'There's five of you man, but I'll get you, wait and see.' The victorious Lennon went back to playing cards. Next night, again visiting the flat for cards he was jumped by all five members of the Graduates. Inexplicably, Lennon took his pasteing like an earned punishment.

But taking stick from the Germans was something he found less easy. Paul and George had been picking up a few words of German, Pete Best had German 'O' level, but John resolutely learnt nothing of the language, preferring to live with his prejudices about the people who had followed Hitler into a war and the mechanised elimination of millions whose only crime was their race. Yet, he was enjoying himself. The violence had an uneasy glamour to it, making even the fracas in the Grosvenor Ballroom seem tame. Punters who got out of hand were expertly rolled, kicked and savaged with the aid of coshes and flick knives by the waiters and bouncers – often at a signal from Koschmider. It was the Reeperbahn way of keeping order. The only thing they worried about was who would pay for damage and if this could be taken care of, then all was sweetness and light, for a time at least.

One night at the Kaiserkeller, a German head popped through the curtain owned by a well-lubricated client who in faltering English urged the band to 'mak show, mak show.' Lennon took a swipe at the perfectly framed target with his high heeled cowboy boot, the German disappeared from sight with a scream. The leering smile remained unaltered on Lennon's face. The next set for the band began. When the same German came thundering toward the stage – urged on by his businessman friends – intent on vengeance, Lennon was too quick for him, a well-placed shove with his boot into the German's face sent him reeling away again in agony, this time Lennon threw a knife from a table after the vanquished figure. It was all a day in the life. Events – especially under the influence of the pills – proceeded at a dizzying pace. Another night at the Kaiserkeller, the band were sitting with the local gangsters and their women – Hamburg had become a haven for arms smugglers and the more undesirable elements who fled through Berlin to the West and easy money. As they smilingly obliged by drinking the beer their hosts pressed on them, no one took any notice of the man who approached their table and then suddenly revealed a tear-gas gun which he shot into one of the gangsters' faces. The man's visage was transformed into a blood-streaming wreckage. Waiters appeared to carry the groaning victim away. The young men sat palely at the table, stunned. However, they went on to give their usual spectacular show. It was the way to stay alive, their passport in a world of incipient violence carried out for reasons they did not understand. The women besieged the young innocents as enthusiastically as the others. On one level they were sophisticates who could mould the emotions of their audience with their music. On another level, they didn't even realise that the women making eyes at them were indulging in a welcome break from importuning a long procession of tired businessmen and starved sailors. The group were showered with drinks, women's favours and presents. John acquired a new Rickenbacker guitar which he could previously only have dreamt about. Bettina, his barmaid girlfriend, also supplied him with the increasingly necessary pep pills. It was perfect freedom, everything was easy with no questions asked; the greatest risk came from VD, rife in the port, but it seemed a small risk to run for the suddenly easily available sex.

There was a new set of followers the Beatles were attracting. John named them the 'exis'. They were middle class intellectuals who followed in the wake of Klaus Voorman, a designer. He had discovered them one night after a row with his photographer girlfriend Astrid Kircheer. She had fallen in love with the raw vitality of the group and in particular the darkly clothed, stylish, intense Stuart Sutcliffe. Within two months they were talking of getting married and Astrid spent her time photographing the Beatles – finding the subterranean depths of their magnetic personalities in her photographs. The Beatles took warmly to this patronage after the grosser attentions of the Reeperbahn rock fans. They were astounded that intellectuals could find them significant. Something was happening to them as they welded themselves into a unit which they could not perceive but which penetrated the defences of their audiences. It was that elusive, untrappable 'star' quality which could break through on a guitar in a Beatle harmony, an elemental pulse that man had known in the jungles, a knowledge of the body and its senses. It had been exported to America with the captured slaves, prevented their spirit from breaking as they toiled in the fields and now it was liberating the post-war generation as they kicked off the regimentation and deprivation of the war when nearly two million Germans had starved to death among the ruins of a technological nightmare run riot; where men had become merely pawns controlled by killing machines. It was a call from way back in time, almost but not quite extinguished in a great black and white totalitarian society dedicated to death and destruction which contaminated all who came in contact with it, even as adversaries.

The pills, combined with the drink, took their toll on Lennon the man, but not the musician. He could be found off stage foaming at the mouth from total excess but then go out and wow the audience with a foot stomping act which set the Kaiserkeller alight. Word spread of the group; Peter Eckhorn, who ran the rival Top Ten Club invited the band over. They were sitting around at first, watching Tony Sheridan perform. Unknown to them, Bruno Koschmider had a very reliable spy there who dutifully reported back that the Beatles had actually played with Tony Sheridan. This – as had been carefully written into the contract – was strictly forbidden. Koschmider suspected that – like Tony Sheridan – the Beatles were about to leave him. The end of their second contract was nearly up. He placed a discreet call to the police. The 17-year-old George was arrested for being under-age and deported. Next Paul and Pete Best followed, after their dingy rooms behind a cinema screen experienced a small fire. John made his way back by train alone. On arrival he told Mimi to pay for his cab. He was broke. 'What happened to your £100 a week?' asked the sharp-tongued Mimi. For a week John stayed at home feeling very down.

◀ Brian Epstein developed an all-consuming passion for John Lennon which was legitimised by his becoming the Beatles manager.

8 'I Could See It In His Eyes – He Was Fixated'

It was several weeks before the gloomy disappointed members of the group got together again. McCartney and Harrison signed on for jobs, Lennon could rely on the support of Aunt Mimi – he liked his home comforts and working at an ordinary job was not something that entered into his calculations, no one ever got rich that way. The faithful Cynthia could in any case be relied upon to provide enough money for cigarettes and booze – he had written to her every day from Hamburg just as he had promised. She gave him security and a loving acceptance – as a doting mother would. It was the introspective side to him, as was the period of seclusion while he recharged the battery that drove the loud-mouthed, aggressive, lunatic musician side of his nature.

To add to the trail of disaster as the year came to its end, Allan Williams' new venture – a purpose-designed showcase club for live rock – burned down after just six days of business. Significantly it had been a roaring success.

Fortune arrived in the shape of a railway clerk nearly in his 30s, a confirmed bachelor called Bob Wooler. He had, on the strength of his ready way with words and an encyclopaedic knowledge of both pop records and local groups, been given the DJ's spot at the large twice-weekly dance show at Litherland Town Hall. Sitting in the Jacaranda picking up the gossip as the groups came and went, he heard about the Beatles and how they had taken Hamburg by storm. His informants were Derry and the Seniors – a group good enough to be taken seriously. The DJ had his doubts, he thought more highly of Gerry Marsden and the Pacemakers, but after 'phoning the promoter Brian Kelly, from the Jacaranda – with the Beatles waiting for the promised break – he was able to get them a gig for £6; they were back in business, even though at a far lesser rate than in Hamburg.

Bob Wooler prepared the poster in his usual meticulous way, playing with the words – a link with the equally pun-addicted Lennon. Litherland Town Hall became Lively Time Here, it was a trick John was to use years later with 'Lucy in the Sky with Diamonds' to get round a censorious British Broadcasting Company. The only following the Beatles had acquired since their return from Hamburg was the 'in-crowd' who frequented the Casbah, the mother of Pete Best's in-house club. But it helped to spread the word. Bob Wooler, who had burned his boats by giving up his job to be resident DJ at Allan Williams' new Top Ten Club, prepared the group. He wanted to impress his new boss.

'When the curtain goes up Paul, I want you to go straight into the first number, no warming up, I'm just going to say "And now everyone, direct from Hamburg – The Beatles".'

It was – in retrospect – to be the watershed, but at the time as with so many historic occasions, it seemed like a thoroughly good night just after Christmas day – Tuesday, December 27 to be precise – but the season's festivities had put the customers in a good mood ready for this new band from Germany. It came to the time for the star turn, the groups of leather-clad rockers and long-coated Teddy Boys eyed the young girls tottering around on their stiletto heels, in teasing tight jumpers which accentuated every bone in the pointed brassieres. They returned their attention to the drink, wondered why the curtain had been drawn. The group waited behind it, desperate for a success which showed they would survive after the disastrous deportation.

'Ladies and gentlemen, boys and girls, direct from Hamburg, the fabulous Beatles!'

Crash! Paul hit his bass guitar and they were off into 'Long Tall Sally', hitting that same driving beat they had used to overwhelm the stoney-faced Germans, turning the amplifiers up full blast, John tearing at his vocal chords. The noise hit the dance hall like the shock blast from a bomb. The whole audience surged forward towards the stage, the bouncers moved in looking for where the fight had broken out, but no, it was the band that had caused all the commotion. After eight hours non-stop playing in Hamburg, the group had no trouble in putting on a manic hour and a half for the fans, they drove the girls into screaming adoration, it was ecstasy enacted on stage, raw explosive sexuality such as Liverpool had never dreamed in its wildest wettest dreams. When the group came out, their van was daubed in lipstick messages from worshipping autograph-hunting girls. They were stunned. Firstly because most of the beat fans were mean moody young males. Secondly because it had never been like this the last time they played Litherland, then they had been jumped by a gang, and Stuart Sutcliffe had received a savage kick to the head.

Shortly after this, Bob Wooler was offered the DJ spot at an underground club in Mathew Street in the city, called the Cavern. Entrance (cost 5 pence) by membership only, cost of membership 5 pence (10 cents) a year. The first booking the group received was for a lunchtime session of two 45-minute sets for £5. They had at last found a spot in the middle of the city where they could perform. Previously they had surreptitiously played rock at the Cavern when its manager had insisted that he wanted Jazz played, particularly the Trad Jazz that was fashionable but as the 'Beat' fad gathered momentum, the Cavern under manager Ray McFall, fell into line. There were now literally hundreds of beat groups in the Liverpool area. What the customers wanted was the raw rock 'n' roll numbers they were hearing on the American-originated singles – 'Money', 'Please Mr Postman', anything by Little Richard and particularly Chuck Berry. It was black American music given a new raunchiness by the Hamburg-inspired interpreters. The Cavern was small, just a large arched basement in a warehouse with two smaller arches, one used as the reception area, the other as a dance area, the main archway being taken up with chairs. Soon the Cavern was packed out. One lunch time Aunt Mimi ventured down to this Hades to see what the errant nephew was up to in his lunch hour. John suddenly spotted her in the great ruck of girls barely out of school – though the club did try to operate a 'no under 17s' policy. Disgust was written over her fine boned face, the face that shared enough of his features for him to be mistaken for her son; he definitely took after his mother's side in looks, having some of that dreamy quality Julia radiated.

'This is nice John,' Mimi told the 20-year-old. On her irate way out she came face to face with George's mother, Mrs Harrison.

'If you hadn't encouraged them, they wouldn't have come to this,' she told her sharply and was off. It was definitely not a place respectable people should be seen. As far as she was concerned John should still have been attending Art School, but Arthur Ballard's valiant attempts to defend Sutcliffe and Lennon were fruitless, even though

Sutcliffe was a brilliant student. Ballard, in any case, felt no warmth for Lennon, the perpetual joker with the cruel tongue who only spoke to shock and who held himself aloof from all but his drinking companions – Tony Carricot and Jeff Mohammed. It was assumptive to say he was even close to them. Lennon's failure in the lettering examination – even though Cynthia had done most of the work on the paper – had proved to be the signal for his premature departure. In retrospect, his tutor thought he might have made a very good illustrator.

It was just as well Mimi did not stay in the club long enough to see how the girls offered their services to the group members – and how some of the women were to be seen engaging in trade later in the day around the narrow streets of the dock area. For a person from Woolton it was Sodom and Gomorrah, for the Beatles it was an early taste of the perquisites of fame. Something had happened to them in Hamburg, they had become desirable because they had learnt to sell their wares. They were also desperate to return to Hamburg. Allan Williams set about drafting a letter to the German Consul's office in Liverpool to see if he could get them a work permit after a call from Pete Best's house won them the promise of a job at Peter Eckhorn's prestigious 'Top Ten Club' in Hamburg – and with the promise of £200 ($380) for the group each week.

In April, 1961, the Beatles triumphantly returned to Hamburg. The Top Ten was a more glamorous and larger venue than the Kaiserkeller. The audience had more of what John termed 'exis', who mingled with the groups of aggressive 'rockers', the gangsters, the sailors, the 'tired' businessmen, the hookers, the amateur good time girls, in fact the astonishingly cosmopolitan audience that was Hamburg at this time as news spread abroad of the money and work available in Germany's richest city. It was a harbinger of the wealth that was to wash across a still war-depressed Europe. In France, even in Paris, it was the norm for people to look downtrodden and depressed with equally nondescript clothes while the old wooden metro carriages and road transport juggled and jangled along their way. John Lennon tasted the new incoming affluence and found it good. He had never been one to refuse the consolations of the good life. Although sharing a room with George in bunk beds provided by the Top Ten Club was hardly luxurious. He took to using even more pep pills than previously, along with even more drink. By the time

Cynthia came across to see him, he was in full flight. She watched with the involuntary fascination of a rabbit caught in car's headlights as a manic figure took the stage at the Top Ten, so drunk that he was frothing at the mouth, so pilled up that he threw himself around the stage, rolling and writhing as he immersed himself in the music. By the end of the show he was sitting on the edge of the stage wearing nothing but a toilet seat around his neck. Had Cynthia known about the time he had picked up a transvestite and then spent the night with 'her' it is doubtful if she would have been so indulgent towards him. Or if she had known about his pill-supplier, Bettina. But to Lennon it was not even unfaithfulness. Bettina supplied the pills and the kicks. Cynthia provide the love and the mothering. Women to Lennon – like most men of his time – still fitted into the Victorian world. There were nice girls and there were the others, who in the final analysis were to be used. John later was to realise he had picked a model of Aunt Mimi, except that Aunt Mimi did not entirely approve of Cynthia. While Cynthia, in her turn, was to blame Aunt Mimi for some of the skeletons John carried round with him from his childhood.

Neither woman would have been terribly amused as the pilled-up zonked-out Beatles urinated from manager Peter Eckhorn's balcony one Sunday morning onto some nuns walking by on their way to church. None even looked up. And while Mimi was to claim John had been religious and was voluntarily confirmed in the Church of England (he was in the confirmation class but there is no record of his having been confirmed) she would not have been amused by his donning of cardboard white dog-collar and erection of an 8 foot cross on the balcony so that he could preach to the 'multitude' below. Especially as the figure on the cross had a French letter attached to it which had been inflated to a gigantic size by the simple expedient of being filled with water. It was an echo of the younger Lennon at Sunday School. One day he had cut out white cardboard dog-collars for the whole class. When the teacher had come in he had turned the deepest purple, then seen the funny side of being faced by an entirely earnest group of youthful vicars. The 'congregation' had to keep the dog collars on all the lesson.

John took Cynthia on a tour of his Hamburg – not having learnt a word of German it was his view of the city rather than its people – the wide Elbe estuary with its ships from the nations, the riverside walk taken by the Hamburgers on a Sunday morning, the magnificent wide open squares and buildings of the rebuilt town. After the grime and decay of Liverpool it was a scene of hope, of rebirth and transformation out of the ashes of the past. And none was to become more phoenix-like than Lennon as he tried on and cast off any number of differing lifestyles. Each taken up with zeal, just as soon to be dropped and forgotten.

Cynthia had the dubious pleasure one evening of seeing the police move in to break up some rival gangs at the Top Ten. Again she watched with that horrified fascination which was liable to grip her at the sight of raw violence. The truncheon-waving police felled the offenders with a teutonic efficiency while the Beatles played on. On her return, John sent across his earnings each week unopened. He could get by from the food and drinks pressed on him by admirers, some hookers, some gangsters. He also took to visiting a strip club where he would play his guitar for pin money while the girls got down to the bare essentials. The pay was certainly better than the ten shillings (one dollar) a session Allan Williams had payed. John got Stuart Sutcliffe to write to Williams telling him he would not be receiving his £15 per week commission since they had fixed up the Top Ten Club themselves. The fact that Williams had arranged their work permit was conveniently overlooked. When a dirty deed had to be done, Lennon preferred to do it through an intermediary. Quickly and finally.

The group returned to Liverpool in July. There were to be two more visits to Hamburg. The group – and Lennon in particular – had a love-hate relationship with the 'fucking Nazis' as he would bawl at them. Once they were banned from performing for three days, so vitriolic had Lennon's abuse of the German audience become, but John was able – when faced with a stronger opposition – to switch on the smile, the joke, the magnetic charm and so ease the tense situation.

The first person to notice this eerie hypnotic quality Lennon possessed and had by now passed on to the whole group, was DJ Bob Wooler. He wrote his appreciation of them in the first beat newspaper to come out in Liverpool, also in July. The paper was produced and edited by an old Gambier Terrace flatmate of John's, Bill Harry. Wooler's article ran:

'Why do you think the Beatles are so popular? They

resurrected rock'n'roll music, the originals of which are to be found in American Negro singers. They hit the scene when it had been emasculated by figures like Cliff Richard. Gone was the drive that inflamed emotions. The Beatles exploded on a jaded scene. The Beatles were the stuff that screams were made of. Here was the excitement, both physical and aural, that symbolised the rebellion of youth.

'Essentially a vocal act, hardly ever instrumental, they were independently minded, playing what they liked for kicks, kudos and cash. Privileged in having gained prestige and experience in Hamburg. Musically authoritative and *physically magnetic*, example the mean, moody magnificence of drummer, Peter Best – a sort of teenage Jeff Chandler. A remarkable variety of talented voices but when speaking possess the same naïveté of tone. Rhythmic revolutionaries. An act which from beginning to end is a succession of climaxes. A personality cult. Seemingly unambitious, yet fluctuating between self-assured and the vulnerable. Truly a phenomenon – and also a predicament to promoters! Such are the fantastic Beatles. *I don't think anything like them will happen again.'*

Wherever the Beatles played in Liverpool now there were large crowds, still more males than females; an atmosphere was building up around them. There was Pat who with her schoolfriend would follow the band from dance hall to dance hall. 'They were fab,' she says, 'that's all you can say. I'd do anything to bring back those times again.' There was Eddie, working as a comi-waiter at Liverpool's Adelphi Hotel for the sum of £2 19s 6d a week ($6). He thought it was the greatest time of his life. Suddenly the natural ebullience of Liverpool had found an outlet. The Beatles that year played the Cavern over 200 times, such was the frenetic pace they were working at. But it seemed less like work than sheer fun. They would riposte with their audience, bite into a sandwich in-between songs which varied from all-out rockers like 'Ready Teddy' and 'Peggy Sue' to the more cloying and richly sad like 'A Taste of Honey'. Never again was their music to be as rough-edged and wholly different as this year. They had seen success beckoning when they had filled Bruno Koschmider's club for him, now they were recreating the same magical effect in the city where they had spent years trying for a break. Gradually it dawned on the Beatles that they had changed.

John Lennon knew he had changed – the blind rage that had possessed him after his mother's death was turning to a sardonic amusement with the world and a determination to sample its pleasures. As their local success grew, the girls suddenly became available, the money began to arrive steadily and even at this stage in greater profusion that they could ever have hoped for in a steady job. When asked, all said they were going to the top. John Lennon believed it fervently. It was his route of escape. Stuart Sutcliffe remained in Hamburg after their early summer visit, he had given up music to devote himself to art. Paul had taken over the part he had been vying with Sutcliffe for – bass guitar. The cleverest Beatle was gone. John wrote long letters of 20 and more pages to him, just as he had done every day to Cyn. But unlike the randy writings he had sent her, these letters to Sutcliffe were full of his deepest feelings and his most secret self, veering between maudlin self-pity and daring speculation. They confirmed each other's dire analysis of the state of the world. Sutcliffe took the role of Jesus Christ in many letters, John at first thinking he was replying in the same joking spirit, took the role of John the Baptist the man preparing the world for the coming of a great leader. Suddenly, John realised Sutcliffe was not joking, it coincided with an explosion of huge canvases where surrealistic modernistic shapes swirled about in chaos – the pictures had the Messianism of someone who knows he will be dead in a year, John poured out his all:

> I can't remember anything
> without a sadness
> So deep that it hardly
> becomes known to me
> So deep that its tears
> leave me a spectator
> of my own stupidity.

The Beatles had acquired 'French' haircuts in Hamburg under the influence of Astrid Kircheer, the young photographer, who flattered the Beatles by photographing them week after week, revealing images of them that spoke of an existential side to their natures they had been hardly aware of and deeply suppressed – it being thought queer to have any sensitivities. So the Beatles wore leather on stage at the Cavern, rather than the bell bottom trousers of their 'exi' fans in Hamburg, that would have been a sure mark of effeminateness.

One member of their audience on a typically crushed Cavern session was the proprietor of a record shop called NEMS. To his staff he was a dapper, public-school educated, polished, young man. Out of their sight he changed into a deeply unhappy man in his mid-20s, seeking a relationship. And since his one steady girlfriend had gone, that relationship had to be formed with a man. The doorman asked Epstein if he could help, since he looked so out of place. No, Epstein replied, he had just come for the show.

From the moment the furtive figure of Brian Epstein saw the black leather clad shape of the sardonic, joking, superior Lennon, he was fixated. He could not take his eyes off him. Epstein was also bored, his record shop was a big success, he needed other diversions. On his furtive trips to the Cavern he began to make enquiries. He got chatting to DJ Bob Wooler about 'the boys'. Wooler, who was also homosexual, quickly realised what Epstein was after, but he played along with the innocuous queries. He had already noticed the older, better dressed man standing there in the crowd of teenages, his eyes unwaveringly watching Lennon, beads of sweat pouring from his brow. Wooler mentioned that the band had no manager, while he got them gigs when he could. Wooler suggested that Epstein speak to Allan Williams their old manager.

Epstein made an appointment to see Williams at his club, the Blue Angel. He asked about the business of managing a pop group, whenever the name Lennon cropped up, his eyes bulged, his brow sweated. Williams showed Epstein some contracts. Lennon was impressed by the well heeled, Zodiac car owning, record shop owning Epstein. When he mentioned managing the group, Lennon decided to find out what Epstein had in mind. What Epstein had in mind was bed, and the relationship was all but consummated. From then on, Epstein's large untapped flood of frustrated love was turned into making the Beatles a success. The group signed a contract giving him 25% of their earnings after he had refused to take 20%. In exchange, Epstein promised to put a lot of his money into promoting them. An only partially satisfied passion had been sublimated into an overwhelming desire for success.

◀ EMI's recording studios in London's plush St John's Wood suburb. They are 200 miles and several thousand light years away from Liverpool.

9 'The Boys Want You Out Pete'

Before Brian Epstein had found his forte running NEMS record shop in Liverpool's main thoroughfare – Whitechapel Road – he had first worked in the family furniture store. Here he had discovered his talents for selling and for window display. An unsettled period at the Royal Academy of Dramatic Art had not quenched his fascination with the theatre, but it was its atmosphere, its costumes, its 'larger than life' quality he loved, above all the chance to lose himself in a shared make-believe.

Although it took him some weeks into the beginning of 1962 to get the wary Beatles to sign the contract (which in his heated state he omitted to sign himself), he had set to work to find them a record company. John Lennon had said 'yes' first of all, when Epstein had agreed not to change their music. Paul McCartney was the most reluctant, even at the age of 19 he was the more business orientated. But Epstein – to who the Beatles were really John Lennon – had what he wanted, John's agreement to be managed. It legitimized their relationship in the eyes of the outside world. And in early 1962 to be a practising homosexual was illegal in Britain.

The first Epstein moves pained John most of all. For the new manager wanted them out of the black leather which so disconcerted him. It was the Beatles' uniform from Hamburg, where they had acquired the French hair cuts and black leather of Astrid Kircheer and her 'existentialist' friends – like Klaus Voorman who was to remain a friend of Lennon's for many years and Jürgen Vollmer, whose picture of John in Hamburg provided the cover for his *Rock 'n' Roll* album in 1975. What the salesman and packager in Epstein saw was that the record-buying public and the fans at the dance halls were not the same people. The rough house image had to be polished and smoothed if the group were to grace the record turntables in ultra respectable English living rooms – whose ambience had changed little since Victorian times, heavy curtains and lace netting to keep out prying eyes, comfortable tasteless furniture, an emphasis on solidity and continuity. As though the loss of influence of the British Empire had never happened.

Epstein set forth his terms. The Beatles had to become punctual (Bob Wooler had despaired of ever getting them on the stage and found it even harder to get them off), they had to stop eating and drinking and carrying on ribald conversations with the front few rows of the audience. Worse still, he wanted them to limit their act to an hour, to have a repertoire of their best songs and stick to it. Previously, the group would play a number for 20 minutes or more, experimenting all the while, their music on stage would never be as free and vital again. They had to smooth off the rough edges of their songs and simply repeat them, again and again and again. With that, they were going to be saying goodbye to the sweet bird of youthful joy, from now on their music was going to become work. It did not happen overnight, but in that decision to limit their playing time came the inevitable consequence of lack of opportunity to try out new numbers. And any artist standing up in front of the audience can see the almost palpable waves of communication between him and them.

But for John Lennon, unlike Paul and Pete Best, the requirement that stuck in his gullet was that the group should wear suits, shirts and ties. Epstein explained it was the only way they would look professional – and he knowing little about pop music protocol, based his judgement on the Shadows, the former backing group of Cliff Richard, the only music group who played as such without a lead singer. Like Cliff Richard, the Shadows were whiter than white and played the kind of music that parents could approve of their children hearing.

However, one small straw in the wind for '62 was that the first day of the year they were giving an audition in Decca's London studios in West Hampstead. Epstein had chanced on a Liverpudlian who worked as a PR man for Decca and he had put in a good word for them. It was yet another in the long chain of coincidences that carried the Beatles magically along in the bitterly competitive battle between the thousands of aspiring beat groups assaulting the stolid British record companies. Wholly out of character with the lack of dynamism shown by these companies, (and the resultant total domination of the British pop charts by people like Del Shannon, the Everly Brothers, Little

Richard, Chris Montez *et al*), Decca had sent up a young assistant A & R man to the Cavern who had put in a glowing report. Epstein told the group to concentrate on the standards they still largely sang, though their repertoire of own compositions continued to grow. 'Red Sails in the Sun Set' was sung by a McCartney who was so nervous that his voice he was sure would crack at the next note. George sang 'The Sheik of Araby'. Unbeknown to the group, another set of hopefuls were being auditioned that day, Brian Poole and the Tremeloes. Pop at this time was still a small business in money terms. Investment had to be kept low if a profit were to be shown. Dick Rowe could only afford to promote one new group. The decision was made – Brian Poole and the Tremeloes won out. Coming from nearby Dagenham, they had the inside track.

Dick Rowe became the butt of the music business for this first refusal. They were, he explained, out of tune on the demo tape he heard. But he was a man who learnt from his mistakes. The next year he was in Manchester judging a contest with George Harrison. They joked about his turning them down, Rowe asked if Harrison knew of any good groups. He was told to go to the Station Hotel, Richmond, to hear a group called the Rolling Stones. 'The Rolling What?' asked Rowe. But he went to Richmond and signed them up. Thus, are fortunes won and lost.

Although all the Beatles, and John in particular, were convinced that the big time was about to happen, the news when it came from Decca some weeks later was a bitter blow. But they had weathered worse – the only time they had ever thought of abandoning hope was after the deportation from Hamburg. In Liverpool their following and prestige continued to grow. A poll in *Mersey Beat* at the beginning of the year to find the most popular group had the Beatles as the winners miles ahead of Gerry and the Pacemakers. A good proportion of the 5,000 copies of *Mersey Beat* newspaper had found their way into the Beatles' hands. The poll forms were carefully filled in with main rivals Gerry and the Pacemakers listed last, signed in an imaginary name and dutifully returned.

After the Decca bite of the cherry, Epstein repeatedly trudged around the other London record companies with the same desultory Decca audition tapes. Columbia, HMV, Pye, EMI, in fact all the labels Brian Epstein had in his record store, turned the group down without so much as an audition. Over a cheerless cup of tea, when they met Brian

on another of his depressed arrivals back at Lime Street
Station in Liverpool, John joked they would have to go on
Woolworth's own label, Embassy. You couldn't go much
lower than that. The pressure was on Epstein to deliver.
Although Lennon admired his suave manner and public
school ease, Epstein knew that the basis of their relationship was that he had to succeed. Someone told him that
it was more professional to present record companies with
a demo record. In a flash, he realised his mistake, he had
appeared amateur to the London big wheels. He cried off
from managing the record store one more time – meeting
with exasperation from his father who had only allowed
him two half-days off a six-day week to promote this latest
fad. His destination was the huge HMV record shop in
London's Oxford Street. He had found out that a tape could
be turned into a record for just over £1 ($2). It was worth
the train fare. As he headed south once again, he was not
clear what he would do with the demo record once he had
it, but an instinct for doing everything by the book told him
he had only to create the demo for the tide to turn. He also
had some of the group's own compositions on tape now,
including John Lennon singing 'Hello Little Girl', a number he had written when aged 18.

The man who discovered the Beatles for the world and
indeed changed its values, has no name. His job was to
turn amateur's tapes into discs. He had heard thousands of
hopeful singers, composers, instrumentalists giving their
all, convinced that stardom beckoned. But it had given the
engineer an ear for what was a notch above the rest. As he
listened to the group the man from Liverpool in his smart
suit was eagerly extolling, the engineer let out that he
thought they were very good. An idea occurred to him.

'I could introduce you to a music publisher if you're
interested Mr Epstein.'

Mr Epstein was more than interested, though he did not
let it show.

'On the next floor there's Ardmore and Beechwood, if
you like I'll give Syd Coleman a ring.'

Syd was as enthusiastic as the technician. He said he'd
like to publish the original compositions 'Love Me Do',
'P.S. I Love You', 'Ask Me Why' and 'Hello Little Girl'. Better still he had a friend on the recording side of the business who he could speak to.

Brian Epstein revised his plans to return to Liverpool that
day, first thing the next morning he was meeting with

George Martin, head of Parlophone at the young age of 36. Although Parlophone was part of the mighty EMI, the label concentrated on what can only be called the obscure, as it tried to find its own niche among the big boys. George Martin came from a poor background but the war had changed his fortune, made him an officer, paid for a classical music course learning the oboe on leaving, and so taken him to the very respectable British Broadcasting Company. He had then become an assistant to the aging head A & R man at Parlophone, who after a management shake-up retired. Martin had concentrated on producing comedy records and had taken some risks by putting out some anti-establishment comedy by young Cambridge graduates at the Establishment Club in London. One of their number had been David Frost who was starting to become big.

Although George Martin had no attraction to pop music (the nearest he had come to pop was a mildly successful jazz/fun record 'You're Driving Me Crazy' by the Temperance Seven) he did realise that if only Parlophone could come up with a group like Cliff Richard and the Shadows they might transform the label from utter obscurity overnight. The fact that Martin had turned down Tommy Steele, who had gone on to be one of the most popular British entertainers, made him more than usually open to the out of the ordinary. Pop fans were so fickle that it was no easy task second guessing what they would turn to next. These dreams had been taken as far as actively looking for a group, then when a 'phone call out of the blue from an old friend came through, it made the rather unbusinesslike and undynamic Martin think 'What if . . .'. In show business as in no other business, everyone but everyone is waiting for Lady Luck to come riding by with her bounty of plenty.

George Martin listened to the record assiduously with his trained musician's ear. He caught the signs of lyricism in McCartney's rather high voice, while George's guitar-playing was technically, he realised grudgingly, highly proficient. The jaunty voice of Lennon singing 'Hello Little Girl' was his idea of what a pop song should be like, simple, catchy, and utterly meaningless to a 36-year-old. But if he knew next to nothing about the market for teenage records, that did not stop him from deducing that here was a group that had mastered its craft. And Martin, whose father was a carpenter, had nothing but contempt for anyone who had not mastered their trade as lengthily and laboriously as himself. He agreed to an audition. Epstein's pleasant manner reminded him of Cliff Richard, he wondered if the group were as personable.

After all the rebuttals from the London record companies, Epstein's spirits soared. He telegrammed the group in Hamburg where they had been since April playing at the Star Club, Hamburg's biggest, run by the owner of many of the Reeperbahn's strip joints, Manfred Weissleder. They began furiously writing new material. Epstein flew across, negotiated a new fee for each of the group of £85 ($160) per week, fixed up some return dates and then brought them back for a June 6 audition.

As the van driven by Pete Best's friend, Neil Aspinall, arrived after the 200 mile journey from Liverpool to Abbey Road, the group were a little apprehensive. Situated in London's plushest suburb, St. John's Wood, the studios appear from the outside like a residence for a Victorian gentleman. They exude an air of quiet privilege. The dapper tall Martin with a clipped voice rather like a BBC radio announcer, was an impressive figure. But as soon as John Lennon, in particular, heard that he had worked with the Goons (a manic comedy team) and Peter Sellers, he warmed to the man. Martin was courteous if a little taken aback by the clowning antics of Paul, George and John. Pete Best was his usual taciturn, moody, handsome self and said not a word to Martin all through the audition. Martin put the group through a rigorous test. The old standards 'Red Sails in Sunset', 'Besame Mucho' left him unmoved. The number that stood out for him was 'Love Me Do' in which Paul and John chimed in perfectly together so that the intense inner unity of the group showed momentarily through with that peculiar appeal which comes from complete harmony. But it was a bird seen on a far horizon. The rational analytical side of Martin saw nothing extraordinary, nothing that cried out for a gamble with the company's money. He searched for the leader to build the group round, preferring Paul, then realising that it could destroy the delicate balance the four had come to. But Martin's craftsman's ear detected the technical inadequacies in Pete Best's drumming. He was laying down a very solid dance beat which almost dominated the guitars. With pop groups like Cliff Richard, the music was notably subordinate to the singer, the guitars only being allowed to take off at the ends of choruses, while the drum played an even more subsidiary role. Martin told Epstein that he couldn't record with the drummer, he was fine for live appearances but he would supply a very experienced session drummer for recording purposes.

In Hamburg, Pete Best had been the only one not to indulge in pep pills or in many of the pranks so beloved by the other four members of the group. He had refused to go in for the French haircut, keeping his Tony Curtis mane above the dark broody looks which drove the frauleins wild. In Liverpool too, Pete Best was the object of many female desires, besides acting as the booker of dates and fixer until Brian Epstein had come along. Stuart Sutcliffe had the previous year decided his career lay in art and had been accepted by Hamburg's top art school to study under Scotsman Paolozzi in his master class.

Paul took over his spot on the bass guitar which he had long been after, having once come to blows with Sutcliffe. He also was never slow to attack Pete Best's drumming, being accomplished himself on the drums. A chance to play as the backing group to Tony Sheridan on a record for the German label, Polydor, had been the excuse to bring in Ringo Starkey – as he was known from the number of rings on his fingers – from Rory Storm's group The Hurricanes. The record was called 'My Bonny'. The resulting effect of the highly competent music backing is remarkably like the Shadows except that unlike that group the Beatles allow the music to take off briefly mid-way.

Now with the word from 'The Man', as Martin had become, the knives flashed. George, Paul and John agreed that their drummer of the last two and a half years had to go. It was John who finally got through to Ringo at a Butlin's holiday camp where he was playing a summer season. He was offered £25 ($45) a week and accepted. Brian called Pete Best into his office one morning. As he was breaking the news, Paul McCartney rang to ask if the dirty deed had been done. A white, shaken Pete Best lurched out, he had been oblivious to all the signs, and became convinced it was his popularity with the Liverpool girls which had caused McCartney in particular to act. John became involved with the pressing problems of Cynthia (of which more later) just as George Martin finally at the end of July came through with a four-record contract.

'Love Me Do' was recorded on 11 September, 1962. George Martin had arranged the session drummer and was surprised to see Ringo Starr (as he had just become) in place of Pete Best. After fifteen takes George Martin was satisfied with 'Love Me Do'. John's addition of a moving harmonica riff – the instrument he had taught himself to play around the age of 10 – had given the song an extra dimension. Backing it was 'P.S. I Love You', a McCartney composition.

As Christmas 1962 approached, the record crept into the top 20 at No. 17. It was the highest it ever reached. 10,000 copies of the record gathered dust in NEMS' storeroom. It was the number Epstein had been told would guarantee a chart entry. Paul McCartney was found to be living on the odd sandwich. He explained that someone had to pay for the mountain of records Epstein had bought. From fixing a poll to fixing a record chart is an easy progression. A small American record label – Vee Jay – put out 'Love Me Do' in the States. It was never heard of again. As the new year of '63 came round it began to snow, and simply never stopped. Britain was in for 'The Big Freeze'.

◀ An early publicity picture that found its way into the bedrooms and hearts of a very different generation of women.

10 Cynthia Joins The Club

On August 23, 1962, unbeknown to the world at large, and unattended by Aunt Mimi, John Lennon took a bride, one Cynthia Powell, at Hope Street Register Office, where 24 years before his father had also taken a bride. At the time Cynthia was some two weeks 'late', Brian Epstein had taken out a special licence to get the marriage ceremony performed quietly to avoid gossip and the 'shame' that attached itself to illegitimate birth. It was, besides, easier to have designs on a married man, even if he was 21. When Cynthia had broken the news, John had thought carefully for what seemed an age to the nervous, tearful Cynthia and then announced they would have to get married. Events happened to Lennon and after dating 'Miss Powell' for three and a half years it seemed the next logical step. Although Cynthia was reduced to signing on for dole money at this time, the just-agreed record contract with Parlophone boded well for the future. John disappeared down to London for the recording session of 'Love Me Do'. Cynthia on her 23rd birthday was confined to bed in her one-room flat, losing blood, desperately trying to save the baby. By the time John returned, the crisis had passed.

Brian Epstein gave the couple a flat he kept near the Art College for his own liaisons. The first time they had a reasonable place to stay (on one occasion at Cynthia's digs John had had to hide under the bed clothes when the land-lady unexpectedly called for her money – in those days sex still happened very much in private between consenting married adults of different sexes). But John and Cynthia had touched bottom, soon from being broke, with a child on the way and on the dole – Cynthia was spotted by one of John's aunts collecting her meagre unemployment pay – the couple were gathering the fruits of success. But for the child who had seen his parents pulled apart by war, misery and lack of money, it was a heeded warning. Lennon threw himself into making money with a determination that was

awesome. He said later, 'I always knew I would be rich.'
Brian Epstein, behind the confident facade, was still prepared to book the group into any dance or show for Liverpool wages – a minimum of £30 ($55). So by the time the
Beatles' second single was released on January 12, 1963,
he had signed them up for a tour backing Helen Shapiro,
glad to give the group exposure behind the enormously
popular 16-year-old who had hit the big time at 14 with her
deep powerful voice. She was believed to be (incredibly)
now over the hill. Prior to this, the group had returned to
Hamburg for their final appearance over Christmas at the
Star Club. This was the time the 1977-released *Live at The
Star Club* album was recorded. Behind the appalling sound
quality it is possible to discern the unison of the Beatles'
choruses. The camaraderie they had built up over their
time in Germany, particularly in a strange alien environment, was to prove an invaluable protection from the
incredible pressures that were about to surround them.

Unhappy with the EMI publishing company, Ardmore
and Beechwood, who had put out their first record, Brian
Epstein was sent along by George Martin to see old friend
Dick James, newly set up as a music publisher after a long,
if unspectacular, career as a singer. Brian asked what
James could do for him with his hot property after he
played him the 'Please Please Me' record. James rang up a
friend who produced one of the very few pop programmes
on TV, *Thank Your Lucky Stars*. After hearing the record
over the phone, the producer, Philip Jones, booked them.
The format of the show was that a panel judged the new
records. It included a delightful girl called Janice who con-
sistently gave more top marks than any other panellist
('Oi'll give eet foive' was her wonderful catchphrase in a
perfect Brummie accent). The upshot was that the show
had a large teenage and young 20s audience, a perfect
showcase for a record that was released the next day,
especially in a by-now snowbound, stay-at-home Britain.
After seven weeks 'Please Please Me' had reached No. 2 or
No. 1 depending on which of the two rival music papers
you followed – New Musical Express or Melody Maker.
The song, like 'Love Me Do' stayed 18 weeks in the charts,
but this time the Beatles could promote the record themselves as they toured the country backing Helen Shapiro.
As the 'caravan' trailed through the snow from Bradford to
Doncaster, Carlisle to York, Southport to Sheffield, they
began to observe the same effect they had produced on

Liverpool audiences. The fans were shouting for them. And just as they had tried to push out the leading act on their very first tour of Scotland, so they pushed out Helen Shapiro. All through her finale the audiences screamed for the Beatles to come back on. John and Paul, working incessantly on songs while in the bus between destinations, came up with what was to be their next single and unchallenged No. 1 – 'From Me To You'.

> 'I've got arms that want to hold you
> and keep you by my side
> I've got lips that want to kiss you
> and keep you satisfied'

Following the lyrics of 'Please Please Me' – 'please please me, oh yeah, like I please you', the message chimed in perfectly with the aspirations of a receptive young audience. It was still the age when women were meant to endure the attentions of their menfolk. That the women should enjoy sex was not mentioned by their mothers (most of whom did not anyway, they were too repressed) but the lyric contained a further admonition, the girls were expected to give as good as they got, and this Lennon plea for the women to assume an active sexual role found a ready response in the hundreds of parties and booze-ups that the young were staging up and down the land. The teenage consumer market was turning into a teenage way of life, they sought fun, could not remember the grimness and scarcities of the war too well and anyway preferred to forget. The Cuban missile crisis had taken the whole new generation to the brink – to gaze at the world left in smoking, contaminated ruins. The people's reactions had been mixed, some had hurried on down to get laid as the West counted its last hours on earth, it had been a pretty close-run thing. But the young, having shared the same out-of-control vehicle as it hurtled towards the most spectacular crash of all time, found little point in planning to give away their most precious possession sometime in the far-off future. At the parties the girls boldly brushed their breasts against the boys, drank the beer, fell onto the bed or floor as everyone paired off for a deep intense 'coming together' where the boys found out how far they could go and the girls wondered how long they would take. A new LP played over the bacchanalia:

> 'She was just seventeen, you know what I mean . . . we

danced through the night and we held each other tight . . .'

'You never even try girl, come on, come on, come on, come on, come on, come on, come on, come on, please please me oh yeah, like I please you. You don't need me to show you the way love . . .'

'You'll never know how much I really love you
You'll never know how much I really care

Closer let me whisper in your ear
Say the words you long to hear . . .'

'There'll be no sad tomorrow
Don't you know that it's so . . .'

It was not the raw sound of Hamburg or Liverpool – quite. But even though Brian Epstein and George Martin had sought to smooth, polish and make commercial the Beatle message, it was impossible to eradicate the soulful longings of McCartney and the lusty phrasings of Lennon. The heady atmosphere of the Reeperbahn 'assignation' bars was transported into a thousand parties and a million living rooms. Sex was the message, buttered up as songs of love but when you are young, at a party, drinking as much as possible in as short a time, when the pounding beat and singing harmonies tell you words you want to hear, it becomes like a spell. A call to celebrate life, to live in the now, just as the writer of most of those lyrics did. He sought escape from the miseries of a lonely childhood. His audience felt the need to take what they had strived for all through the disciplined fifties when they had been told that if they worked hard the world would be full of opportunities for them.

After the successful facing down of Russia over Cuba, the West could relax, let its guard drop, it felt strong and business appeared to be supplying the money to make enjoyment possible. The mood was one of being in good cheer. George Martin had in April quickly released the Beatles' first LP, *Please Please Me*, trying as far as he could to recreate a Cavern performance with its 'ecstasy on stage' as compere Bob Wooler had called it. It was the music that had the girls trying to touch the Beatles after the show, to even – if they were incredibly lucky – 'get to know them better'. One girl, Maureen, had been dared by a friend to kiss Paul, after she had done so she waited to kiss Ringo after the show. At another session Ringo danced with her. They began going out. As she waited for another show to end, a girl came out to her sitting in the car.

'Are you Ringo's girlfriend?' she asked.

'Yes', replied Maureen.

A hand grabbed at her face, the fingernails tearing into her flesh as the girl screamed with fury. Maureen frantically wound up the window as her assailant sought to destroy her in blind atavistic fury.

What had already happened in Liverpool the previous year, now began to spread out over Britain. *Please Please Me* quickly was riding high at No. 1. It stayed in the charts for over a year, the constant background to a year that became more bizarre as it progressed, A government minister was caught out in his predilection for call girls. Two of them, Christine Keeler and Mandy Rice Davis, set the nation agog as the 'goings on' in high places became public knowledge and rumour upon rumour spread as to the precise nature of the 'goings on'. It was as if the whole country had suddenly discovered sex.

John, that most prolific of artists, was to be less so on the physical plane, but his first born struggled into the world with the cord to the placenta entwined around his neck. It was a long arduous delivery which Cynthia unfortunately had to go through alone in Sefton Hospital, the same hospital to which John's mother had been taken after the car fatally struck her. Her famous husband arrived from London after a week, adored the baby who was named John (as his father and great-grandfather were) Charles (after Cynthia's father) Julian (the nearest they could get to Julia) Lennon. He had arrived at 7.45 am on April the 8th. John Lennon arrived at the hospital in thin disguise, the private room was quickly surrounded by fans. He asked Cynthia whether she minded if he went on holiday to Spain with Brian Epstein. She was too dumbfounded to protest.

Brian, in his turn, was too elated that the third single 'From Me to You' and the *Please Please Me* LP were out and doing famously, to really care what people thought. He and John sat around in cafés while he asked his close companion to appraise the boys who walked past. Lennon played him along, theirs was an intense relationship, he could make Brian squirm if he wanted by denying him whatever he asked; Lennon used the power it gave him to the full. He wanted to know every detail of the man who was organising his group and to be sure he had him in his power. The fact that Epstein was madly in love with him was a definite asset. He knew all about the lost weekends when Epstein would disappear, the occasional beatings-up when he gave way to his impulse to go after a particularly rough type. But elegance, good breeding and a homosexual inclination were his ideal. Becoming a pop group manager had been simply his way of getting close to just such an object of his desires.

After supporting Roy Orbison on tour during May, the group gathered for an all-out celebration on Paul's 21st birthday. The fans would have besieged his Forthlin Road terraced council house, so the festivities were held at an aunt's house. Drink flowed all day. 'From Me to You' was No. 1 with no doubts about it this time. They had broken through the single hit syndrome which had cast up and then cruelly cast down so many pop hopefuls. The Beatles knew they were going to be around some time, although their masters, EMI, patiently waited for the bubble to burst as they rushed out the third single in six months.

The drinking went on all day and into the evening. Cavern DJ Bob Wooler joked to a drunken Lennon that he had been having a homosexual affair with Epstein. Lennon lashed out in blind fury, the chubby Wooler was clubbed to the ground, in the Liverpool fashion the boot went in – repeatedly, to the face, to the ribs – the berserk young man of 22 with the world at his feet had to be dragged away from his victim. It was an occasion that haunted him to very near the end of his life, why had he completely blown his top? Everyone was sworn to secrecy. Brian Epstein paid over £200 ($390) to Wooler whose face was twice the normal size the next morning, and whose every rib ached. The macho hero's mask had been temporarily stripped away, and the tangled confused person beneath searching for love, any kind of love, had lashed out in self-defence intent on destroying before he himself was destroyed.

Aunt Mimi had taken pity on Cynthia, she was delighted to heal the rift over the marriage, and it was with her that Cynthia stayed until her mother returned from Canada. Mimi, who was to stay John's lifelong friend, made no complaints as Julian screamed much of the day. It meant she saw more of John. Then Cynthia moved back to her mother's house in Hoylake. Denying to ever more persistent reporters that she was married to John. It was thought it would ruin his appeal to the girl fans. By November the secret was out. The fans did not mind at all. The newspapers had invented Beatlemania after a show at the London Palladium in October when it was expected – but did not happen – that the same frenzy would take place in London as in the provinces.

'She Loves You' – the most successful and ebullient of all the early Beatles singles – had been released at the end of August and sold over 1.3 million copies. The song summed up the lovable mop tops for the public. They were incredibly happy, successful and jubilant because they were loved and loving in return. As Lennon said later, if he'd only had that love in his early childhood he would not have needed to be going out to look for it. It was simplistic, but it had an element of truth in it. He, as the rest of the group, felt themselves fulfilled. In 1963 they could still move around more or less as they pleased. They were taken by Brian Epstein down to the Station Hotel in Richmond to see a group called the Rolling Stones who were producing near riots with fans swinging from the roof supports. With the leather-coat-clad Beatles in the audience, Mick Jagger felt embarrassed at his poverty and looked anywhere but in their direction. John and Paul finished off a song for them in ten minutes 'I Want to Be Your Man', it was the beginning of a long friendly rivalry. Jagger cut his first record with this Lennon-McCartney composition and found his group had taken off. In return, he showed the still very provincial John Lennon around the London he had got to know as a student at the London School of Economics. Jagger was at this time entirely into Rhythm and Blues and Muddy Waters, but his funky sound was soon to join the Beatles' second UK album *With The Beatles* as the accompaniment to the wild wild parties that were being held around an increasingly swinging London. The Little Red Rooster and the man who wanted to roll over Beethoven were to become long lasting friends and rivals. Each in his way had more than a touch of genius.

LEASE PLEASE M

Recorded by **The Beatles** on PARLOPHONE

Paul

Ringo

John

George

◀ It was to take the public a long time before they could successfully identify each member of the group on record, so together had they become in their harmonies.

11 'The Beatles Are Coming'

The carefree days when the group could go out relatively untroubled by fans were about to come to a sudden end. In retrospect, Lennon looked back on when he could tour round with Eric Burdon of the Animals, Mick Jagger, Brian Jones and Keith Richard as a small élite group of new musicians and think of it as his happiest time in London. In November, he moved Cynthia and Julian down to the big city, the secret was out that he was married so there seemed little point in Cynthia hiding away in Liverpool. Money was beginning to flood in, it was estimated each Beatle was earning £5,000 ($9,000) a week. But it seemed slightly unreal. Walking along the street with a potential business deal in the offing for a film, George suddenly took to the gutter to busk. Lennon disdainfully tossed a few coins his way. John and Cynthia took up residence off the Cromwell Road near the Air Terminal in Kensington. Soon the fans had discovered where they lived and the block was under siege with Cynthia on the fifth floor in a flat without lifts. She was virtually a prisoner with a fractious baby. Beatlemania started in earnest when the group arrived back at London's Heathrow Airport to find thousands of fans screaming, bellowing out their names. It was deafening and gave an eerie presentiment of what the next three years were going to be like. But for the present they loved the attention, none more so than the short-sighted, slightly chubby John Lennon. He sensed the power his pen had created, now he could begin to write out his messages to the world. John the Baptist recognised that his following was gathering.

The Beatles second LP, *With The Beatles*, was released in December along with 'I Want to Hold Your Hand'. Advance orders shot it to No. 1 while the LP with sales of tens of thousands gained a place in the singles charts. Still nothing happened for them in America.

Alan Livingstone was head of Capitol, EMI's American label. Three times he had rejected the Beatles' singles. Now Brian Epstein and George Martin tried again. But a strange phenomenon had begun to take hold of America. First one small radio station and then another began to play 'I Wanna Hold Your Hand' as the DJs pronounced it. The record was promoted by word of mouth, Capitol had agreed to put out the record, the earlier songs had gone to Vee Jay Records and Swan, two very tiny labels. 'She Loves You' had risen no higher than No. 116. In an effort to make amends, as radio stations began pushing the record intrigued by the insistent negro-type beat and the lusting voices of the Beatles, Capitol worked over Christmas pressing a million copies. $50,000 were allocated to a publicity hype that sent out Beatle wigs to every DJ in the country. Epstein flew over to set up a two week tour, he had been working on it since June '63. Sid Bernstein managed to contact him to agree a New York concert. Bernstein had booked the Carnegie Hall months earlier on the strength of the Beatlemania reports he had read in the English newspapers.

Meanwhile the year opened with the Beatles playing France for three weeks at the Paris Olympia. Their hotel was the Georges Cinq, Paris' finest. One evening the news came through that was to make even the Beatles silent. They simply sat in Epstein's room overcome. 'I Want to Hold Your Hand' had gone to No. 1 in America. No British group had ever done it. The next day Lennon put in one of his more unusual requests to roadies Neil Aspinall and Mal Evans.

'Go and get a dozen of the top hookers and bring them back to the hotel.'

Neil and Mal were used to going to fetch girls from the fans gathered outside after a show for their masters, the accommodation in the dressing rooms being what it was, the fans' adoration often turned into what in Liverpool parlance is called a 'knee trembler' in some convenient cubby hole or washroom. This request was more unusual since it was only midday, and even though they knew Lennon was a man of gargantuan appetites, particularly for sex, they still wondered about the dozen women ordered for so early in the day, especially for someone who hated rising in the morning. However, although they were treated as equals (Neil Aspinall had been a friend of Pete Best and an accounting student before becoming road manager, and Mal Evans had been a part-time bouncer at the Cavern) the two roadies were also expected to carry out to the letter the most bizarre Beatle whim, and as the money coming in grew and grew, so the requests became more bizarre to divert their easily bored employers.

The women were duly gathered and John ushered them into one of the hotel's high ceilinged, beautifully appointed rooms. Brian Epstein had a long series of business meetings at the hotel as he set up the final details of the American tour the next month. As each appointment arrived John waylaid the man with a 100 franc note and with his famous leery grin indicated the room where the women waited.

'This one's on John Lennon', he said with a knowing wink.

The manipulator was delighted to see how even fixing a Beatle deal could be reassigned in priority when a man found himself confronted with some of the most beautiful – if not chaste – women in Paris. The arrangements for the American tour were in any case perfect.

On February 7 a Boeing 707 in the Pan Am fleet took off inaudibly from London's Heathrow Airport. The engineers had not discovered an answer to jet roar, it was simply that the wild shriek of thousands of bereft fans drowned out all other sound. Every seat on the plane had been booked by people who wanted a slice of the Beatle action. Particularly businessmen who wanted to merchandise goods with the Beatles name. By the year end $50 million of such goods had been sold. Brian Epstein was besieged by notes asking for his OK. Apart from avoiding shoddy goods, Epstein was happy to give his imprimatur. His lawyer had set up a subsidiary, Seltaeb, to handle such rights through a personable Chelsea socialite called Nicky Byrne. But his lawyer, David Jacob, like Epstein, Jewish, middle-class and homosexual, had given away a fortune when he asked for only 10% of any income made by Seltaeb. Recognising the wealth to be amassed, Nicky Byrne set himself up in style in New York and proceeded to only deal with company presidents. His partner Lord Peregrine Eliot helped to provide the front so beloved by American big business. Epstein, in comparison with Byrne, thought very small. On the strength of deals already accomplished, Byrne arranged a welcoming committee to beat all welcoming committees as the Beatles flew on innocently across the murky Atlantic. A free Beatles T-shirt was promised to anyone at the airport. Touts urged school children to head out there from the suburbs. The radio stations repeated the offer every 15 minutes. 200 press men were joined by 4,000 deleriously shouting fans as the plane touched down. The four Liverpool lads were put straight into a press conference as demented American girls threw themselves against the plate glass, the only thing separating them from the idols they had had many a wet dream over. Each thought that their idol – be he John, Paul, George or Ringo – could see and hear only them. So they screamed out their frantic welcome – the Beatles waved back bemused. So this was America.

One girl did manage to get approvingly noticed. She was suspended from the spectators' gallery, her arms held on to stoically by two friends, as she screamed 'Here I am'. The hard-boiled reporters were a pushover compared to the fleabitten, tough as old boots Fleet Street brigade. John led the gang in a vicious send-up of American banality.

'Will you sing something for us?'

'We need money first' replied John, his acid wit ready to be unleashed at each unfortunate victim. He only had to be himself.

'How do you account for your success?'

'We have a press agent.'

'Was your family in show business?'

'My dad did say mother was a great performer.'

   'What do you think of Beethoven?'

'I love him – especially his poems.'

Brian had arranged Cadillac cars for each of the Beatles to take them to the swanky Plaza Hotel. Super cool American girls drove alongside the motorcade and shouted their greeting. At the hotel there was a mad football crowd. The four lads, with Cynthia in tow, sprinted through the police lines.

The first show in Washington produced the same screaming they had heard on their tours of the English provinces, but it was more intense and wild, the Americans were going to do Beatlemania really big, the band played on with their set show of half an hour, finishing on their show stopper 'Twist and Shout' when Lennon's voice threatened to tear itself apart. It was all Lennon on rhythm guitar and Ringo on cymbals. The screams fell momentarily only to come back with roars of sexual pleasure in full public view. The long-suffering cleaners came across sodden knickers and damp seats cleaning up after the show. But it was only a two show rehearsal for the return visit to the USA in August when they would play 24 venues. Two appearances on the Ed Sullivan Show drew an audience each time estimated at 70 million. *Meet The Beatles* their first Capitol LP zoomed to No. 1, the previously unheard of early Beatle singles chased 'I Want to Hold Your Hand' up the charts, while the *Please Please Me* LP was hastily re-released by Vee Jay Records. America had fallen in two short weeks, The Beatles were shortly to be even bigger in the States than they were already in Britain.

Somehow, on a two week tour that became ever more surrealistic, crowded and chaotic, the dynamic duo of Lennon and McCartney – pilled up to cope with the enormous demands – composed some more songs for their next LP while in America. 'Can't Buy Me Love' was one of these songs. Despite denials, it is about a prostitute. 'I may not have a lot to give but what I've got I'll give to you'. One of the ways the pent-up energies of the group were released after the cocooning existence of getaway cars and heavily guarded hotel rooms was through the services of the best call-girls in town. The idolisation of the unbelievably successful, rich, handsome young men meant that any foible was acceded to, while the local dignitaries looked on in fascination and awe, that no-one spilled the beans for so long – it was left to Lennon himself in one of his characteristically sharp interviews – can only be attributed to the common reluctance to end the dream-like existence where money cascaded over an ever growing entourage of journalists, business associates and self-important host town dignitaries. Although each of the group was allocated a room in the hotels, privacy became impossible with the constant siege of the agog world. The girls were shuttled from room to room, journalist to journalist, anyone touched even at three removes by the Beatles had become magical. And a great ball was had by all.

The songs Lennon and McCartney miraculously worked on amid the hubbub had to be ready for a film which was shot between their return from the States and setting off on another worldwide tour. The job had got too big for Epstein, he could not break his Liverpool habit of booking the group work for as far into the future as possible – always expecting the bubble to burst. He could not believe in spite of the evidence of his eyes that the Beatles had become a self-perpetuating phenomenon that was setting the world alight with their sheer joie de vivre. Nicky Byrne in New York had presented him with a cheque for £10,000 as part of the proceeds of the merchandising deals. Epstein told him to take his cut, unable to comprehend that this was his paltry 10% on just one deal. He offered to employ Byrne for £1,000 a year. The sharp, street-wise Chelsea socialite realised Epstein was out of his depth, and not even in it for the money. Epstein stood by the stage as the group played crying tears of joy. He had become another fan who dreamt of one day going to bed with John Lennon. The untouchable, unreachable idol created by his own love. Woolworth meanwhile was negotiating to put Beatle counters into its stores to sell off merchandise like the Beatle wigs that were pouring out of the factories in tens of thousands. Even Paul Getty was spotted wearing one. The deals being negotiated were in the multi-millions, then word spread that the Seltaeb concession might not be legally watertight. NEMS was seeking to renegotiate the Beatles' royalty. A flurry of lawsuits began between Nicky Byrne and his partners, between Epstein's NEMS and Byrne's Seltaeb. Approximately $70 million of orders for Beatles goods were cancelled by the big American chain stores. A lot of fingers got badly burnt. The name Epstein became synonymous with ruin for these entrepreneurs.

For the Beatles and John Lennon success and work multiplied geometrically. The songs from Paris and New York became the sound-track of *A Hard Day's Night*, the third LP – it was their happiest and most romantic, written in the full flush of success, the first where they wrote all the songs.

'If I fell in love with you would you promise to be true and help me understand?'

'I should have know better with a girl like you that I would love everything that you do. . .'

'I never realised what a kiss could be, this could only happen to me'

'In this world there's nothing I would rather do cos I'm happy just to dance with you'

'She gives me ev'rything
and tenderly
the kiss my lover brings
she brings to me . . .'

'Bright are the stars that shine
dark is the sky
I know this love of mine
will never die'.

The words are those of one who has been elevated to
another realm, he beams back from there the songs of
heaven. The adulation of young womanhood breaking out
of a centuries-old constraint has propelled the recipient
into a paean of love to a generation. The writer of the lyrics
is whisked from the film to the next world tour, beginning
in Denmark and Holland. 100,000 people pack the streets
of Amsterdam, girls dive into the placid canals flowing
under toytown humpback bridges, their idol is escorted to
the redlight district where in the streets that have been
preserved from the port's rough-tough buccaneering days
he is delivered to the sailors' comforters. As dawn breaks
over one of Europe's most beautiful cities the old sea dog's
son crawls out on his hands and knees into the daylight,
demented from pills and drink. Seven days later he is in
Adelaide being greeted by the largest ever crowd to have
met them – 300,000. Aunt Mimi, who has been brought
along, flies home, the intensity is too much even for her.
Then it is back to Britain for the premiere of the film to rave
reviews, on release in America the girls begin screaming
as soon as the fab four appear on the silver screen, they
have become utterly unreal and offer instant happiness. In
August the most spectacular tour of pop history gets under
way. On the second night in Las Vagas John is smuggled
out of his hotel to gaze in the desert night air at the unlit
top floor of the Dunes Hotel where Howard Hughes has
the whole storey to himself. It has been one of John's
dearest wishes to see the lair of the famous multi-
millionaire recluse for himself.

The next night he is driving the youth of Seattle into an
orgasm of pleasure, the screams reach fever pitch as soon
as the group walk on stage, he launches into 'Twist and
Shout' and as his rhythm guitar drives along the screams
get louder and louder and louder . . . his power is absolute
. . . a thrust of the shoulder sends paroxysms of pleasure
through one vast united quivering audience, it is a sexual
ritual of Dionysian frenzy and he is happy, giving white
people back their soul.

Cripples are wheeled to their dressing room – as though
a touch could cure them – their hotels are besieged with

girls trying to be delivered in parcels, girls climbing up air conditioning shafts to reach them, their rooms become the setting for satyricon, sex, drink, pills, instant pleasure and gratification. The one thing Lennon, McCartney, Harrison and Starr cannot have is themselves. The world believes it owns them and neatly seals them off from painful reality. Only the best call girls will do, only the top names at the Civic Hall can speak to them. Fear irrationally grips Harrison at Denver, he is convinced the plane will crash. But the machine just keeps on rolling 22,000 miles in 32 days, 31 performances, it is only possible thanks to the proving ground that was Hamburg.

Two weeks later Brian sends them out on a month's tour of England. John hardly recognises his own son, who is now living with Cynthia in the lush outer London suburb of Weybridge in a mock tudor mansion. It is aptly called the stockbroker belt. The 'orphan' has arrived – except that this orphan's father has reappeared, won back by his son's fame. It has been nearly twenty years.

◀ America fell into a worshipping, Dionysian frenzy before the four young
men who had become gods.

12 'Help!'

During the filming of 'A Hard Day's Night' early in 1964 a
grey-haired man, not very tall, had managed to track down
his lost son. A woman he worked with at the Greyhound
Hotel, Hampton on the outskirts of London, asked if the
Lennon who was in the Beatles pop group was his son.

'He's got your singing voice, but you're the better singer'
she told him.

Alfred Lennon, who was now working as a porter for £10
a week after leaving the Merchant Navy, thought about
the woman's words. Since John had run after his mother in
the summer of 1946 Alfred had seen nothing of him. It had
been an incident he preferred to forget – especially as he
was *persona non grata* with the boy's aunt, Mimi. Taking
his courage in both hands, Alfred pushed into the dressing
room, past the crush, past the security men, telling them
proudly he was John's father.

'John, John, it's your father', he smiled, revealing badly
stained, crooked teeth.

'What do you want?' scowled the 23-year-old. He had
got where he was without his father's help. He owed him
nothing.

'Isn't it enough just to be your father?' asked Alfred.

'I'll get in touch, leave an address, look we're filming.'

Later a letter arrived at the Greyhound. It opened 'Dear
Alf, Fred, Dad, Pater, Father, Whatever . . .' Inside the letter was £30, John Lennon like his father was always a soft
touch and very generous.

The only sad song on the *Hard Day's Night* album was
entitled 'I'll Be Back', the boy who had run after his mother
now tried to explain why,

'You could find better things to do, than to break my
heart again,
This time I will try to show that I'm not trying to pretend,
I thought that you would realise,

that if I ran away from you,
that you would want me too
but I've got a surprise . . .
I wanna go, but I hate to leave you,
you know, I hate to leave you'

But reconciliations after twenty years are not that easy to make. While Lennon was writing that his father didn't have to work again, paying £12 a week to set him up in a flat in Kew, Lennon the public figure was claiming in various interviews that his father was a drunk, little better than a bowery bum . . . that he had slammed the door in his face the one time he had called at his palatial Wcybridge home (a story put out in the later admitted-to-be-fake story of his childhood in an authorised, sanitised biography). He was making a harsh savage indictment on a victim of the war. The next year he teased his father into making a record 'That's My Life', it would prove that he had done what his father could not do. Freddy was happy to join the parties out to London's clubland, telling the waiters 'I don't pay, I'm John Lennon's father.'

It was to take a long time for Lennon to get to know his father, till his death in fact. Aunt Mimi, who to this day claims she only ever met 'Lennon' twice, had constantly berated the erring adolescent with the jibe that he would turn out as useless as his father. Only in 1977 with his father a day away from death was he to finally learn the truth, in the meantime he was to seach the world for a worthy father figure. And that meant conquering the world, with everybody joining his gang.

At the 1964 Hammersmith Christmas show at the Odeon, the Beatles made the acquaintance of a group called the Yardbirds and a guitarist in that group called Eric Clapton. It was a fateful meeting, for George Harrison in particular. Eric Clapton had for years been whooping it up at the parties which took place all over the green London suburbs of Wimbledom, Surbiton and Richmond boasting that one day he was going to be the best guitarist in the world. In the ultimate duel he was to later shoot it out with the Beatles' lead guitarist for the hand of a model – Patti Boyd – who had had a small part in 'A Hard Day's Night'. The living testimony of that battle is the extraordinary unrepeatable guitar work on 'While My Guitar Gently Weeps', although it was his LP Layla which finally won this prize of a woman over.

The year of '65 saw John Lennon filming for four months with fashionable director Dick Lester in a full-colour extravaganza, *Help!* It was all good fun, Lennon became bored, he felt like an extra being shunted around, but he went along with it. Co-incidentally (and in the Beatles' story, that word acquires a new dimension) there was a sequence that had the fab four being pursued by a strange Indian. George was fascinated by the sound of the sitar used on the film sound-track, his musician's ear and his mystical Piscean tendencies detected one of the ancient traditions of the East in its vibrant ethereal sound.

But it was a dinner held by the group's dentist that more immediately affected George – and John Lennon. He and Cynthia were used to the bizarre, and dinner parties always seemed to end in the surreally bizarre. There were laughs aplenty being entertained by comedian Peter Cook with his 'stooge' Dudley Moore, there were dinner parties where the hostess would make for Cynthia while the host set about seducing John. But the most bizarre experience of all was to follow the simple serving of coffee. On the mantelpiece were lined up four cubes of sugar, the host ceremoniously dropped the lumps into the guest's coffee and sat back watching while they drank.

George, who had persuaded Patti to move in with him the previous year, was the first to feel a flood of energy gripping him so that he unconsciously began grinding his teeth together. The colours in the room became intense, the dentist seemed threatening, sinister, mocking.

'Let's get out of here' he said to John.

John, used to keeping the world outside on the perimeter of the magic circle of the Liverpool lads, instantly agreed. He had no great love for Londoners.

'I advise you not to leave' said the dentist. That decided it, George and Patti, John and Cynthia abruptly left. George got into his mini, the lights of passing cars seemed incredibly bright. As they drove off, they saw the dentist get into his car.

'That bastard's following us' John muttered to George.

'Hey, how do we get home?' asked George, feeling as if the car was flying, so smooth did it seem, the car was driving itself at an incredible speed.

'The Ad Lib, go to the Ad Lib.'

That was their regular nightclub haunt, it was expensive enough and exclusive enough to protect them from being surrounded by demented fans.

George found his way slowly through the streets looking for a safe familiar place in what had become a vast, bewildering, strange city. They drove along Regent Street with its shops loaded with expensive goods.

'Let's get out and smash all the windows' giggled Patti, beginning to enjoy the ride.

Cynthia fought to keep control of herself, her mind fluttered from one sight to the next, it was impossible to filter out the world that was bombarding her senses.

George found the club. They got in the lift, a red light on the floor indicator suddenly beamed at them.

'There must be a fucking fire, look at that fucking red light,' John said panic stricken.

The women began screaming. They were trapped in the middle of a fire in the worst possible place, a lift between floors. The doors suddenly opened and they rushed out. They were at the entrance to the club, there was after all no fire. John suddenly thought this was how they described experiences on opium, where everything had a larger than life clarity. He made his way to a seat, the music sounded like music from heaven, he listened, overcome. A singer came over.

'Can I sit next to you?' the singer asked.

'Only if you don't talk', said the shell-shocked superstar.

Cynthia soon suggested they leave.

'Can you still drive?' John asked George. All four seemed to be the only alive people in the place, the rest were curiously unreal, unaware of the great flood of life energy everywhere.

'I'll try', said George.

They drove out from London, south west towards his Esher home, 12 miles away. The car speedo said 10mph but they seemed to be doing more like 1,000. The green suburbs started to appear.

'Let's get out and play football' suggested the bright cheery Patti.

No one else could take it as lightly, they were too over-come. At last George's house came into view. It seemed huge and yet floating on the earth's air like a submarine. John went inside this strangely alive machine, feeling he was steering the ship. He began drawing on scraps of paper writing 'I agree, I agree.' He doodled, fascinated by the fact that a pen could make marks on the marvellously white paper. Next morning the effects of his first trip began to wear off. It took him two months to recover. Cynthia had been terrified, she had seen John in weird hallucinatory ways – as a slimy snake, as a mule with dagger-like teeth who leered mockingly at her. It was not the man she knew and loved.

It was not until August after a spectacular performance at the Hollywood Bowl that they ventured to try the drug again – this time deliberately. For most of 1965 they were on a milder mind-bending drug, cannabis. Bob Dylan had introduced Lennon to the pungent smelling weed that relaxed inhibitions the previous year on their first major American tour. *'Help!'* with its giggling co-stars was largely made while they were stoned. On the surface, at least, the group were moving from success to success. In March '64, John had published his collection of macabre stories and pictures possessed of a mordant wit, it revealed to the critics that a rock-star could also be intelligent. The book gained him a spot on Peter Cook and Dudley Moore's TV comedy show where he read some poems. The critical acclaim took Lennon by surprise, yet from then on he began to seek acceptance by London's avant-garde. In June '65, he published a second book of similar fantastic creations, *A Spaniard in the Works.* The establishment in the form of the recently elected Labour government which had been out of power for 13 years, signalled its approval of 'working class' culture by awarding the group the decoration of Member of the British Empire, MBE. It usually went to distinguished – if minor – civil servants and war heroes. Lennon later told the press that they had a quick puff on a joint in the Palace's lavatory but it was untrue. They were too over-awed. John decided that the Queen really thought she was different from other people, he was genuinely reluctant to accept the medal, but went along with the group.

'How long have you been together now?' the Queen politely asked Paul.

'Oh, many years' said the 23-year-old Paul.

John Lennon in the summer of '65 was putting on weight (his small pot belly embarrassed him), he was drinking a lot, smoking a lot (as were all the Beatles, between them 250 cigarettes a week) eating a lot and copulating a lot – mostly not with his patient, unsuspecting wife, who was still upset that John had not invited her to the Palace. He was more in love with the Beatles than he was with her, she told him, and she tried in vain to persuade him to take a family holiday. He preferred to have the other Beatles around. Ringo was also living on the private estate on St

George's Hill, while George lived just down the road in Esher. Paul was sharing the house of the Asher family and the affections of their teenage actress daughter, Jane.

Yet behind the confident bravura he exuded to the world, John Lennon felt all the insecurities he had had since childhood. The riches were not that easy to earn, it meant he had almost no private life – and at this stage he was still an intensely private person, only really opening up with the other group members, roadies and wives/girl-friends,. There was an early pact that the four would not pursue each other's women, and the greatest rebel of them all had to remind George of this rule when he was very innocently proposing to take Maureen out for a trip.

Outside of this family circle, only young newly liberated women impinged on his consciousness. It would be an over-simplification to say that Lennon was over-sexed, he simply gratified his desires and had, besides, behind the impassive exterior an overwhelming need for love. His songs bear testimonies to what the world would call one-night stands but to a man on a conveyor belt that was moving faster and faster the liaisons were much more, they were above all the raw material for songs, brief snatches of love after the loneliness of single childhood.

'Hey, you've got to hide your love away.
How can I even try
I can never win,
Leaving them, seeing them
in the state I'm in
How could she say to me
Love will find a way?
Gather round all you clowns'

The man with the mask of a clown, the loser, the man sear-ching for love is how Lennon portrays himself. It perfectly co-incided with the hopes and fears of his audience – the vast numbers of newly affluent young who casually cou-pled and uncoupled at parties – celebrating their youth. But youth above all has the ache to find a mate – to create the youth of tomorrow, with the new freedoms that mate could come from anywhere, instead of round the corner, so the search was harder, wider and the sights were set higher. Lennon might have been a married man but he was also still the incurable romantic searching for the per-fect love.

'Although I laugh and I act like a clown
Beneath this mask I am wearing a frown
My tears are falling like rain from the sky
Is it for her or myself that I cry?'

'She's sweeter than all the girls and I've met
quite a few (poetic understatement)
Nobody in all the world can do what she can do'

But in a sign of what has to come later, the lead song for the happy-go-lucky second Beatle film is a cry for help. Like most of Lennon's songs it means exactly what it says because that was his need, to express what he felt, and expressing his feelings had to come in songs because normal means of communicating were almost totally blocked. It had been his strategy for survival as trauma had followed trauma. Stuart Sutcliffe was not the last or first of those closest to him for whom he could not grieve or in fact show any emotion; in his tragic view of life the clown had to laugh as the alternative to crying.

'When I was younger, so much younger than today
I never needed anybody's help in any way
but now those days are gone I'm not so self assured
now I find I've changed my mind
I've opened up the doors.'

John was to look back on this period as his 'fat Elvis period' but to the outside world one pinnacle of success was scaled only to be followed by the surmounting of a higher one still. Analysing pop lyrics for content was still regarded as futile although The Times music critic William Mann had the previous December discovered that the Beatles had used the same chords as Mahler at the close of his work 'Das Lied Von Der Erde'. But then William Mann was one of the few music critics to enthusiastically welcome the *Let It Be* album of later years.

Help! premiered in July to rapturous reviews, the accompanying album shot to No. 1 where it stayed through the summer. In August the Beatles returned to America, to play a more manageable 12 performances in 10 cities. John regarded the record-breaking 65,000 crowd at Shea Stadium as the highspot of the group's career, for many years the show held the record for the highest gross in entertainment history, $304,000. For two nights New York went wild, wild, wild as only New York can; during the performance McCartney had to hurriedly tell John (as far as he could with the deafening noise in the background) to cool it as Lennon whipped the crowd up into a frenzy that in the days of the worship of Dionysus was a prelude to the demented women tearing the god limb from limb – a ritual that satisfied the most atavistic instincts of mankind. The group were taken from the stadium in an armoured car, racing down one way streets at 50 mph, leaving before the encore which never took place, to the refuge of a hotel where they could not move from their rooms as besotted screaming girls fought to touch their idols and receive their magical Midas glow of success. The lines of cripples bore testimony to the godlike status they had assumed, but John the Baptist could not face the ugliness of the deformities – cripples became a code word for any unwanted intruder within the magic circle.

EMI in 1977 produced a wonderful record of this most momentous of tours in *The Beatles at Hollywood Bowl*. It preserves for all time what already seems incredible – that four young men could whip that audience into a totally united, delirious, ecstatic unison where a catch of John's rasping voice could send the women into fresh transports of pleasure manifested in an even higher scream while George in 'Dizzy Miss Lizzy' had the corporate body surging and sighing as responsive as any lover with the lead solo, da-da da-da da-da dah, da-da da-da da-da dah, followed by John flying as he sang 'You make me dizzy Miss Lizzy, with your rock'n'roll.' The screams had become a drug, the power overwhelming, when they eventually had to step off the magical machine there were certain to be withdrawal symptoms.

But John and George were beginning to embark on a different exploration – an interior one. After the Hollywood Bowl concert they went to a party given by young actor Peter Fonda. Many of the guests were on LSD. Fonda kept coming up to the 'tripping' George, John and Ringo saying he knew what it was like to be dead. Roadies Mal Evans and Neil Aspinall were also tripping. It seemed inconceivable to John that anyone could miss the fact they were high as kites. A representative of the British press, Don Short, was there. Neil Aspinall was instructed to get rid of him. Mal Evans went off to play snooker with him – the balls were as big as footballs, to his opponent's astonishment Mal cleared the board in one break, something world champions occasionally manage once or twice in the

course of a year. In the California hills the night air spark-
led with the light of the stars – it had always been the place
where America took everything to the limits. John Lennon
believed in plunging in headfirst and thinking about the
consequences later. He was about to take the world with
him into a new fantasy.

As the year came to its end, a breakthrough in the
cheery, foot stomping, party times recordings occurred. LP
number six, *Rubber Soul,* had some perfectly beautiful
songs, an Indian sitar for 'Norwegian Wood' and the
haunting 'In My Life', a song to match Paul McCartney's
'Yesterday' from the *Help!* album. As always, the
tremendous rivalry for leadership of the group, begun in
Hamburg, continued. Lennon and McCartney were at
once best buddies, collaborators, rivals for women, com-
petitors for attention and a lyricist and musician who could
swop roles. They made other famous partnerships seem
simple, so labyrinthine were their connections and also
their differences. But the songs tumbled out one after the
other. At the same time as *Rubber Soul* came the single
'Day Tripper' whose drug hints were at this time completely lost on an innocent, adoring public and establishment. It was a Beatle private joke, they felt invulnerable.
While the togetherness the three 'Irish' musicians had
developed in Hamburg manifested itself in beguiling,
eerily perfect harmonies. McCartney had always simply
wanted to fill the world with music, this did not mean
however that he was inferior in his lyrics. Lennon was
more word orientated, his overwhelming need was
expression and the person who showed him the way was
Bob Dylan on 'Mr Tamborine Man'. 'Yesterday' was written and performed almost solely by McCartney. However,
simply the fact that Lennon was there to criticise if McCartney went off-beam prevented the song descending into
mawkishness. 'Nowhere Man' was a craftsman's song, as
John Lennon sat around the house musing to himself
between tours.

> 'Doesn't have a point of view
> knows not where he's going to
> Isn't he a bit like you and me?
> Nowhere Man, the world is at your command'

The fêted rock star dwelt on the power he had, the question was what he was going to do with it. But there were
the odd moments of satisfaction, in thinly veiled lyrics he

told of an encounter that had to be suitably remembered and perpetuated. The girl in the song probably to this day plays the record every week, so sweet was the evocation he achieved with George's nascent abilities on the sitar hinting of the experimentation and direction that were to come.

'We talked until two
and then she said
'It's time for bed'.

After many many takes he had got it. 'Norwegian Wood' The bitter sweetness of love gained and gone. Being a rock star had its compensations. They are all through *Rubber Soul*, a harmonisation that speaks of a band perfectly together – for although they liked afterwards to complain of the touring it had forged them into a unit so that they could read each other perfectly, only they had experienced the adulation of the whole world and no-one would know the flood of power that released in each. John Lennon, Nowhere Man, continued to ponder what he could do with this power.

◀ The film 'A Hard Day's Night' had girls screaming in the American cinemas as soon as the fab four appeared.

13 'We're More Popular Now Than Jesus'

An 8-city tour of Britain in December '65 was living proof that Beatlemania continued unabated, but the problem was that the cinemas and theatres only held a maximum of 2,500-4,000 people. It was simply not economic for the group to tour their own country any more. At the time, they thought the money was flooding in – and so it was, but EMI kept most of it. They were on 2d (one cent) royalties, twice what they had originally signed for when they recorded 'Love Me Do', but still a derisory percentage of the retail price of their records. It does much to understand the acrimony that was to follow if it is realised that between 1962 and 1970 the Beatles' record sales were worth £17 million or in today's money £60 million ($110 million) yet the four members of the group were only worth in total £1 million (£5 million – $9 million) in 1968. In raising their take to two pence a record EMI had signed them on for five more years. The year after this contract was renegotiated (in 1967) 30% of EMI's profits came from the Beatles, and EMI in its turn completely dominated the record market taking an unprecedented 40% share. Put another way, one in eight of all records sold in Britain in 1968 were Beatles records. Brian Epstein, always scrupulously fair, had allowed the Beatles to be treated like any other group whereas he was managing a social phenomenon. The Abbey Road studios today are an eloquent testimony to the transformation the Beatles wrought for EMI. Once inside the 'English country home' entrance you realise you are in a large corporation's nerve centre with commissionaires and receptionists leafing through long lists of internal 'phone numbers. On the notice board are newsletters with 'Pension Fund News' – living proof that some have yet to receive their largesse from the golden bonanza that came out of one artist's inspiration. Once inside the building the Beatles were treated just like any other corporation employees – their fellow executives were glad to note they had no 'side' to them – they came just to do a job of work. Down winding corridors lay the Number One and Number Two studios, as large as school gymnasiums and with a similar air of having seen much strenuous activity, equipment left where it had last been used. Old mikes from the days the Beatles recorded lie forlornly at the sides of the studio floor – for the studios have hardly changed in the last 20 years and have the peculiar 'faded' air that today hangs over so many British companies. Now, anyone can use the studios, while EMI waits forlornly for another Beatles group to arise. They never will.

Yet in this corporate rather ramshackle structure, the group put together its masterpieces. Their memory is revered by those who were priviledged to be there at a time 'when we were all together, all sharing in the excitement they were creating with hundreds of fans screaming outside the doors'. Today 'normality' has returned, it is just a place of work, fearful of what the recession in the music business will bring.

What Brian Epstein really cared about above all was presentation and style. Beatlemania was becoming transmuted into what was chic and trendy, it fitted in with the times as skirt lengths shortened, hair lengthened and the merry-go-round of partying became more frenetic in a London that was beginning to get known as the place to be for anyone connected with the arts. Epstein let it be known that unlike those scruffs 'The Rolling Stones', the Beatles washed their hair every day, were always immaculate in their stage clothes and ever more full mops. They were scrubbed, cheerful and he was careful to project – harmless. The Stones in contrast were the sort of group who gave rock music a bad name – rebellious tough guys blatantly inviting the all too willing women to spend the night together. For John Lennon, the rebel and man with a chip on his shoulder, all this hurt terribly. The Epstein mould fitted uneasily and yet Epstein was the one person who could cower Lennon with his icy manner. He knew Lennon knew about his 'after dark' side, but then so did he know about Lennon. It was Epstein's problem that he could never reconcile the public persona – drenched in expensive toilet water and looking perpetually as if he had just stepped out of a bath – with the private side that sought momentary comfort from rough trade pick-ups who occasionally would beat him up. It was a very English hang-up – only in his case magnified.

During the first half of the year the frenetic pace slowed. John Lennon had time to enjoy the fruits of success, he was becoming incredibly generous, feeling at once guilty at having so much money and at the same time having no trouble in spending it. Cynthia worried that their food bill came to £120 a month (£600 − $1,100 today), but John poured money into the house which had cost £30,000 and to which he added another £30,000 of improvements, hiring contractors who turned every room into a showcase, while he and Cynthia and Julian lived in a room at the back where glass sliding doors opened out over a superb view of the rolling Surrey Downs from the hilltop position. The effects of LSD that he had experimented with the previous year, were now investigated with more thoroughness, he would sit for hours at a time gazing into the distance, not speaking to a wife he never rowed with but who was increasingly simply not on his wavelength. The world envied the Beatles their sudden wealth and simply thought they were happy.

But for John Lennon, writing music was his reason for existence, so he wrote. The group now had as much time as they wanted in the studios and they used the freedom it gave them well. The early songs had been simple two-track recordings, one track recording the music, the other the vocal. Now two-track grew to four-track and then to eight. George Martin, their producer, could control the level of each instrument, he created a demand for stereo simply by playing around with how he put the music and words down, switching a voice from one speaker to another, putting drums on one side, lead guitar on the other. It was not true stereo effect, it was playing around with the speakers, but it was light years ahead of what everyone else was doing. The Beatles increasingly took control of the sessions.

George Martin simply fulfilled their need for someone with a musician's training to achieve what they heard in their heads. Even the cover design for the record was left in their hands, for their August release − Revolver − they used Klaus Voorman, who they knew from Hamburg, he had been one of Astrid Kircherr's 'exi' boyfriends before she took up with Stuart Sutcliffe. Klaus had by this time moved to London to play as a member of Manfred Mann's group. However it was his artistic talents and perception they were interested in. It was Astrid Kircherr who had persuaded Stuart Sutcliffe to adopt a 'French cut' hairstyle, to wear black leather and collarless jackets and he in turn had persuaded the others, John Lennon held onto his older rocker image longer than Paul and George. Pete Best – the handsomest – had refused to change. The image Klaus Voorman now saw is the most explicit reference the group had yet given that they were entering a 'mind-expanding' phase. As if in an Hieronymus Bosch painting the various members of the Beatles clamber through their by now tangled locks – they are entering the 'beautiful people' stage.

The new single of June – 'Paperback Writer'/'Rain' – gives the announcement of the new direction.

> 'Can you hear me that when it rains and shines it's just a state of mind?'

Returning from the studios at Abbey Road, Lennon in a very stoned state was looking for a distinctive ending to the 'Rain' recording in his own home studio. He played the tape backwards, liked it and finished the record with it. No one demurred – experimentation had begun to be welcomed. Strange clubs were opening like The Electric Garden in London's Covent Garden where a group of art students from North London called The Pink Floyd were about to play in the cavernous depths of an old warehouse. The fabulous four were to be found at the more exclusive and chic clubs like Sibylla's and Blases, but word spread quickly that new movements in music were afoot. John, always the fastest to extract the mood of the hour out of the air, experimented feverishly. He wanted to stay out there in front.

The acid trips were producing a mystical bent to his song lyrics – he had, he was to discover, always been that way inclined. Now the closet poet came right out with his visions which the mass market found utterly incomprehensible. The music though they could respond to. For 'Tomorrow Never Knows' on *Revolver* he wanted the sound of a thousand monks chanting to back up lyrics taken from the Tibetan Book of the Dead:

> 'Turn off your mind relax and float down-stream
> it is not dying, it is not dying
> Lay down all thought surrender to the void
> it is shining, it is shining'

The void was a Buddhist concept, which had become synonymous with surrendering to the ultra powerful effects of LSD, the illuminations were often religious as can be seen in 'And Your Bird Can Sing'. He is vying in competition with another 'voyager' to see who can get 'there' first

'You say you've seen seven wonders
And your bird is green
But you can't see me
When your prize possessions start to wear you down
Look in my direction
I'll be round'

The bird as symbol of the spirit is universal but for a pop singer to use such imagery was too much for the pop critics, they wrote that Lennon's lyrics had become impenetrable. The Beatles and in particular John Lennon were off and away, scuttling for the new high ground while the record engineers and producer George Martin simply did as they were asked. 'She Said She Said' talked about the first deliberate LSD trip in California the previous year when he had got into his own childhood which, he had been astonished to find, had been quite alright. He happily remembered playing in the woods and parks of Woolton, in places like Strawberry Field.

'She said you don't understand what I said
I said no no no you're wrong, when I was a boy
everything was right, everything was right.
She said I know what it's like to be dead
I know what it is to be sad'.

Lennon was beginning to rediscover what he had had; an infinite capacity when young for day dreaming. And the ever-faster roller coaster of touring had found its antidote, just as the tensions between the group had begun to surface:

'Please don't spoil my day, I'm miles away
And after all, I'm only sleeping
Keeping an eye on the world going by my window'.

The growing bands of pot smokers recognised the imagery on 'Tomorrow Never Knows', the Beatles were leading them down new paths and they happily followed the pied piper. London swung, op art dresses slashed to near the thighs saw the young women blossom out as had never happened before. The pill promised emancipation from fear of pregnancy although not many women were actually using it. But the old inhibtions and morals crumbled as it became screamingly obvious to women that they wanted and enjoyed sex.

In America in August there were any number of young women prepared to demonstrate that. As a quipster joked after one Shea Stadium Show, 'there wasn't a dry seat in the house'. Bob Wooler's long-ago perceived orgasm on stage had progressed to a vast jelly-like organism that quivered in screaming ecstasy as a band in its centre harmonised, exhorted and colonised its every individual part. To the Beatles it was madness, one night the fans got around the getaway car and proceeded to pile on top of it, the bodies getting higher and higher in a fever pitch until the limosine's roof collapsed. Fortunately, it was a decoy. John was asked if he was worried about the damage.

'No', he laconically replied, 'it's not our car'.

But in the generated hysteria they each became prey to irrational fears. Earlier in the year Lennon had given a lengthy rambling interview to Maureen Cleave who was the first national journalist to travel up to Liverpool to speak to the new group called the Beatles. In the interview Lennon was characteristically acerbic and manic, predicting the imminent demise of Christianity and – wearing his John the Baptist hat – saying that 'The Beatles are more popular that Jesus now'. Just prior to the greatest moneyspinning tour of them all, a crusade began after *Disc* magazine blew the remark up into a main headline. At the end of July Beatles records were being ceremoniously burnt across small town America. Lennon was shocked, it was the physical burning that offended him, verbal violence, he realised, turned very quickly in America into the real thing. Brian persuaded him to eat his words and say he hadn't really meant that. Even though he had. He was nursing messianic ambitions now, visions garnered on his frequent trips. His home was deluged by books about Jesus and Christianity and he refined his theory that there had been many Jesuses and what their message was. 'It hurts people to hear the truth', he bitterly observed, 'and it's not nice to get bitten when you say it'.

In his fears he waited for some lunatic with a gun to appear. The first death threat had been in Paris in '64. Some nut had sent a note saying he would be shot at 9 o'clock. A jittery group played through the appointed hour, Jeanne Dixon had predicted their plane on an American tour would crash, roadie Mal Evans even made a will, fellow groups refused to travel with the Beatles. It is alleged that the plane crashed two years later killing all on board. But prior to the American tour they had played Hamburg at the Ernst Merch Halle and been received like long lost sons. John was re-united with Bettina the bar maid and took in the whole sleazy world of the Reeperbahn again. 'Don't listen to our music, it's gone right off' he apologised to his old friends. The gig, as was customary, was drowned out. The Germans went wildly and grossly emotional – something they do when saying good-bye to old friends. Lennon curiously felt as though he had returned home. In Tokyo there were no riots, it would have been a severe loss of face for the organisers but in Manila, capital of the Philippines, they decided to ignore an invitation from the President's wife to a reception. As they left, apologies unaccepted, there was no police guard, they were kicked and punched and jeered as they ran for the plane. Brian Epstein had to pay out £7,000 (£35,000 – $65,000) in tax money to the government collector on the plane before being allowed to fly out. The pressures grew and grew, particularly for Epstein who, in San Francisco at the very last Beatle concert on August 29th, stood dejectedly by as the group played itself out of live performance. He could often be observed with tears coursing down his cheeks as he watched his dream in action, the dream he had put his heart and soul into creating. Back at the hotel a boyfriend robbed him of his case at knifepoint. He had to let it go, but inside were pictures and papers that would blow his respectable front and nice guy image forever. The police were called in and got the boyfriend but the incident played on his mind. The next month he took a large over-dose of pills in a suicide attempt, but was rushed to hospital in time to save him.

The Beatles, after years of living in each other's pockets, came back from touring to a life of individuals. The adjustment was hard to make. John Lennon was invited by the by now rich and famous director Dick Lester to star in a film as Private Gripweed. It was called 'How I Won the War', an obscure anti-war movie in which Private Gripweed shorn of his flowing locks and wearing steel rimmed 'National Health' glasses gave a credible performance. Right from 1965, he had been for speaking out against the rapidly escalating Vietnam War, but Brian Epstein had persuaded him to keep his mouth shut – more or less. The only way he could achieve this was by being permanently stoned on drink and drugs. The humiliations became more goading – the politician's wife who threatened to reveal all if the group weren't woken up to meet her. The hopeless cripples in ever more profusion whose mothers demanded these incarnations of a Lennon nightmare be kissed. No one ever did reveal the incessant stream of milling girls being laid all round the group's besieged hotel rooms, it was ancient Rome and the young Emperors were sated and fêted as only that civilisation could have done.

Spain was a release. By himself with Cynthia, Lennon had time to think on the interminable periods between takes. A mysterious event occurred at about the time that Lennon was to write his greatest song. He had rented an old voluminous villa which used to be a convent. Joined by Ringo and wife Maureen they decided to hold a party for the film crew and actors to liven up the rather spooky atmosphere of the long empty property. Just as the party was getting underway, a terrible storm raged as can happen in Spain very suddenly. The electricity failed but a huge supply of candles was quickly distributed and with these burning from every nook and cranny the hall became transformed into a warm welcoming place. Someone began to sing and immediately everyone there, standing in their own little groups, joined in. For half an hour they sang as if powered by a choir of angels – as if the spirits of the nuns were there – it was sublime, out of this world. As though on cue, the lights came back on, the singing ceased. It was a religious experience that sent John Lennon's mind casting back to the last time he had had such feelings – as a youngster wandering through the woods that came to the back of Mimi's house, the grounds of Strawberry Field. He began writing, seeking to pin down that elusive other-worldly quality he had just experienced again.

Back in London he found a host of invitations to private views at art galleries. He began going two or three times a week, London was becoming a hive of artistic activity – the mini skirts had ushered in a peacock era for both men and women. Patti Boyd, George's live-in lover, led the way in beads, gypsy skirts, kaftans, shorter and shorter skirts, free flowing long hair; the King's Road became continental, the crowds promenaded up and down admiring each other's displays of finery. Tourists flooded in to see what *Time* magazine had christened swinging London. Everywhere arts clubs, galleries, bistros, magazines, boutiques, unisex hair salons, discos and clubs opened their doors to the newly affluent young determined to enjoy themselves while faraway in America the youth heard the increasing rumbles of a war that was sucking away the men through the hated draft. To avoid it became the objective of the college kids particularly.

One invitation invited Lennon to John Dunbar's art gallery, Indica; he was a friend and the former husband of Marianne Faithful. A show was being presented called 'Unfinished Paintings and Objects by Yoko Ono'. John's interest was taken by the announcement that there would be a woman in a bag, it sounded like the latest sex quirk in an underground scene where just about anything now seemed to go. John thought it would be a happening – a New York concept where the audience and the performers became intermingled and things were expected to 'happen' in the ensuing remixing of the elements. It was the night before the event. There were a couple of arty types lying around on the floor. An apple was offered for sale, price £200. That struck Lennon as funny. There was a ladder leading up to a canvas on the roof. Lennon seeing very little else to do climbed up the ladder which was near the entrance. He took hold of a small magnifying glass hanging at a corner of the canvas and looked for the message. It said simply 'yes'. He felt relieved.

John Dunbar had a quick word with Yoko Ono, explaining he was an immensely rich and powerful Beatle, then introduced her to the great man. The shy Yoko handed John a card which said 'breathe', John good-humouredly panted and left, rather disappointed there had been no sexual happening in black bags. He could hardly have known that was to come much later. Before that there was to be the summer of love.

◀ John Lennon was later to call it his 'fat Elvis stage'. As the success grew,
he became more insecure, and troubled.

14 The Summer of Love

Coming events cast their shadow before. There were very
early signs that 1967 was going to be different – very
different – from all that had gone before. For London. For
the world. For the Beatles. For John Lennon.

By the year's fantastic end he would have guaranteed
his financial security for life – and this was always his most
pressing preoccupation for reasons that we will explore
when he steps off the bandwagon he had created and
starts to come face to face with what made him run so hard.
In the course of the year all the seeds were sown for his
future work. In retrospect the signs are clear indeed, at the
time nothing was anything like as clear cut. That was the
magic of the year – everything was in a state of flux
beneath a calm, ever complacent, surface. The seeds that
were planted would grow luxuriantly – in fact their
growths are today inextricably woven into our lives – but at
the time they were tossed carelessly and effortlessly where
they would fall. It seemed natural in the swirling cavalcade
that the Beatles first attached themselves to and by the
year's end had managed to take over. 1967 was the Summer of Love and the year of the Magical Mystery Tour.

A decade and a half later is is difficult to conjure up even
in the imagination the atmosphere of London as the year
opened. On the surface the war had been decently laid to
rest and an unprecedented prosperity had come to the
land. No one had consciously tried to alter their lives to
take in this new situation – change is not actively welcomed in England and takes place mostly unremarked, it is
a country which prides itself on continuity and its 1,000
years of uninterrupted rule (the Civil War having been
well forgotten). The ravages and traumas of the Second
World War had as we say been decently buried in a quiet
corner of the nation's subconscious. Employment was at a
peak with a little over half a million unemployed which
caused some concern, but not much. The Labour govern-

ment had been returned a few months before with a massive majority and people were expecting they would be able to get on with their own lives with any changes from Harold Wilson's white-hot technological revolution being to their benefit. Yet at the same time that experimentation was welcome, no one believed that the changes would affect them personally. What is significant is that change was going to be allowed to happen, even if its import was dimly understood.

It is Friday night, January 1967. Tottenham Court Road is becoming quieter as the cinemas send their respectably dressed patrons home. *Who's Afraid of Virginia Wolf?* with Elizabeth Taylor and Richard Burton is still playing to full houses. The young men in the street are mostly in their weekend suits while their wives and girlfriends totter along on high heels suitably wrapped up in heavy – though not glamorous – coats. Proceeding along the road in the direction of the newly built GPO Tower, which rises like a space gantry to 600 feet, you come across an extraordinary sight: a crowd of several hundred young people are quietly filing into a door which leads down into a cavernous basement. They look like a crowd of film extras (in fact some are actors with Peter Brooke) and are garbed in gypsy dress. Trailing furs and bells, floppy jeans leading the eye away from outrageously long hair, the women dressed as if from a fairy tale, long dresses, vibrant colours, silks and laces much in evidence, eyes heavily made up, hair long and free instead of being tightly coiffeured.

You have stumbled upon UFO – a phenomenon extraordinary even by today's standards and at that time incomprehensible to a very conformist society. Downstairs the women smile at everyone and always accept an invitation to dance. Young men strip off to the waist and dance all night with a tribal abandon to the other worldly pounding sounds of groups called The Pink Floyd and The Soft Machine. As dawn breaks and the hundreds of revellers flow out into the street, Suzy Creamcheese whispers seductively over the loudspeaker system suggesting that people, 'Take a trip into the countryside'. Most extraordinary of all – for 1967 was a violent era whatever rosily coloured memory may say – there have been no fights all night, only an incense laden atmosphere of sheer enjoyment. It is as though there is a shared secret among the people present, as indeed there is.

In February that year the Beatles released one of the

most evocative and elusive songs they were ever to make. 'Strawberry Fields Forever'. The lyrics John Lennon had written were both hauntingly distant and immediately present, while the music rippled and cascaded dazzling with its colour and richness. Years later, after the critics had interviewed the lyric writer and explored his background more fully, it would be possible to say that this was a brilliant evocation of John Lennon's childhood. At the time the wonderland peopled by strange phantoms, an ever present land that co-existed alongside the everyday, could only fascinate with an unexplained power.

The double 'A' side single had Paul McCartney singing about 'Penny Lane', accompanied by piccolo trumpet. He, too, under the influence of the LSD had begun re-exploring his early years. It was the most accomplished single the Beatles ever released. Yet it was the first single in 4 years to not achieve the No. 1 spot in Britain, sticking obstinately at No. 2.

Almost as much time was spent on Lennon's best ever song – with its brilliant marriage of word and music – as had previously been expended on complete LPs. Both Lennon and McCartney lavished attention on their productions. Plans for a new album at the end of '66 were abandoned. Perfectionism was all. Lennon after playing around with many versions of 'Strawberry Fields', strumming to Paul who would then respond, decided there were two different versions he liked. One had driving guitars, the other orchestral backing.

George Martin, who was more attuned to McCartney's professional composer's attributes, was told peremptorily by Lennon that he wanted the first half of the guitar version and the second part of orchestral version.

'It's not possible', said Martin, 'they have different tempos for a start.'

'You solve it,' said Lennon, the least technical of the four, and now quite sure who was in control. Martin had been proved wrong before, he had the disadvantage of being a trained musician. Even Dylan found the Beatles' chords outrageous. Lennon, Martin acknowledged, was a 'true original'. He speeded up the first tape, slowed down the second. Where John came in again with

'Let me take you down
cos I'm going to . . .'

he made the join as near inaudible as makes no difference.

The strange slowed down voice of Lennon and the haunting flute added to the 'other dimensional' effect of the
record. It had come miraculously right. Lennon at the
height of his LSD experimentations went home happy.

John Lennon's wife Cynthia saw the period rather differently. Her husband, who was always his own man, had
seemed to suddenly tire of a life that was becoming a
gilded cage. The previous year he had been content to
write and compose, to socialise with the other Beatles, to
buy an endless succession of gadgets which he and his
next door neighbour Ringo Starr would play with and
quickly forget. Undoubtedly the art school rebel should
never have moved into the exclusive St George's Hill
estate in the first place. The superbly equipped new
houses looked out from their hill over the rolling downs of
the English green belt, an area around London where
building is strictly controlled. The gardens were suitably
large, the roads private and protected by a gateman but
their neighbours were naturally uncommunicative.

As 1967 broke Cynthia was mystified. To her they had
everything. A palatial home, their Beatle friends nearby, it
was an extended family which wanted for nothing. For a
girl from the right side of the water in Liverpool who had
found herself pregnant while on the dole it was a fairy tale
ending. So it seemed to the world as well, the dream of
affluence come true, proof that talent could carry even
those from the most ordinary of backgrounds into the privileged world and comforts of the élite.

Yet for John Lennon it was not enough. The money he
possessed did not bring the degree of respect he expected.
He was besides unclear of whose respect he really sought
– a problem he was to spend many more years attempting
to solve. What is worth noting at this stage in his development – he was 26 – is that he was prepared to live among
stockbrokers and that in spite of having been in London
since first hitting the pop charts he was still an outsider living well out from the capital among strangers. John was
shrewd and his ambitions had yet to be fully achieved. Far
from being the carefree happy troubadour he projected to
the world, he was actually prepared to sacrifice almost
anything at the altar of success. What he saw as success is
what distinguished him from almost anyone else – he
wanted to change the course of the world. He knew himself to be an artist of genius yet received small confirmation of this from the intellectual circles he actually wished

to be accepted by. Most writers in the weekly magazines and the unique British Sunday 'quality' press regarded the Beatles still as the objects of teenage girls' wishful dreams with nothing exceptional to say.

There was one area of intellectual ferment in the capital that did attract John Lennon. The London Underground. It communicated in the pages of a newspaper called *International Times* – any resemblance to the London *Times* extended no further than the title. Lennon soon sent along a donation of £1,000 to aid the cause.

The name Underground aptly describes the invisible web of influence that spread rapidly through the capital. There appeared to be an instant solution to the world's ills. John Lennon, never a man slow to adopt a cause, had become a fervent believer in LSD as the Vietnam War rumbled on ominously thousands of miles away. Its reverberations stirred Lennon's generation's memory of, while very young, growing up in bombed streets. Few more so than the 'orphaned' Lennon, child of one of the many wartime marriages when only today mattered and who felt in the grip of evil forces beyond his control.

'Strawberry Fields Forever' competed on the juke boxes and radio waves with a sudden explosion of new and strange sounds. Jimi Hendrix with his mocking 'Hey Joe'

'Hey Joe where you gonna go
where you gonna run with that gun in your hand?'

and the raunchy sophistication of the Rolling Stones.

Things are different today
I hear everybody say
the pursuit of happiness
is just a bore
so she took an overdose
no more feeling so morose
no more running for the shelter
of her mother's little helper.'

As the new consciousness swept over Britain and America, the Beatles retired into the Abbey Road recording studios where they logged an astonishing 1600 hours putting down the tracks of their next album. (Their first album had been recorded in a day, change in the music industry was taking place at a breakneck speed as it gave the first hints of becoming a multi-million dollar business).

Home life for John Lennon was becoming increasingly

bizarre. Now when he returned home it was not to play the role of husband, instead he brought back crowds of strangers from whatever club, flat or pub he had been in. These strangers were invariably glassy-eyed and their only desire seemed to be to smoke, indulge in their private fantasies and finally to 'crash' on the plush carpet. In the morning they would expect to be fed before leaving without having offered to help in clearing up the inevitable debris. Cynthia obliged with the aid of the ever helpful Dot who she had known since her student days in Liverpool. Cynthia had nothing in common with these London people and no wish to get to know them. For her husband it was different.

The dedicated artist who was never far from the surface pounced on the new lifestyle and mood, it expressed all his old rebelliousness which had been so assiduously covered up by Brian Epstein as he groomed the Beatles for stardom. Though it has been said that the Beatles and the Rolling Stones led the youth culture it was vehemently denied by the groups. Later in the year at Mick Jagger's drug trial he was to carefully disclaim any responsibility for his fans. Lennon played on a mocking Stones' record to the judge, 'We Love You'. The judge had no doubts that Jagger had a following and that he shaped the fans' behaviour. Lennon, as we will explore, quite certainly aimed to influence, in subtle yet highly effective ways, he had a strategy which was applied with consummate artistry, and if the message was beautifully presented it was a message nonetheless. However, at this crucial point in time it is more accurate to say that the Beatles were making the transition from a provincial pop group with a worldwide following – inspired by their projected ingenuousness which had a basis of truth. They were learning the required attitudes of their peer group – the London scene – and none sought more enthusiastically than John Lennon to gain acceptance by what he saw as the new emerging movement. He knew besides that this would be the market of the future, the Beatles needed to change direction commercially as well as artistically if they were to stay on top. Lennon, as cannot be stressed too often, had much greater ideas than merely surviving. He had started the group, and he was determined to lead them in a new direction, one that fitted his own personality and would allow him to use his own voice. In the words of the time he now wanted to let it all hang out. This was a deeply personal need and it also fitted the mood of the times exactly. The world was at last prepared to face some more bizarre pictures of itself. The strain engendered by the group presenting itself as happy fun-loving mop tops had created a mood of tension. In 1967 this tension proved helpful in powering their creative output, in fact the energy released was overwhelming.

June 1, 1967, is arguably the most important landmark in the history of pop music. The rock'n'roll era commenced with 'Rock Around the Clock', with its opening up of the whole world of African tribal music and the unfettered emotion that went with it. *Sergeant Pepper's Lonely Hearts Club Band* was a record which came exactly at the right moment.

Even if it had not been released, the summer of '67 would still have been bizarre by any standards. But its release lit the powder keg that propelled pop into a whole philosophy and way of life. From now on it was a chal-lenge, the vanguard of a movement for change.

The Beatles had total creative control with the new record, and this included the cover design. Little more than a year previously their record producer, George Martin, was still only an employee of EMI, drawing a straight sal-ary with no royalties, while the Beatles were to that orga-nisation just another pop group, even if a spectacularly profitable one. The wise heads in the company daily waited for the bubble to burst, as all the other pop bubbles had burst. What they had left out of their calculations was the sheer drive of the Beatles, Lennon in particular had to achieve greater and greater success. Why he did not know, what it could give him he had not analysed but he knew he was only really now exploring his talent. The voice he had found still beguiles our perception of the world today.

Sergeant Pepper's Lonely Hearts Club Band was Paul McCartney's concept and inspiration, he in turn was influenced by the acid rock coming out of California, espe-cially the Beach Boys' *Pet Sounds*. Lennon, however, wrote more of the song lyrics than Paul. Many of these are about loneliness – Is it worrying to be alone? – but the record is suffused with an optimism in the future that perfectly reflected the mood of the summer that early June. The 'hangers on' who had repelled Cynthia Lennon were also responsible for wafting John Lennon on a cloud of mari-juana smoke into the preoccupations of youth. The 'vibes' were almost palpable and besides the airwaves were being besieged by the broadcasts of pirate radio stations with a seditionary message. So although the BBC banned the playing of 'A Day in the Life' which the Beatles unconvincingly argued was not about drug taking, the music was still everywhere.

Woke up, got out of bed
dragged a comb across my head
found my way downstairs and had a cup
and looking up I noticed I was late.
Found my coat and grabbed my hat
made the bus in seconds flat
found my way upstairs and had a smoke
and somebody spoke and I went into a dream . . .

The middle part of the song lyrics was supplied by McCartney from a work in progress, it uncannily matched the mood of Lennon's first draft. It was his archetypal theme, the worlds of the imagination, the daydream, where he had lived so much of childhood, only now he wanted to take the whole world there. And it seemed that anyone under 35 was prepared to follow.

Pop record covers up to this time had been merely considered protection for the record inside. But for *Sergeant Pepper's Lonely Hearts Club Band* the Beatles took just as much trouble with the cover image as with the music. A collage of pictures showed more than 50 seminal influences upon them, and by inference their audience. Significantly, among the stars from Hollywood's period of worldwide domination, there were four Indian saints pictured – but that was next year, a very long time in 1967. It is also well worth noting the pride of place given to the Rolling Stones, for they lived in each other's pockets. The harsher, more 'black' music the Stones favoured was soon to find its way into the Beatles' music.

The mood created by playing *Sergeant Pepper's Lonely Hearts Club Band* is one of relaxation. It is designed to end the hectic night out with a quiet smoke as dawn breaks through the window and the loving couple make their intoxicated way to bed and dreams. It was how the Beatles relaxed and it had temporarily solved the tensions and stresses, the moods and fears, brought on by the frenetic years of touring. For John Lennon in particular it seemed the answer to the discordancies he was only too well aware of inside himself. Creating beautiful music was one outlet, smoking another. But in the music lyrics a further persona has been created who is hinted at and, as was the way with

Lennon, he would soon be revealed completely.

The banned 'Day in the Life' was the most dazzling of a dazzling collection of songs and music. Part of it ironically describes the death crash of a brewery heir high on LSD. The sardonic writer in John Lennon gives him the distance to see the futility of it all, and to see the contradictions in the way the privileged élite in England were hurling themselves into the revolutionary lifestyle the Beatles appeared to be condoning. It was a temporary phase, as people were to soon realise, but at the time it appeared that all the old barriers in English social life were crashing down, the divisions between the classes, the divisions between the sexes (there was probably never an easier time to find women eager to comfort their men – or acquaintances) and as so often happens it was the attitude co-inciding with the means given by the pill.

The austerities of the war – and with it the pronounced emphasis on duty and obligations – were being swept away as swinging London was born. While in San Francisco the great 'acid rock' bands like Jefferson Airplane, Country Joe and the Fish and The Grateful Dead were also taking off. All the currents came together. A new affluence for the young. Women's liberation from the fear of pregnancy. The rumbling reality of a new war growing all the time in far off Vietnam. The old, the young decided, had to yield to the new. In Britain this meant shaking off the stiff imperial attitude as the last colonies were granted independence. In its place came a new imperialism, a cultural one. Britain was briefly a powerhouse of a new philosophy, and the astonishingly subtle Lennon was determined to be the first spokesman.

He was to later feel the need for a partner in his grand vision. For the moment he was content to let the more commercially acceptable music and words of Paul McCartney provide the vehicle for his own ambitions which were evolving at a speed that frightened the rest of the group and the establishment which still appeared to smile benignly on the mop heads. What follows will show that John Lennon was well aware of what he was manipulating, he had found his cause. It is also worth nothing that he had already met and kept in contact with Yoko Ono, though it is almost certain that it was a relationship of mental rapport and followed the only path that John Lennon knew. Yoko as the relentless pursuer, and he the star, who backed one of her art shows 'Yoko plus Me'. Many times this strange woman in black came to his Weybridge house and found no audience. To John Lennon it was merely a dabble in the avant garde world, a harmless diversion.

After Yoko had met him for the second time at a gallery cocktail party for Claes Oldenbürg, she had gone to him like many in the underground for 'support'. As she explained, conceptual artists like her did not get very much money from an uncomprehending public. Her film Yoko No. 4, showing 365 bottoms had caught the mood of the capital and established her name, she sent Lennon her book *Grapefruit*, which had been published in 1964. It was made up of zen-like sayings and instructions. Its innate contradictions appealed to the author of *In His Own Write* and *A Spaniard in the Works*. Yoko, continuing the campaign, one night stepped into the car with John and Cynthia after they had attended a meditation meeting. Cynthia for some reason immediately thought the game was up, John had found an intellectual equal. No such thought had yet occurred to the bored Lennon, he was well used to being pursued relentlessly. When Yoko called at the house in vain she left calling cards saying 'Watch all the lights until dawn' or 'Dance' or 'Breathe'. Eventually Yoko had a backer for her show. An intrigued but puzzled backer. For a woman who had tried to commit suicide and was obsessively devoted to her art it was all the encouragement she needed. Lennon would provide the launching pad for her art. Pure and simple. The telephone operator who had given her his private number had made the link that was to reverberate around the world.

◄ The woods of Strawberry Field children's home ran up to near the back of Aunt Mimi's house, it was his spiritual home while young, here was one place he could be himself.

15 'If You're Lonely You Can Talk To Me'

The finale of the *Sergeant Pepper's Lonely Hearts Club Band* album was a true spectacular. Into the confines of the Abbey Road studio were packed an orchestra, its conductor wearing a red nose, Mick Jagger wearing a party hat just like everyone else, and presiding over the proceedings the peacock clad Beatles. George Martin had passed on to the orchestra the requirements – they were to start very softly on *pianissimo* and progress – each at his own pace – to *fortissimo*, a sound blasting away the limitations of the physical world. They were cued in by cellos and violas echoing John's voice as he intoned, 'I'd love to turn you on.' As with everything else on the album, the climax went splendidly. Then, just after the album was released the Beatles participated in a worldwide satellite link-up in which some of 'All you need is love' was recorded live before the people of the world. It seemed John Lennon could do no wrong as the song became the anthem for the world's youth. In America where the inroads of the draft worried the young, the Beatles were elevated to the position of leaders – and perhaps saviours. The juxtaposition of a meaningless death in Asian jungles and the wondrous vistas opened up in Pepperland struck a deep chord. They seemed equally real alternatives, as in so many other wars the presence of violent death brought out the counter response of affirmation of life.

But as the summer turned to autumn and then to winter, the original clear vision became clouded as people began to work out how they could reach 'there.' The proffered solution from the Beatles was 'a magical mystery tour' – Paul McCartney led the group in producing their own film. It had flashes of originality but was well ahead of its time and left the critics bemused. A national showing on NBC was cancelled on the strength of the universal panning given by the critics. John's contribution to the concept of the film and also its accompanying music was small in quantity. But he came up with 'I Am The Walrus', a brilliantly original piece of surrealism that appeared to mock the straight world from some distant vantage point. The first two lines were written on LSD on two consecutive weekends. So soon after declarations of the visions the group had seen on drugs, there was Lennon mocking 'choking smokers'. He was now into something else, as so often he had picked up and dropped a cause before the great mass following had even worked out the message.

The increasingly powerful voice given to Lennon by the Beatles' success was being put to the test. It was as if the idol now had to be weighed in the scales, it was the price he had to pay for his messianic role. In August '67, Brian Epstein died suddenly, apart from one or two inconsistencies the evidence pointed to an 'incautious self-administered overdose'. It being 1967, there was concern that the 'dark' side of Epstein's life might come out, he was always open to blackmail because of the letters and pictures he carried around, as had happened in San Francisco the previous year. The police found many bottles of pills in the flat, and the coroner was informed by a doctor that 'roughly speaking I would say the overdose was a build-up of bromide over weeks rather than days.'

John Lennon received the news in Bangor, having just been initiated into Transcendental Meditation by the Maharishi Mahesh Yogi. Lennon explained how his new cause had helped in coming to terms with his grief. He did not explain how Brian Epstein was the only person who could control him and the sinking feeling he felt inside as he realised he was on his own. His reaction was to start speaking out more and more plainly, no longer would the message be covered in poetic allusion, John Lennon had lost another paternal figure.

Clive Epstein, Brian's brother climbed into the breach, but it soon became apparent that the NEMS company which managed the Beatles was in serious financial trouble. For one thing, Brian Epstein had spent money on a prodigal scale, so much so that he had had to borrow money by selling off the controlling interest to Australian entrepreneur Robert Stigwood. All four Beatles refused to have Stigwood controlling their fortunes, they then were told by Clive Epstein that they were liable for crippling taxes unless they started investing their accumulated money in new ventures which would qualify for tax allowances. To Paul McCartney, who was now making all the running in the group, it seemed like a dream come true. They were being told to lose money as an alternative to giving it to the taxman.

John Lennon had never needed any encouragement to be generous. In 1965 he had bought his Aunt Mimi a £25,000 house with completely private gardens leading down to the sea. It cost only £5,000 less than his own house, Kenwood. He also payed all the running costs. Now, he felt more kindly disposed to Freddy, his father, who had filled in some of the great gaps in his knowledge of his early childhood. Mimi had never mentioned his parents' relationship. What he learnt for the first time was how in love his parents had been. Freddy at the end of '67 was invited to spend some time at the Lennon household – it caused some consternation with Cynthia and her mother, indeed everyone would knowingly wink and point out that Freddy was on the cadge. Lennon himself had propagated just such an image of his father. Inexplicably, a student John employed at Kenwood as a secretary, Pauline Jones, found Freddy fascinating. John decided to help this along. Over Christmas, with a house full of guests, he sent Freddy into Pauline's bedroom. As Freddy was 56, and the secretary was 19, it seemed an unlikely match, particularly to the girl's parents, they made her a ward of court. With John's help, the couple eloped to Scotland and then set up house in Brighton. A half brother of John Lennon arrived later in the year, but by that time he had expanded his own family more directly. Yoko was pregnant.

On every level, early 1968 was the most creative period of John Lennon's life. The strands of his activities crissed and crossed in a crazy mosaic. He himself described it differently – a confused time on the material level, but a correspondingly rich time for his artistic self.

Prolonged use of LSD over two years had produced a personality that Cynthia could no longer relate to. They mostly slept apart, having gone into a terminal drift; Cynthia had on a few occasions tried LSD to bridge the gap but it widened inexorably with John lost for days in his own thoughts, gazing over the rolling Surrey hills. While he was helping to edit the 'Magical Mystery Tour' film he had even ventured out into Soho cafés virtually undisturbed. He and Ringo had taken their first London bus ride and enjoyed the rare glimpse of freedom. The price he had paid for power became clearer to him. Now he sought to gratify any whim, determined at last to be his own man. Being told he had to run up tax losses only confirmed that he was at last financially secure. On a cold January day he was working with a writer – Victor Spanetti – on a stage adaptation of his book when the unsuspecting Spanetti mentioned for sake of something to say how chilly it was. Lennon never made small talk, every word spoken in conversation was weighed and analysed.

'Do you want to go somewhere warmer?' he asked.

'Sure.'

Lennon picked up the 'phone. By eleven o'clock they were flying to Marakesh in North Africa. On arrival they found it was snowing. Lennon simply laughed: he always followed his impulses, wherever they led him. He also had no money with him, but with his name, signing bills was enough.

It had been on impulse that he had backed Yoko Ono's show at the Lisson Gallery. She had started to ring him after their chance second meeting. First to ask for his song scores for a John Cage book (an experimental musician she knew from New York), then to ask for his backing. After that show she had deluged him with letters, staged her 'Dance Event' dropping in cards through his home's door. Often she knocked for him, but the housekeeper, Dot, always told her he was not there. Yoko threatened suicide in one of her letters if he did not see her. The book *Grapefruit* she had sent to him alternately repulsed Lennon with its trendy avant garde poses and then fascinated the aspiring intellectual side of him, the part that sought acceptance by the avant garde. It occurred to Lennon that Yoko could open up new worlds to him. He invited her along to a recording session. 'Hey Bulldog' emerged in the course of the day. It was a song about loneliness. 'Why do you make it so simple?' asked the perplexed Yoko Ono.

What Lennon did not know at this time was their shared link of an isolated childhood cut off from pre-occupied parents. 'If you're lonely you can talk to me' sang Lennon to the world, as in the studio he quickly put together a craftsmanlike song.' Yoko Ono was determined to take him literally. She felt lonely and had felt so all her life. Her father was very rich, a director of the Bank of Japan, but he had been forced to give up a career as a concert pianist. Her mother was part of the Japanese aristocracy who had little time in between fulfilling her social diary to give much time to her four children. That was left to nannies. Yoko had to make appointments to see her parents in the mediaeval aristocratic tradition of pre-war Japan. For she was born seven years and eight months before John Lennon on February 18, 1933. At the age of three her hands were inspected to see if she had the fingers of a concert pianist. Yoko preferred composing songs to performing them. She realised the only way to get through to her father was to be an artistic success, it was her inherited duty to achieve great things as an Ono. She took on the heavy burden dutifully, death was preferable to disgrace in her culture.

When war broke out (in America) in 1941, it was expected that Tokyo would be bombed. She was sent out with her brothers and sister, Setsuko, to the safer country-side home in the charge of servants. Shortly afterwards the servants abandoned their charges, and the children were left to fend for themselves. Abandoned children, she was to find, are the same the world over.

Sitting in the studio, Yoko pondered on the message the Beatle was singing to her, why had he singled her out to speak to in this extraordinary way? Of course, she was lonely, (and very unhappy), but this man was telling her she could talk to him, loneliness he seemed to understand. Then, he was off, leaving 'the flavour of the month' as the other Beatles referred to her. While John Lennon and his wife sat in the Indian foothills of the Himalayas, Yoko Ono poured out her soul to John Lennon, in long typed manu-scripts, in hastily scrawled notes on the back of envelopes. She had at last found someone she could communicate with, of that she was sure. Her husband, American film maker, Tony Cox, and her daughter, Kyoko, were also in London but Cox had not gained the acceptance for her films she had hoped. Lennon had, after taking her to the recording studios, taken her round to Mal Evans' flat where a bed had been unceremoniously made up out of a couch. But Yoko was not going to become another easy conquest, she slept separately. But to the rock star, his relationship was still one of munificent backer and strug-gling artist with avant garde pretentions – it was a very cerebral link they shared. The slight Japanese-American could enthuse about her work in a manner only given to those whose whole concept of themselves is bound up with what they produce. In this she shared a link with the Beatle who, in spite of himself, just had to keep writing, even though it could be an agony, the writing came from a vulnerable part within. He had spent six weeks while filming in Spain constantly working on 'Strawberry Fields', every moment on and off set he was reworking the idea, this evocation of the visions of his childhood that separated him from everyone else with some hidden knowledge. Frustrations that turned to violence were another link with someone apparently so dissimilar. Yoko, who appeared on occasion to have a bird-like fragility, could be moved to sheer passion. She had once stabbed Cox in his heel with a pair of scissors. Another time she had held him motionless for 45 minutes with a broken glass pressed up against his neck.

The route to India for John Lennon had been circuitous and long. George's essay into LSD had awakened a mystical side in his nature, so that he had first stopped off there on his way back from the Philippines where they had feared they might be killed by the irate mob who were unrestrained by the police. George and Patti Harrison had returned to India again at the end of 1966 to study sitar with Ravi Shankar. In India, music is intimately wrapped up with religion. Shankar had introduced Harrison to his spiritual guide – *guru*. George had taken to a hill in Cornwall for several days, under the influence of a Western 'teacher', on his return to Britain. The equally mystical Patti had in early '67 joined the Spiritual Regeneration Movement, which taught meditation to Westerners. The Movement's leader, Maharishi Mahesh Yogi had then unexpectedly come to Britain in August and given a public lecture at a London hotel. At Patti's insistence all four Beatles were taken along, there caught up in an inexplicable enthusiasm, the four decided to follow him to a three-day initiation in Bangor, North Wales. Mick Jagger and Marianne Faithful joined the pilgrimage. Brian Epstein was scheduled to come along for initiation on the day he was found dead, August 27th.

An astute examination of the *Sergeant Pepper* cover (on which an enormous amount of time was expended) will reveal four Indian saints. Yogananda, his guru, that guru's guru and last of all in the middle of the group a drawing of a man looking skywards. He, explained McCartney, was Babuji, the man who controlled it all, who wouldn't let anyone photograph him.

Now the Beatles were in India looking for this spiritual controller of the world. The heavily scented, slight and carefully pampered Maharishi did not seem to be a spiritual powerhouse, but he did give off a pleasant confidence in the future. George and Patti, John and Cynthia arrived in the neatly laid out ashram – overlooking the river Ganges as it plunged down from the Himalayan heights – several weeks before Paul and Ringo. Donovan, the folk singer, arrived. Mike Love of the Beach Boys, Mia Farrow and her sister Prudence (yes, the one who wouldn't come out to play), Magic Alex, a blond beautiful Greek who entranced John was also there. Rishikesh is dotted with ashrams, and the town is full of Indian holymen. It is high enough up in the mountains to be cool by night, but splendidly warm by day. Deradoon, the nearest town, was a place where John Lennon could actually walk without being besieged by fans. He took to wearing Indian clothes, including a shawl that he wrapped around himself as he rose early to start his meditation. He took the course even more seriously than George. They were required to do meditation morning and evening. The payment of a week's wages was the only payment the Maharishi had required, now they could relax and forget about the world. Lennon turned to writing songs, many of which were to appear later in the year on a double album that contained what he considered some of his best songs. Paul McCartney came and stayed for a month, before setting off to explore India with Jane Asher. Cynthia Lennon found herself and John passing each other on the ashram's pathways, nodding and continuing on their way, absorbed in their own interests. All was peace and calm, there was no suggestion it was actually the eye of the hurricane. Then, with nearly 30 songs written, John Lennon allowed Magic Alex to persuade him that the Maharishi was after one of the girls on the camp, Mia Farrow's disturbed sister Prudence. He told the Maharishi he was leaving, and left in a rush, certain that the Indian yogi would somehow prevent his leaving. He had hoped he would learn how to escape from the restrictions of being a Beatle. On that journey of several hundred miles through village India, their taxi broke down. John Lennon was stranded without money in the middle of a poverty stricken land. He was totally bemused, there was no acolytes to take care of him, no-one even recognised him standing by a dusty Indian road with no idea what to do next. A cab drew up. The Indian passengers offered to take him and Cynthia to the next town. They recognised him, fixed up a cab in the town and sped on their way. The magical effect of being a Beatle had overcome the Maharishi's vengeance. The cab spent hours circling Delhi while they tried to remember the name of the hotel where they were meant to meet up with George. John wanted to get out of India and away from the Maharishi as fast as possible. They took a flight that night and only breathed a sigh of relief when the plane was airborne. In the luggage that had sat stranded by the roadside was the body of songs that came closest to expressing the true Lennon. One was a beautiful, lyrical work called 'Julia' – in memory of his mother. Nature in its radiant aspect had become his mother 'Seashell eyes, windy smiles. Her hair of floating sky is shimmering, glimmering in the sun. Morning moon touch me.'

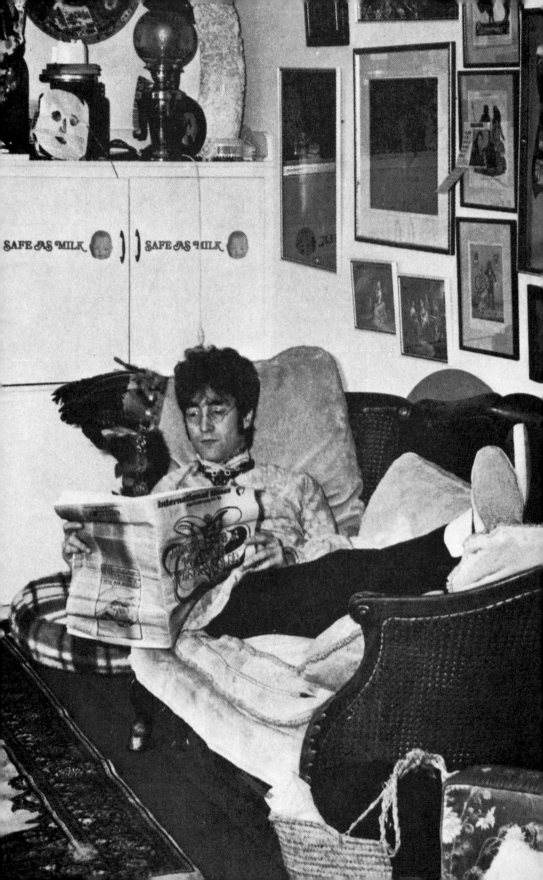

◀ With the arrival of the psychedelic era, John Lennon quickly tuned in to the vibes and read the Underground's house organ 'International Times', once donating £1,000 to it.

16 'Let's Have Some More Babies'

At about the time Paul McCartney and Jane Asher began to fall out over when and how many children they should have, exactly the same argument developed between John Lennon and Cynthia Powell. Although he was later to refer to Julian's arrival as a Saturday night special 'the way most people get here', he could hardly have been surprised since neither he nor Cynthia took precautions, and so after three and half years the relationship had moved on to its next stage. While away touring he could write home and sincerely say how wonderful it would be for them all to be together again – for he missed his son. It was what bound him and Cynthia together as he undertook his mental and physical voyages. In India, he had enthused about seeing Julian again to Cynthia – they had both been deeply touched when the Maharishi had presented an Indian prince's costume to them on his birthday, April 8th. They had been two months at the quiet holy spot on the Ganges – more peaceful than for over eight years. Lennon had established a deep rapport with his environment and broken out of the constraints of a Beatle ego, but it was a fragile flower. The easily-brought-on paranoia inside had sent him racing for the airport faraway in Delhi through a countryside that was both timeless – and for a millionaire – difficult to gaze on calmly as crowds of beggar children looked about for someone to portune for 'paisa' – about the amount the group received in royalty for a single record of 'Love Me Do' sold.

John returned from India enthusiastic about Paul's ideas of setting up a multi-media art empire that would not rip off its artists – as they felt they had been. Apple Corps Ltd. was announced by Paul and himself in New York during May, as they sailed in a Chinese junk round the Statue of Liberty. Cynthia Lennon had not been allowed to make the trip. He had come back from a weekend at a friend's house where he had been surrounded by children fired with the idea (gained under LSD) of creating a similar happy family. Cynthia, in tears, had declined while he continued to dream his drug dreams. They were not sleeping together, now she had pulled out the rug, there was no reason for them to get back. Feeling depressed, John suggested she go to Greece on holiday with friends – Magic Alex, Donovan and his friend Gypsy – negotiations were at an advanced stage for the Beatles to buy up a Greek island and set up a paradise on earth for whoever cared to come out and join them. The Greek military government were favourable to the idea, then on a fleeting visit Lennon suddenly realised they were only going to be used to promote tourism. A wonderful dream died in the making. It was back to work in a recording studio – though it was to be five months before the painfully slow album was complete.

On John's return from India his faithful correspondent had redoubled her literary output. Enormously long letters arrived at the house everyday, but that was not too unusual. An American fan had written to Paul 'This is my 42nd letter to you, if you don't reply soon I shall run out of stamps.' What she and what Yoko did not seem to realise was that Beatles did not reply to fan letters – though when he was so moved John Lennon did read those long rambling missives explaining why the world needed conceptual art.

During Cynthia's holiday absence, John Lennon invited his old school friend from Quarry Bank over to keep him amused. In 1965, Lennon had set up Peter Shotton in business – running a supermarket in Hayling Island – a flat, dreary mudbank of a place in the Thames estuary. It seemed like the Lennon of old when he suggested they get a 'girl' over for the evening.

Yoko Ono, 35, finally got the call she had been waiting for and duly arrived as midnight approached. A pop idol's chat-up vocabulary is strictly limited. They took some LSD. John asked her if she'd like to hear his electronic music experiments 'upstairs'. Yoko Ono took him literally, he played all the tapes through, then she suggested making their own experimental tape. It was dawn before they finally got around to some physical communication.

Yoko Ono had had only two or three liaisons outside of two marriages – neither of which had lasted too long. The first, to a Japanese musician, Toshi Ichiyanani, in New York – to where she had moved with her parents in her late teens – had shocked her family because of his low social status. The break-up after five years had traumatised her. In Japan she read a highly critical review of her work and tried to commit suicide. While she was still under psychiatric care she was visited by an old friend, Tony Cox. In 1963 they married and quickly produced a daughter Kyoko. Yoko Ono having made love to John Lennon, stayed on in the house. The pile of dirty plates in the kitchen grew – she did not take to kindly to housework, unlike Mrs Lennon.

When Cynthia – fully restored to optimism after her Greek holiday – came back to the house with Magic Alex, Donovan and Gypsy she found the front door open. In the kitchen she came across the 'two virgins' sitting gazing into each other's eyes.

'Oh hi', said John casually.

'We were thinking of going off for dinner in town, are you coming?' Cynthia asked, equally normally.

'No thanks', said John.

It was the end, Cynthia felt, she rushed out the house to return days later when she had had time to get a grip on herself. It turned into a confessional with John about what he had done. About what he wanted, most of all, more children. Cynthia was still not sure, then he announced he was going with Paul to set up Apple in New York and that 'no' she couldn't come. Instead, she took another holiday this time with her mother in Italy. Events proceeded at an increasingly breakneck speed. Yoko rang to announce she was pregnant. Magic Alex was despatched to Italy to tell Cynthia that John was suing for divorce and custody of Julian. Cynthia fell very ill, she was only allowed to meet John in the presence of Yoko Ono on her return.

John and his new love moved out of Kenwood, into Ringo's flat in Montague Square, London. Paul McCartney composed his best ever song 'Hey Jude'. It was about the pain of losing love (he had just broken with Jane Asher). The song was dedicated in its title at least to Julian, who Paul had a very soft spot for.

Apple Corps (it was named after a Magritte painting Paul owned) had come into being and word quickly got around the naturally parasitic music press that with the Beatles running their own business it was 'open house'. The principle was that 'the artists' had to be able to get through to 'the top men' who in this case were artists themselves – John, Paul, George and Ringo. The most spectacular discovery who received the most sponsorship was the

Japanese conceptual artist from New York. In June she and John set off in the white Rolls to Coventry Cathedral to plant two acorns for peace in hallowed ground. This was too much for the custodian of the ground. Yoko Ono tore into him with a vindictive fury, John acting as peace-maker at the time, then spending three hours cursing the hapless Cannon Verney in an accent that became deep scouse Liverpudlian. In a fury people revert to the lan-guage of their early childhood, the time when they learned first of all the magic of words. The previous month Yoko and John had met a young Oxford arts graduate, Anthony Fawcett, at The Arts Lab in Drury Lane during a 'Destruc-tion of Art' exhibition. The Arts Lab had been born in the frenzy of activity and creativity that was London in 1966. By 1968 it had become a haven for drug pushers, black power agitators and an increasingly active underground that was now talking about revolution. One of the regulars was 'Michael X', leader of the Black Power movement, sometime poet, onetime heavy for a notoriously grasping slum landlord called Rachman, Michael X was also jailed on account of an inflammatory anti-white speech he had given in Reading. If you shook his hand you were hit by the dense angry waves of energy emitting from him while his face weighed up your worth. He was hanged in 1973, for the murder of a young English woman, Gail Benson, daughter of an MP, in Trinidad. One of his only defenders was John Lennon. His poetry was simple, disturbed and ultra-intense, as was Lennon's.

The summer of love had by 1968 metamorphosed into calls for action. In May in France, President de Gaulle had gone into hiding for five days while students and workers united in an attempt to overthrow the government. Gros-venor Square turned into London's first bloody confronta-tion between police and students as an unprecedented crowd of thousands stormed down Oxford Street and howled at the American Embassy. In Germany, Red Rudi formented strife among the previously docile German youth. In America Lyndon Johnson announced he would not be standing for another term.

John Lennon was deeply troubled. What should be his stance? Such was the Beatles' power, he could have turned a youth feeling its power, cynical of all institutional estab-lishment double-talk, and in America being called to die for their country protecting a corrupt dictator, into an army of dedicated revolutionaries. But Apple was his centre; he poured through the mail and the begging letters, dealt with the endless demands for press interviews, ran the office in conjunction with the ever present Yoko. He concentrated on promoting their first fully public art exhibition at the Robert Fraser gallery. It was called 'You Are Here' and featured 365 helium-filled balloons, each having an address label that was to be filled in with comments by its recipients. A surprising number came back – with messages less than complimentary. He was asked why he was joining forces with a third-rate artist, letters from Army barracks warned of the perfidious Japanese. John Lennon started to feel the effects of race hate. He was pushed back into his businessman's role. An Apple boutique started in December '67 had by July '68 achieved a loss of £100,000. The dream was souring. At last came Apple's first record, 'Hey Jude', and it was McCartney's personal triumph, the whole concept of Apple Corps was his much more than John Lennon's. McCartney was rapidly becoming the one in charge, as he had sought to be since Hamburg, even then they had arguments about who was the leader. 'Hey Jude' was backed by 'Revolution'. Lennon had thought deeply about the position he would take. He was ambivalent,

'Well you know we all want to change the world
but when you talk about destruction
don't you know that you can count me out
Don't you know it's going to be alright'

His advice was for people to change their heads, to attack the violence at its source.

'You better free your mind instead.'

In a year when Robert Kennedy was shot, when draft dodgers multiplied, when the Democratic convention in Chicago was marred unforgettably by police going on bloody rampage, and simmering cities in America were on the brink of wholesale rioting, Lennon had used his power to ask for a much more difficult act than mindless violence, instead he was calling for people to change themselves within. It was a brave, optimistic and wise decision when he could have courted easy popularity. The artist had been true to his vision. A year earlier he had seen how a single full-page advertisement in the august *Times*, largely paid for by himself, but signed by many 'names', had generated a serious debate about the legalisation of marijuana. Power had to be used carefully and well, and since he and McCartney had always believed that power was won by will-power, the challenge was met. The establishment saw his moves towards political radicalism less benignly. In October he was arrested on charges of possessing an ounce and a half of marijuana. The policeman who led the raid, Det. Sgt. Norman Pitcher, was later dismissed from the force for falsifying evidence. John rang Neil Aspinall at Apple from Marylebone police station.

'It's happened', he said 'the worst paranoia you could imagine.'

John took the call at the police station from the head of EMI, speaking as 'Sergeant Lennon.'

Sir Joseph Lockwood advised John to plead guilty. Lennon wanted to protect Yoko by being the only one charged, it would have affected Yoko's visa, little realising how much he was going to need a visa in the future. He was fined £150 and the case was closed. A measure of the envy the millionaire provoked is that the weekly wage bill of the 7 police officers came to £178-14s-6d. 'You are a very holy man', called a woman outside the Court. In the same week, Yoko, who was expecting her baby shortly after Christmas, miscarried. The Beatles' double album came out. Plus a record called 'Two Virgins' which featured on its cover, under a sanitising brown paper bag, John and Yoko in the altogether. The stress and pressure had never been so high even for John Lennon. For six months he had been growing further apart from Paul as they jockeyed for control of the group. Yoko caused resentment with her monopolisation of John in the studio. Previously he and Paul had played each other their first ideas, improved on them, altered them, often amalgamated them – as in 'A Day in the Life' and 'Baby You're a Rich Man', where two songs had become one. Now on *The White Album,* as it became known, they simply approved each other's ideas, there was no criticism, no two-way communications. Lennon was heard to speak in his authoritative, uncensored voice.

Commercially *The White Album* was not quite the monster hit that *Sergeant Pepper* had been. In the UK charts it stayed in for 18 weeks compared to 43 weeks for *Pepper* and 62 weeks for *Please Please Me.* However, it was the first double album in pop (although to describe the Beatles as pop by this time is highly misleading – the music was now at its most experimental, the guitars thundered and jaggered, an enormous amount of energy poured out, thanks to the influence of the underground groups, which had mushroomed all over London). George Martin wanted to cull the prolific output the band had recorded over 5 months, and so produce one commercial record, as had been done with *Revolver*. All the Beatles were in full creative flood for their own various reasons, all refused.

An American called Linda Eastman had flown to London with a request for a photographic session with Paul McCartney. He had seen her in New York (and on the West Coast) when she had passed her 'phone number to him. Their first meeting had been at the photo call on *Sergeant Pepper* when with the help of Peter Brown (Brian Epstein's assistant, then manager of Apple, then American manager for Robert Stigwood) she had been one of 14 chosen photographers. Jane Asher's 'divorce' had made him the most eligible bachelor in the world. She was quickly ensconced in his Cavendish Avenue town house. Paul's hard rockers like 'Helter Skelter', 'Back in the USSR', 'Birthday' and 'Why Don't We Do it in the Road?' were the raunchiest, wildest, most exhilarating numbers he was ever to do. As always he was in competition with John Lennon, who also appeared to have discovered sexual abandon for the first time. As he put it, when he and Yoko weren't in the studio they were in bed. But it was dark horse George who had progressed most musically – and in singing voice. Quietly he fought to keep the constituent parts of the group together as it threatened to tear apart in the spinning vortex created by the wild energy released in the tumultuous year of '68 when all the West's institutions seemed on the brink of collapse. He managed the impossible, pulling the music back to centre through the sheer professionalism of his guitar work. When John Lennon pounded off into a guitar riff that threatened to peter out he was there to take off again with solos that soared. 'Yer Blues' although in theory a song about suicidal feelings, became in the group's hands an assault on all barriers, whether of knowledge, feeling or of custom. The import is genuinely revolutionary in the tidal gusts of power and emotion it releases. Lennon's voice was never more expressive or hypnotic in its range; while he had seldom claimed to be a technical virtuoso on guitar he could make the instrument release his trapped powerful emotions in a raw statement of primal feeling. But what he could do in his music, he could not yet do in his life.

'Happiness is a Warm Gun', rivalling 'Yer Blues' in power, was a brilliant lyric and paean to sexual joys now only disguised enough to make sure it was not banned out of hand. But no one had ever been this explicit before, nor had anyone come up with such poetry:

'She's not a girl who misses much.
She's well acquainted with the touch of the velvet hand
Like a lizard on a window pane
The man in the crowd with the multi-coloured mirrors
On his hobnail boots
Lying with his eyes while his hands are busy
Working overtime
A soap impression of his wife which he ate
And donated to the National Trust'

Most of the Lennon songs had been written from February to April in India, but the worldly, knowing tones of this song are quintessential '68. Like many of his songs, it had been triggered by something Lennon had seen, in this case the front cover of a gun magazine, which said 'Happiness is a warm gun.' ('Being for the benefit of Mr Kite' was an almost direct crib of a poster Lennon bought at a curio shop while out filming a sequence of the 'Strawberry Fields' record promotion). However, that alarming statement has been transformed into a potent sexual allegory 'When I hold you in my arms, and I feel my finger on your trigger'.

But through the lyrics float other Lennons, the raunchy rock star with multi-coloured mirrors on his hobnail boots (the psychedelic voyager in no-nonsense rocker disguise) lying with his eyes while his hands are busy working overtime (the soulful poet who was also the Marco Polo of the senses). A soap impression of his wife . . . which he donated to the National Trust. The god who had thrown away the dream 'because he had become rich and famous and it didn't mean anything' and with the dream, the wife and family. Yet he was troubled, needed a fix (towards the end of '68 Yoko and Lennon got into heroin which quickly establishes a physical dependency and turns the user into a cynical exploiter of any relationship, the drug being all he cares about) his dream girl was instructed once again to 'jump the gun' – John and Yoko were infatuated with each other, and at this time, it was also a very physical attraction. For the time Lennon had found sexual happiness. Mother (Yoko) was up on him (Superior) blowing his brains out.

But right beside Lennon at his most sexually powerful, there was the lyrical Lennon singing in his childlike tones of a lost mother, his hours-long meditations had resurrected her memory and he had transmuted that treasured memory into pure gold. It was the perfect tribute.

What is most astonishing about *The White Album* is the sheer professional versatility of the group, now straining that cohesion built up over a decade by each shooting for their personal summit. There is parody ('Bungalow Bill' was a Lennon pastiche on a fellow Rishikesh meditator who then went off hunting wild tigers), blues – 'I'm so tired' is the meditator agonising – 'it's three weeks, I'm going insane'. 'Wild Honey pie' is a song fragment left in to please Patti Harrison, while 'Honey pie' was in the style of Jim McCartney's 1920's jazz band. George, together with Eric Clapton on lead guitar produced the ultimate in soul searching heart-rending music with 'While My Guitar Gently Weeps.' No wonder the album left the group temporarily exhausted. In terms of value – being a double album – it was the most successful album ever released worldwide.

17 'I'm Down To My Last £50,000'

In 1969, money reared its ugly head among the multiplying monsters in John Lennon's closet. The heroin and the negativity of Yoko were overtaking him, he had always had a chameleon like quality which meant he took the mood of those closest to him. He had been prepared to go along with most of Paul McCartney's schemes since the death of Brian Epstein, being preoccupied with other more important considerations than what a managerless rock band might do next. But Apple had managed to consume £1½ million of their money in its brief existence. The clothes boutique run by some Dutch designers called the Fool was merely a precursor of what was to come. He and Paul had laughed it off. 'I've always been fascinated by women's clothes, I'm a bit queer that way', he explained. One positive reaction to the record cover showing the somewhat drooping breasts, abundant pubic hair and lean behind of one Yoko Ono, together with a limp Beatle cock, was that four main directors of the board of Apple's accountancy firm Bryce Hanmer Ltd refused to handle the business. A young bright accountant called Stephen Maltz stepped into the breach and established as reasonably certainly as was possible that Apple's losses were running at £20,000 a week. It was if anything an understatement. He wrote to all four Beatles. 'Your finances are in a mess. Apple is in a mess'. The news was hard to believe. Since 1963 the Beatles had played over 350 live performances and made £4.5–£5 million (£22–25 million – $40-45 million today) out of a gross of £50 million. The ill-fated merchandising deals had actually benefited them to the tune of £2 million, though the profits for others were incalcuable. That year the royalty payments to Northern Songs, which published their work, produced profits of over £800,000. But the young accountant's warning set Lennon off into panic.

Lord Beeching was approached to see if he could do an axe job on Apple as he had done with British Railways. Lennon, who spoke to him, at least realised what the solution was. Swingeing cuts. Lord Beeching advised him to stick to making music. Paul McCartney meanwhile was buying up more shares in the publicly quoted Northern Songs so that he could 'get a bigger share of the jelly babies'. He was acting on his father-in-law's advice, one Lee Eastman (né Epstein). A predatory character at the Rolling Stones' film *Rock'n'Roll Circus* had been hovering around Lennon the previous December. Lennon had ignored him, even though he had certainly heard of Allen Klein's accomplishment in getting better royalties for the Stones, who he managed, than the Beatles themselves received. In 1967, in return for a 9-year contract, Brian Epstein had negotiated royalties of 10% in place of the derisory 2d a record the Beatles had previously earned from EMI.

In January '69, as news got out of the financial problems of Apple, Allen Klein managed to get through to John Lennon and fix a meeting at the Dorchester. As soon as Lennon learnt how Klein had lost his mother at 4, spent some time in an orphanage and been entrusted to the care of an aunt, the decision was made. Lennon wrote to EMI boss, Sir Joseph Lockwood. 'Dear Sir Joe, from now on Allen Klein handles all my things'. In February, after Lennon's persuasion, Klein was appointed manager when George and Ringo agreed. Paul did not sign the contract, but went along with the majority vote. Allen Klein would receive 20% of any increase he arranged in their earnings.

At exactly this time NEMS, who received a 25 per cent management fee on all Beatles' earnings, was talking to an investment bank about selling out for approximately £1 million. The group were horrified and Clive Epstein intimated he wanted to sell to the Beatles. His brother's death had left him with £½ million death duties. John Eastman, son of Lee Eastman, soon to be Paul's brother-in-law, was judged too young to be handling the negotiations on behalf of the Beatles and with Klein's appointment as manager, friction grew. It was a clash between surrogates for John and Paul. Clive Epstein had given the group three weeks to come up with an offer to match that of the Triumph Investment Trust. Half way through the allotted time, Epstein sold NEMS for a mixture of cash and stock on 17 February, just two weeks after the appointment of Klein. He wanted to return to Liverpool where he still lives today in Woolton, a calm, handsome, wealthy soul who jogged past the author as he was photographing Strawberry Field – Lennon's best song and one which earned the passing runner a small fortune. For him at least the abandoned children's home's magic is real enough.

The outrageous behaviour (by 1969 standards) of John Lennon had also caused their music publisher Dick James to want out. In a secret deal he sold his 23 per cent shareholding in Northern Songs to ATV in the shape of showbusiness impresario Lew Grade. Vain battles by John and his group to get back control of their own songs failed. To John 'it was like playing monopoly but with real money'. However, neither he nor Klein nor John Eastman could get the City of London on their side.

John Lennon kept writing. An early 1968 song, 'Across the Universe' which he considered one of his finest lyrics was recorded for a film *Let it Be* shot over six weeks in January and February. Coming soon after *The White Album*, the band were 'pooped'. The barnlike film studios were no place to try making an album in front of the cameras. The concept was to do a 'full circle of the wheel' recording. They wanted to get back to the urgency and simplicity of their earliest days. 'The One After 909' was revived, a Quarrymen song written when John was 18, and Paul 16. The location moved to Apple, so cold and uninspiring was the scene at Twickenham. In vain, they sought the old magic, recording dozens of songs from their Liverpool and Hamburg repertoire. At the end of January they played their last 'public' performance on the rooftop of Apple. It made the last 20 minutes of *Let It Be* a strangely moving film as the Beatles, now in long flowing locks, fur coats, jeans and an assortment of unmatching, ill-fitting clothes, performed for the last time. Eventually the police moved in to stop a show that later promoters would offer millions upon millions to stage.

Although the album was held till a year later it was not in the end to be the final Beatles LP. That came in July and August when, beset by money negotiations, the Apple staff being ruthlessly fired by the New York axeman Klein, the record companies being pressured to up their royalties, the group agreed to reassemble in Studio Number Two to make an album in the way they used to.

It had been an eventful spring. On March 20th, John and Yoko had married in Gibraltar. Anthony Cox had been paid £6.700 in a divorce settlement, while Cynthia Lennon

had received £100,000 for hers. John had originally peti-
tioned her for adultery with a man she met on her Italian
holiday. The ultra jealous Lennon had believed the story of
Magic Alex, one of the first victims of Allen Klein's axe. But
all that was behind Lennon, he had discovered a new
cause, that of peace. Most of the year was taken up in a
flurry of peace promotions master-minded by Yoko, who
was relentlessly urging him on to greater and greater
efforts in accord with her own driven nature. It began in a
hotel bedroom high up overlooking the newest, richest
part of Amsterdam in the Hilton. As far as the Europeans
were concerned he had taken leave of his senses, the
English in particular were convinced that he had gone too
far and become hopelessly eccentric. But to troubled
America he was still the leader, faithfully reported in the
American press with serious commentary. The British
press were by turns scoffing, cynical and superior, but they
reported the doings – or non-doings – day by day. Yoko
and John, but particularly Yoko, had decided to use the
fame of the Beatles for a worthy end.

Lennon explained when the bed-in for peace took up
residence for 10 days in the Queen Elizabeth Hotel, Mon-
treal, in May:

'We think students are being conned by the establishment. The establishment is like the school bully. It aggravates you and aggravates you until you hit it. And then
they'll kill you.

'You gotta remember, establishment, it's just a name for
– evil. The monster doesn't care whether it kills all the students or whether there's a revolution. It's not thinking logi-
cally, it's out of control, it's suffering from, it's a careless
killer and it doesn't care whether the students all get killed
or black power – it'll enjoy that. We've got to realise that it
doesn't care which way we go. But the only thing it can't
fight is the mind. But the students have got conned into
thinking that they can change it with violence.

'It doesn't make sense because the monster's insane.
The blue meanie is insane. We're the only ones that really
care about life. To them it doesn't matter. Destruction is
good enough for them. It's not just the government, it's
power or the devil or whatever we call it. It doesn't matter
to him. Either way he gets his kicks. And his kicks are control or destruction. If he can't control, he destroys. We're
the only ones interested in life, the peaceniks or whatever.
We've got to make the others aware of it – the ones, the

borderline ones, who don't know.

'Evil, the same thing that's caused it for millions of years. Evil is a way of life. We've got to get through, we've got to get past that. We want to live'.

'We think all of this is wrong. Violence begets violence, it's a universal law. All right, some will say situations vary from place to place and the situation will sometimes justify the use of violence, but that's a compromise and I say peace cannot be compromised. For two million years, we've had violence . . . so what's wrong with peace for a change?'

Phone links put John Lennon in his bed through to the front line, panic-stricken students reported that lines of police and national guard were moving in on their demonstrations. Lennon rose to the occasion, advising them to avoid the confrontation the machine wanted.

It was with some relief that the peripatetic couple arrived at the Abbey Road studios. In May a single 'The Ballad of John and Yoko' had been released with John doing both the vocals and guitar work, while Paul McCartney took care of the drums, bass and harmonies. In spite of John Lennon's increasing fears about the 'establishment' the single reached the No. 1 spot he had come to regard as his right.

> 'Christ you know it ain't easy,
> You know how hard it can be.
> The way things are going,
> They're going to crucify me.'

A poll taken in a pop paper still had John Lennon slightly ahead of Paul McCartney in popularity. Among the younger generation at least his motives were considered good and praiseworthy, although one earnest 17-year-old expressed the fear that he was in danger of becoming confused by drugs. He was in fact about to release a particularly powerful record detailing the pain of coming off heroin, but alongside the personal battle, there was the worldwide battle as half a million American troops napalmed the Vietnamese jungles, and sought out the determined guerilla opposition, it was a computerised war with 'body counts' describing the sorry tangled bodies found after an area of jungle had been blasted, the American army being none too sure if the body count actually included guerillas or non-combatant villagers.

So in July, what was to become the anthem of the anti-

Vietnam war campaigners – 'Give Peace a Chance' – was released. Allen Klein obtained new sharply increased royalties from Capitol – the American EMI-owned record company – and John Lennon knew at last he would never want for money in his life. In May he had purchased a choice 70 acres of the English countryside and a manor house to go with it, Tittenhurst Park near Ascot, 26 miles from London. It had been traditional for the public to be allowed to visit the gardens, John Lennon only agreed that the previous lady owner should be allowed to visit her beloved rhodedendrons. For £145,000 he had obtained privacy and a love nest suitable for a Japanese princess. One room was furnished with half of a chair, half of a piano, half of this and that. It was the *Half Wind Show* that he had anonymously backed in 1967. It was in the peace of this English countryside that he was to write 'Imagine'.

Late in August, Bob Dylan helicoptered in to visit the Lennons on their estate. He had just given a concert for thousands upon thousands on the Isle of Wight. It had been a reminder that the remarkable cohesiveness of the young still held together. But the Beatles, always a year ahead of the game, were putting the finishing touches to their final album, it had been agreed there would be no bickering, the recording was competently and professionally put together, but it lacked fire. George stole the show with his simple mystical 'Here Comes the Sun' and his beautiful love long about Patti 'Something'. Ironically, it co-incided with her steady drift away from him and towards Eric Clapton. George had once years ago taken a girlfriend off him and Eric had never forgiven him, although most of the time they got very, very stoned together, a neat threesome.

'Come together' a number that Lennon had composed to be used as a political campaign song at the request of Timothy Leary's wife, showed he could enter the political field without making any concessions over lyrics. 'Come together over me', had the typical Lennon messianic touch. But all four knew it was the swan song. The 'B' side had song fragments strung together – using up Polythene Pam and Mean Mr Mustard from Lennon's Indian stay. The group played themselves out on their guitars, each taking the lead in turn for the instrumental that followed the prophetic words:

'And in the middle of the celebrations
I break down'

John's burst of lead guitar work came right at the end, the instrument was flying high. Paul came in with their final message

'And in the end the love you take is equal to the love you make, Ah —'

The Beatles were back singing about the redeeming qualities of love. But for the four members of the group there was no longer enough love to go round.

meet it is a humbling experience. The long battles to prove he was a

The Two Virgins. John wanted Yoko naked for the cover, so she naturally insisted that he be naked as well. 'We wanted to show we're not a couple of deformed freaks', he said.

18 'Temperature Rising, I Wish I Was A Baby, I Wish I Was Dead'

John Lennon's decision to buy Tittenhurst Park — with its rare oriental trees protected by the local council from demolition — was the outward sign of his desire to put himself somewhere else. The pressures of the boardroom wrangles, the fear that he could even slip from his millionaire status in a welter of losses and tax claims combined with the agonising withdrawal from heroin and a suspicious wife who saw plots against her from the other Beatles and wanted him for herself — removed from the influence of the 'in-laws' as she referred to them. Shortly before the newly-weds moved into Tittenhurst Park, they crashed in a hired car while visiting one of John's aunts who lived in the remote Scottish Highlands near Durness. John had regularly visited her every Christmas in his teen-age days. He remembered his freedom then. The release of a new single 'Cold Turkey' in the autumn proved to him that he could make it by himself. 'Something' from the Abbey Road album had reached no higher than No. 4 in the charts, as it descended 'Cold Turkey' rose to a credit-able No. 5 while in America it hit the No. 1 spot. Backed by Eric Clapton on a wailing jangling guitar, John Lennon went for the gut:

> 'Temperature's rising
> fever is high
> can't see no future
> can't see no sky
> My feet are so heavy
> So is my head
> I wish I was a baby
> I wish I was dead'

What had to die was the old Beatle, but this was the brutal breaking down of the old image, he was unsure of what would come in its place. He had picked fights with his old best friends, Paul McCartney and George Harrison. Privately they found it the last straw when Yoko had moved her bed into the recording studios for Abbey Road (her back still hurt from the road crash), George had told Yoko to her face that he'd heard from New York that she had 'bad vibes' – Dylan was one of his informants – now he told John that she was simply using him for her own ends. John listened patiently, hoping he would win them over to love Yoko as much as he did. The couple made films together, their first film 'Rape' showing the effects of media intrusion on private lives had received respectable reviews, now at the Institute of Contemporary Art they showed 'Self Portrait' a close up look, head on, of the same character who had graced the cover of 'Two Virgins'. But now shown in a new role, straight and extended, although as the film limped on, the star partially lost his initial cocksureness.

'One could not say this is a film into which a lot of thought has not gone' wrote one reviewer.

It could have been an allegory for the star's manager. He was unsure of which direction to take, but spells of inertia were interrupted by frenzied excitement. In September a call came through from John Brower in Toronto, Anthony Fawcett – Yoko and John's personal assistant and art adviser – took the call. He had been rescued from obscurity when they met him at the Arts Lab the previous year on first venturing out in public together. Halfway through the call, Lennon, who was being interviewed, started to take an interest in Fawcett's notes. He took the call and with a typically grandiloquent gesture said he could only agree to accept seven free first-class tickets to attend a concert in Toronto if his new band was allowed to play. John Brower, to his credit, responded brilliantly by promising that he would arrange all the necessary documentation immediately.

Lennon told Fawcett to get hold of Klaus Voorman (guitarist with Manfred Mann and Hamburg friend of Astrid Kircherr), Eric Clapton with whom John had played during the *White Album* and on 'Cold Turkey', plus a session drummer Alan White. He had formed a new band, just the way The Quarrymen had coped with a last minute gig.

Fawcett unfortunately could not locate Eric Clapton and everyone had to be at Heathrow Airport early the following morning. Mal Evans was detailed to take care of all the logistics of moving over the equipment. The new band's performance would also be recorded for subsequent release by Apple. At the airport, in the cold light of dawn, Fawcett anxiously checked his watch. One hour before take-off and still no sign of the Lennons or Eric Clapton. He put a call through to Tittenhurst Park. The cook answered. The Lennons were still in bed and could not be disturbed. Frantic, Fawcett managed to get the call transferred to the bedroom. John apologised. He hadn't managed to wake up. Besides Yoko wasn't feeling too good. Could he cancel the flight and the show, send apologies, usual sort of thing, signed with love and peace?

Ignoring his master's instructions, Fawcett tore round to nearby Ascot. The couple had now breakfasted, Lennon was wondering if they could go out on the next flight, they would just about make the concert in time. The missing Eric Clapton came through on the 'phone, he really wouldn't miss this gig for anything. The old energy gripped Lennon, the show was on, and he leapt out of bed.

As the Air Canada flight's progress across the Atlantic was broadcast to the North American continent, the freeways leading to Toronto from the rest of Canada and from the Niagara Falls border with America became snarled with automobiles carrying would-be concert goers. The Varsity Stadium became a scene of indescribable chaos, it was as if Beatlemania had never died. Black market ticket touts could name any price.

Switching straight back into his American tours persona John led a sprint for the waiting black limosines at the airport, and unlike the other members of the group appeared unaffected by the fans who surged over the car at the stadium. He fired out his orders, realising the mayhem there could also be backstage.

'Gimme a private room, Eric we gotta rehearse, where's my bloody amp. Hell what are we gonna play?

As Eric Clapton bent over his guitar picking through the chords, Lennon decided on the same warm-up numbers the Beatles had always used. He couldn't remember the words of 'Cold Turkey' or 'Give Peace a Chance', his two latest records. Yoko wanted to do her own numbers. He felt sick in the guts and went to the rest room to vomit. It could be the undoing of the whole legend, a singer who couldn't even remember his words and a group who'd never even rehearsed together.

Clapton took him by the arm and led him on stage where the sea of faces transformed Lennon into the all-powerful performer able to mesmerise his audience with a single gesture, the same as at the Star Club when he had been incoherent off-stage and could still go out to wow them. He kicked off with Elvis' 'Blue Suede Shoes' then 'Money' – that had always got them going, followed by 'Dizzy Miss Lizzy' which had been responsible for more wet seats than any other Beatle number in performance. Lennon paused, dare he now throw off the Beatle John and become just John Lennon? He went into 'Yer Blues' which Clapton had already played with him during the *White Album* days. The effect was sensational, Clapton believed in the free-ranging spontaneous playing that the Beatles themselves had used in the pre-Epstein days. Next 'Cold Turkey' had Lennon screeching out his agonies of withdrawal – no one in the stadium realising it was also the pain of withdrawal from the Beatles – Yoko dashed off stage to get lyrics for her two numbers. The band went into 'Give Peace A Chance' and the whole Vietnam protest generation joined in. As the deafening roar of the crowd died down, Yoko took to the front of the stage to sing 'Don't Worry Kyoko', followed by a freaky, screeching rendition of 'John, John, Let's Hope for Peace'. Lennon had proved he could live apart from the Beatles as the roar of approval went on and on for five frantic minutes.

The peace campaign gathered pace into the autumn, as John was urged on by the iron determination of Yoko. He hit on the idea of making a very British form of protest. His chauffeur, Les, was despatched to Poole, Dorset, where Aunt Mimi kept his MBE medal above the television. She was out but Les managed to get in and take the medal, which was just as well, for it is unlikely Mimi would have given this seal of Establishment approval to him. The driver's destination – in his white Mercedes – was the Central Chancery of Orders of Knighthood, St James's Palace. 'Hokey Pokey' – as Mimi called Yoko – and John Lennon composed a note to accompany the medal:

'Your Majesty,
I am returning the MBE in protest against Britain's involvement in the Nigeria-Biafra thing, against our support of America in Vietnam and against 'Cold Turkey' slipping down the charts.

With love,
John Lennon of Bag.'

The British press thought Lennon had finally flipped his lid, and duly printed their views. Philosopher Lord Bertrand Russell praised the deed. But the frenzy of Yoko-style protest and assault on the complacent consciousness of the establishment continued. Posters were put up in a dozen cities across the world announcing:

War is over if you want it.
Happy Christmas from John and Yoko.

Continuing at the same frenetic pace, John decided to take the peace campaign on stage at the Lyceum Ballroom in London's Strand. It was to be England's last public performance by John Lennon, fortunately recorded and put out on the *Some Time in New York City* LP. The personnel of the ever-changing group was Delaney and Bonnie (discoveries of Eric Clapton), the Who's drummer, Keith Moon, keyboards player Billy Preston, George Harrison – who had been playing heavily disguised behind a huge beard on a Bonnie and Delaney/Eric Clapton tour of the UK, Alan White on drums and Klaus Voorman on guitar. The proceeds of the performance were earmarked for UNICEF. Lennon opened up with his all-powerful 'Cold Turkey' but the next number proved too much for George. Halfway through 'Don't Worry Kyoko' – who Yoko had hardly seen since her elopement, nor incidentally had John seen much of Julian – Kyoko's mother burst out of a white bag to begin shrieking and wailing, to accuse the audience of having murdered Hanratty. The Plastic Ono supergroup left the stage – and George at least was never going to let her perform with him there again.

Just before Christmas, Yoko and John took off for Canada where veteran rock and roll star Ronnie Hawkins played host to the travelling circus that the John Lennon roadshow had become. Telephone engineers laid on extra phone lines to the house on the outskirts of Toronto as the world's media trooped in and the campaign for peace was conducted across the continent by phone. He was also hard at work signing a collection of lithographs, Bag One, which were to be sold in sets of 14 inside natty white cases. It had been a major project John – with Antony Fawcett's encouragement – worked on intermittently over a long period, he was unsure of what value his art had. The best lithomakers in Europe were called in to print the plates of Yoko and John engaged in various exotic positions of love-making. It was said, by a woman reviewer from one of the more staid English 'papers, to be a tender essay on the delights of conjugal love, in particular oral sex. 296 of the 300 sets were sold from a New Bond Street gallery when the exhibition opened. John's personal cut was £35,000 from the £150,000 gross. An obsenity charge thrown out by the magistrate helped to keep the interest going. What anyone could find obscene in a lithograph of Yoko masturbating, John Lennon was at a loss to explain. Why so many scenes of oral sex? he was asked. 'Because I like it.'

However the signing of the lithographs was cut short by a phone call from Ottawa. Would John like to talk to President Trudeau about his peace campaign? A commission appointed by the government to find out whether marijuana should be legalised also wanted to speak to him. In addition, Marshal McLuhan, media expert and author of *The Medium is the Message* engaged in a TV debate with Lennon, notable for his first ever anti-drug reference. 'Speed kills', he said in response to a question about drugs. It was a slogan from London coined to explain the inevitable behaviour of people who took methedrine, a stimulant that quickly convinced its takers that everyone was plotting against them and turned close friends into police informants, chance strangers in the street into police tails.

The considered view of Lennon about drugs was that marijuana should be legalised, and all the others banned. The fifty minute meeting with Trudeau did little to harm Pierre's 'swinging' image, John had hired a train that took 3 days to make the appointment on December 22, one of the proudest days of his life. In Britain, he was regarded as cracked, in Canada – a haven for draft dodgers from across the border – his views were taken completely seriously. Trudeau was impressive and came out after their talk to be photographed with the odd couple. In John Lennon he had engendered a deep respect.

Back in London, John and Yoko took up more of the injustices in the world. The American Indians had been the victim of genocide, they said. Black Power leader, Michael X, like his American counterpart, Malcolm X, was quite clear in his message that Black Power wanted to overthrow the whole paraphernalia of white exploitation – yet because he was usually to be found in the company of white people – especially young white women – it was somehow presumed the 'Underground' would be spared when the assassins were sent out to do their work. Although various armed and very mean-looking black men rendezvoused with Michael X during his meetings with the whites, Lennon and Yoko found his cause worthy of support. The Black House received funds from 'the prince of peace' as a fervent admirer had described him in Toronto. Yoko herself had been the object of much racial disparagement, which took the form of subtle jibes like 'Nip' when she and John walked through the crowd. Indeed, all the hurts and injustices of the world found their counterpart in the increasingly confused interior landscapes of John and Yoko's minds.

At the beginning of the new decade she was in Denmark in the remote hamlet of Aalborg where her ex-husband Tony Cox was living with Kyoko in a farmhouse. She wanted Kyoko back, and was certain it would be easy to arrange, she had always been able to dominate him. Now, although he had been given custody of the child, the loss to her had only just begun to sink in. She was stunned to find that Cox was adamant, she could not have the five-year-old. He harmlessly filmed John Lennon having a bath with the child splashing away. Allen Klein was called over to see if he could prevail, yet not even the master wheeler dealer could fix it. A deep depression hit Yoko as the reality sunk in, she had gained a Beatle but lost her own flesh and blood. A girl in the nearest hairdressing salon received a call to visit the farmhouse. There she removed the locks of John Lennon and Yoko Ono; a woman often lops off her hair when losing a love, John joined her in the ritual mourning. Then, the couple returned to the empty acres of Tittenhurst Park depression deepening all the time.

In a contest between two wills as strong as those of John and Yoko, the only solution was for one partner to sink into passivity and inertia. This was the role Lennon now took, for someone as event orientated as himself it was a dangerous inactivity. His chameleon-like nature, his ultra sensitivity that for so long had tuned into the mood of the world at large, now became overtaken by the grief and rage of the former psychiatric patient. The rows and sullen silences were frightening to the household of cook, two secretaries, live-in couple as caretakers and Anthony Fawcett, personal assistant. Visitors were rare, the workmen furiously remodelled the house Lennon was spending hundreds and thousands upon, including the installation of an artificial lake. When the kitchen where they mostly lived came to be renovated, he moved out to the Inn on the Park hotel with Yoko.

To John Lennon the on-coming black mood could be easily explained. He had been 'living at 20,000 miles an hour, and at this rate I won't see 40.' But even the passivity could break down. One morning at the end of January he had woken up with the words of a song ringing around his head.

'Instant karma's gonna get you, gonna knock you right on the head, get yourself together you're gonna be dead . . .
We all shine on, like the moon and the stars in the sky'

He furiously wrote down the words as they just came like all his best songs did. The flow was back, he wanted to capture it in its first full flood. Sitting at the piano in the kitchen he sang the melody line again and again until he had it. The white Mercedes was ordered to take him into town, a piano was bought from a music store by a customer who stayed in his car and simply selected from the shopfront display. At Apple the musicians were booked, Alan White, drums, Klaus Voorman, guitar and also George Harrison. Phil Spector, who Allen Klein had brought over to produce the long moribund *Let It Be* tapes was hurriedly summonsed from the Inn on the Park – he had produced 'Will You Still Love Me Tomorrow?' by the Shirelles, and the Teddy Bears' 'To Know Him Is To Love Him', two great songs from the days when American pop ruled the world. By seven o'clock they were in the Abbey Road studios. After several hours of experimentation they had the basic tracks laid down on tape, then Lennon decided what was lacking was a big chorus. The roadies were despatched to the Speakeasy nightclub to bring back anyone who wanted to sing. Then he launched into a super powerful rendition of the song, pouring out the energy he could always summon for his music. 'Instant Karma' was in the can. It only later occurred to him that he was prophesying his own imminent meeting with the result of his own actions, and the prophet was right.

'Who do you think you are, a superstar?'

◀ Apple proves rotten to the core, and even in 1982 no one seems too eager to take over the luxurious office accommodation.

19 Pain

Five million copies of *Abbey Road* were sold in America thanks to unchecked rumours that Paul was dead, which found proof in only his back being shown on *Sergeant Pepper* and being bare-foot on *Abbey Road*. *Sergeant Pepper* had only sold four million – and Allen Klein had in his own inimitable manner extracted a 67 cents a record royalty out of Capitol. EMI boss, Sir Joseph Lockwood, agreed to twenty five per cent royalties on Beatles records. It was to transform the four's finances. At first when Klein had marched in to demand higher royalties Lockwood had said 'fine if there's something in it for both of us.'

'No you don't understand', said Klein, 'we're going to get more, you're going to get less.'

'Get out,' said Lockwood.

Accordingly, Klein trailed out the room with McCartney turning round to give a 'it's nothing to do with me' shrug. Half an hour later Klein rang to apologise for his sharp manner. Lockwood wasn't surprised.

'I've met his type before,' he said.

But he had little bargaining strength. The Beatles had agreed to write 70 songs at the time Epstein had renegotiated their royalties to 10%. They only had to release what became *Let it Be* to have fulfilled their contract – indeed it was the main reason the album had to come out, not as Lennon claimed that he wanted the world to see the group with 'their trousers down', to see there was nothing there any more. During these negotiations Klein had persuaded Lennon to keep quiet about a plan he had formulated on the plane to Toronto for the concert – to start a new band. He had later thought that the last thing he wanted was to trap himself in another group but had told Paul McCartney he wanted a divorce and hadn't spoken to him since.

By March the isolation he and Yoko had retreated into was becoming overwhelming in its intensity. Day by day she became more destructive and emotional, then they discovered she was pregnant again. The miscarriage late in

1968 had been a deep shock. Yoko had previously had an abortion while married and had needed surgery after the miscarriage. If she was to successfully carry a child through to birth, John Lennon realised, she would have to calm down. At exactly this time a member of Apple on business in the States had mailed a book to Tittenhurst Park called *The Primal Scream* by Dr Arthur Janov, a superstar American psychiatrist.

Janov's message rang bells in John Lennon's head. The hidden hurts of childhood were buried under a self-protective false personality. Neurosis could only be escaped by finding the forgotten needs which had been suppressed, and the most basic need for a wholesome self was love. False needs were created to hide the ache of the real need. Twenty books were ordered from a New York book store. 'Phone calls were placed through to California, would Janov come to England and take John and Yoko through his therapy?

Janov agreed, sending in advance his instructions. They were to retire to separate rooms, give up smoking, drinking and any drugs, they were to ignore the 'phone, not watch TV, nor listen to the radio. The 'patients' would be left facing themselves instead of being distracted out into the world. Janov arrived and began with the man who wanted to stop being a Beatle and become John Lennon. It had taken years for the fans – except the most ardent – to say for certain which Beatle performed which song, while in the early days they had seemed four parts of one fabulous entity. This Brian Epstein image beguiled Lennon just as much as the world.

'Look at me, what I am s'posed to be
what I am s'posed to do'

asked Lennon on the record that was to come out of this therapy *John Lennon/Plastic Ono Band*.

The primal scream, said Janov, occurred when the patient in going back into his childhood came across that false adjustment to the world around the ages of five to seven where he gives up trying to obtain the love he cannot obtain. After a few days Dr Janov had two very shaken patients, now he wanted to separate them more drastically – physically. They checked into different hotels in central London, where the screams of hurt and rejection echoed through the lush but soulless rooms.

Janov told Lennon one of his problems was facing up to

his guilt at not being a good father to Julian – he was recreating exactly the same situation that had occurred between him and his father. Lennon arranged to see Cynthia and went over, glad at the chance to be together again with Julian. While at Cynthia's a 'phone call came through from Tittenhurst Park. Yoko had taken an overdose. He hurried back, it was the last time he saw Cynthia. Yoko – shaken by the therapy – could not bear the threat that John would return to his former wife. About this time Freddy Lennon and wife Pauline paid a visit to Tittenhurst Park with their young son David. A large part of John's painful memories were to do with his missing father, now he had learnt to feel the pain of that separation and the anger that naturally accompanied it. One particularly vivid memory he had dredged up from deep down in the repressed layers of himself had been an incident that happened in the fateful summer of 1946 when he was at Janov's critical age of five. He was playing on the beach, happy that he would soon be setting off for a new country with Freddy instead of staying with Aunt Mimi. Freddy had let him wander off while he went for a drink with his navy pal who he planned to emigrate with. The young boy, short sighted even then, had stumbled into a great hole on the shore and couldn't get out. For hours he struggled afraid he was left for dead. Eventually the search party scouring the beach found him, it had been a close run thing, he had been nearly buried alive.

Freddy was taken aback by his son's furious greeting, he positively screamed when he saw the new family Freddy had acquired. A wave of rage and fury swept over him.

'Get out of this house. When I was a child you left me to perish. If you don't go now, I'll have you buried in a slab next to the car on the lawn.'

Freddy left, noticing the battered Austin Maxi John Lennon had driven into a ditch the previous summer while visiting one of his mother's sisters. He was not to know that the Janov-treated John Lennon had just relived the time he had nearly died in that pit – apparently forsaken again by his father. Alfred and Pauline now made their own way in the world, to help them get started in married life John had been paying the rent on their flat by the sea.

It was a time of separations and new beginnings. Paul broke the silence of nearly five months to announce he was leaving the Beatles and was going to bring out his own LP *McCartney*. The other three members of the group sent

Ringo round to ask him to delay release of the album until *Let it Be* had come out. The long-suffering McCartney who had struggled hardest of all to keep the group together threw Ringo out of his Cavendish Avenue home. A perceptive feature writer in 1964 in the conservative *Daily Telegraph* had predicted the Beatles would break up when the male bonding was broken by the four marrying very different wives. The previous year Paul and John had married within a few days of each other. Their wives encouraged them to believe in themselves, they could make it alone. Lennon had accused McCartney of trying to take over leadership of the group, of hogging all the 'A' side of singles, of calling the group in to make albums at a few days' notice so that he got the lion's share of the new songs with Lennon hurriedly writing a few songs to make up the required number. It was untrue – apart from the songs for *Magical Mystery Tour* where Lennon's only contribution had been 'I Am The Walrus' – one of his very best in any case – a count of the songs on *Sergeant Pepper, White Album* and *Abbey Road* reveals an equal contribution. Lennon had berated McCartney for putting out what he considered lightweight numbers such as 'Ob-Bla-Di, Ob-Bla-da' and 'Hello Goodbye', while McCartney had vainly resisted 'Revolution No. 9' – Lennon's vision of what a revolution would be like – going on to the *White Album*. Each in actual fact felt stifled by the direction the other wanted to go, the musical compromises that resulted in the Beatle sound had become increasingly hard to make. Lennon wanted to give primacy to his lyrics which could then be received by a wondering intellectual élite. McCartney, distrustful of the avant garde, wanted to communicate his music to the greatest number of people possible. The world needed music, that was his philosophy. Ringo Starr, the impassive observer of both musicians, had been convinced that on one occasion McCartney had failed to carry it off with a new composition. In the lift he found himself whistling it. 'That's one thing you have to give Paul,' he said in mock chagrin, 'he writes bloody catchy tunes.'

After Paul's phone call, John Lennon shut himself away for days. Dr Janov advised John and Yoko that they should continue the course in California. This time Lennon managed to get a temporary American visa. For four months he and Yoko rented a flat in Bel Air, and twice a week attended group therapy sessions which usually ended in tears. When he returned to Britain, recharged, he set to work on his first solo album, saying of the primal therapy treatment 'Janov showed me how to feel my own fear and pain. Therefore I can handle it better than I could before, that's all. I'm just the same, only there's a channel. It doesn't just remain in me, it goes round and out. I can move easier. I still think that Janov's therapy is great, you know, but I don't want to make it a big Maharishi thing. If people know what I've been through there, and if they want to find out, they can find out, otherwise it turns into that again. Primal therapy allowed us to feel feelings continually, and those feelings usually make you cry. That's all. I was blocking the feelings, and when the feelings come through, you cry. It's as simple as that really.'

He did not say that there had been constant rows between Yoko and Janov and they had broken off the treatment. It was in character. He had seized the opportunity to leave the Maharishi after being the one who had plunged most fanatically into hours of meditation. The accusations against the Maharishi had created a doubt, when he saw that even George took them seriously he had left, it was as if he were looking for the perfect father and at the first sign of imperfection thought his father must be somewhere else. As indeed he was.

John Lennon/Plastic Ono Band is a brave, honest record, utterly different from all that had gone before. But it also fitted a pattern. John Lennon had always wanted to expose society by exposing himself – it had even been so when a national newspaper had been helped to expose the beatnik 'horror', with Stuart Sutcliffe and himself two malignant symptoms of the disease. Now, with minimalist backing from Alan White and Klaus Voorman, and himself on piano and vocals he told the world who he thought he really was.

'People say we've got it made
Don't they know we're so afraid'
'I learned something about my ma and my pa
they didn't want me so they made me a star'

John Lennon hardly ever changed his lyrics to suit the public – although the song sheet on 'Give Peace A Chance' says 'mastication' while he actually sings 'masturbation', but the honesty employed in his song 'Mother' is that of a man reliving the most traumatic moment of his life when he had to choose between his parents at the age of five. As he sings

'Mother please don't go'

he is there once again watching his mother walk out of the door, unable to bear the past. The whole album has an apparently unrelieved sombreness as John Lennon takes us through his various hells, but it is necessary because he has realised that to make it

'First you must learn to smile as you kill
if you want to be like the folk on the hill.'

He is the working class hero, the abandoned child trying to acquire the middle-class ways of his prosperous aunt who never talks about his 'disgraced' parents and who never answers his questions about them.

He believes that 'love is free, love is living, love is needing to be loved.'

'You sit there with a cock in your hand
don't get you nowhere, don't make you a man.'

But the final conclusion is 'it's gonna be alright', there is the grand perspective.

'Don't you worry about what you've done, no remember, remember, the fifth of November.'

Boom. The explosion to end all explosions is the cause of the angst of humanity, the underlying backdrop to individual pain. The real fear the neuroses disguise.

'They're afraid of everyone
afraid of the sun
isolation
the sun may never disappear
but the world may not have many years isolation.'

Lennon was later to say that 'if the Beatles or the sixties had a message, it was to learn to swim. And once you learn to swim, swim.' Characteristically he put it better on the record.

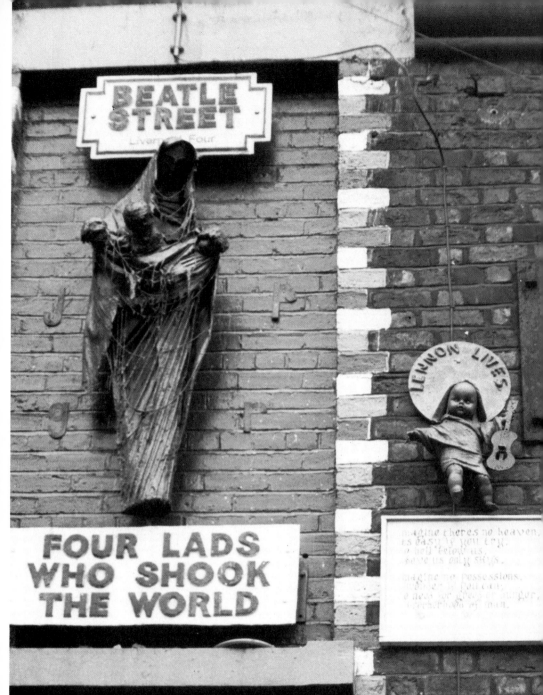

◀ A recording studio was built at Tittenhurst Park and it was here that 'Imagine' was recorded in the summer of 1971.

20 Imagine

If the beginning of the decade had seen the actual end of the Beatle partnership between John Lennon and Paul McCartney, it was the end of 1970, December 30 to be exact, that it took on a legal reality as McCartney initiated proceedings to have himself released from Allen Klein's managership. He had been advised by Lee Eastman that the only way he could achieve this was by suing the other three Beatles as well as Klein. The court cases were to go on for years.

McCartney tried ringing Lennon, then writing, he had been out of favour since doing a self-interview on his first solo album release in which he had told the world he had no regrets at the break-up. Love sometimes manifests itself through an excess of hate, and so it was between them. Lennon was later to comment 'If you can't fight with your best friend, who can you fight with?' They had been living in each other's pockets for thirteen years and had shared experiences no other mortal on earth could even conceive. It was not only the public who sometimes found it difficult to sort the two out, the roles had merged, now Lennon started setting up McCartney as the little queer, the mean-minded businessman. he replied with a cryptic card asking 'How and Why?'

Paul in return replied. 'By all signing a piece of paper agreeing to dissolve the partnership because we don't have a partnership anymore.'

A further card arrived at Cavendish Avenue – 'Get well soon. Get the other signatures and I will think about it.'

To get to the top and stay there, Lennon was to reveal, the Beatles had to be the biggest bastards in the world. Certainly the acerbity released by primal therapy turned Lennon into as big a threat to the Apple staff as Allen Klein. Quickly he got rid of Peter Asher, brother of Jane, and Ron Kass – between them they had sold 16 million records. Peter Brown and Neil Aspinall, the friends from

Liverpool, were not re-elected to the Apple board at Klein's instigation, but they were saved, all other friends who telephoned their old friend John Lennon got no reply as the smart Georgian office block in London's swanky Saville Row turned into an abattoir. Lennon decided he had been taken for a ride by his old friends and now acted with utter ruthlessness. One day on a whim he fired the whole press office and replaced them with Les Perrin an altogether straighter character than the expansive Derek Taylor. Even the indefatigable personal assistant Anthony Fawcett jumped whenever Lennon barked out a 'shurrup' to some unfortunate Apple person.

'It's alright Anthony, you haven't been fired,' soothed the quietly spoken Yoko.

After *John Lennon/Plastic Ono Band* was released and rather predictably failed to ignite the public imagination the way was clear for dark horse George Harrison to take over the running with an unprecented triple album that was easy to fill because he had so much work unused from the Beatles years. It was a huge success, especially one number 'My Sweet Lord' which set a new tone of optimism for early 1971. It is not often that decades announce their flavour so early, but 1970 had been a strange year. A Conservative government had managed to get elected in spite of all the opinion polls (or perhaps because of) predicting an easy victory for Labour. The public tired of the socialist experiment that also included the four 'working class' lads from Liverpool. Strange undercurrents were at work, in America the Vietnam war obstinately refused to go away, it simply became more and more futile as well as ruinously expensive. It set off a burst of inflation that undermined the wealth of America and with it that country's unchallenged leadership. After the supreme self-confidence of the 60s with the face-down of Russia by Kennedy, a new mood of doubt and a hankering for the old safe values began to creep in.

After the release of *John Lennon/Plastic Ono Band* the couple at Tittenhurst Park were astonishingly quiet. Lennon had set himself a new direction with his stark realism and uncompromising stance. Above all his imageless biting lyrics. The poet had retired to the background as the angry confused man behind stepped forward. But it was all an attempt to lose the Beatle image; he was bored, getting fat and lonely in the rolling acres of his English country home, it was easy for Yoko to persuade him to go to her old stomping ground of New York where she felt she would be able to find some role for herself in the avant garde art world. Most people in England, it seemed, hated her, she had even seriously thought there were plans afoot to murder her as the Beatles realised John Lennon was determined to leave the group – and Paul McCartney in particular. Yoko's second pregnancy had ended in the same disastrous way as the first, while arch-rival Linda McCartney presented Paul with a bouncing daughter.

In New York, Lennon felt a sudden influx of energy. The city struck him with the same sense of excitement that London had first done. He recognised it as the centre of the artists' world and gave a long thoughtful interview to the serious rock journal *Rolling Stone.* In America he was treated as a significant artist. The British by contrast he said, regarded him as someone who had met Paul McCartney and got lucky. In his interview Lennon set about putting the record straight saying it was Epstein and McCartney who had forced him into the 'fab four' image with suits and ties and a political consciousness only slightly above that of a moron. He shocked the world by telling of the sexual shenanigans that accompanied the tours, said he had always needed a drug to survive – that did not go down well in the city where the battle over the Beatles' fortunes continued, over a million pounds in royalties were held by EMI until in March the judge appointed a receiver who froze all funds being paid out of Apple pending the wrangle being resolved. It effectively ended Klein's managership but it also meant that the four ex-Beatles with their vast outgoings were suddenly having to be conscious of money, threats of huge arrears of tax to be paid convinced the prodigal Lennon who vastly enjoyed being rich that he had been swindled, that he had to keep on making records and needed some cash. It was as McCartney had sung on Abbey Road 'only funny pieces of paper' they received, instead of money.

McCartney's second album *Ram* features on its back cover two beetles screwing, while in the song lyrics were references to 'too many people going underground.' John's first single of '71 had been a militant cliché-ridden anthem – 'Power to the People' – that had all of Yoko Ono's abrasive qualities and none of John Lennon's deft touch. He lived in two pairs of 'bib and braces' jeans, occasionally donning military uniform. The clown had gone to be replaced by what the public saw as a dangerous malcontent.

Yoko learnt in April where former husband Tony Cox had taken her daughter Kyoko. 'The best babysitter in the world' was showing unwelcome signs of independence. She determined that the six year old would be better off living with her. John Lennon she knew had a way with children and although he spoke on the phone to Julian he still felt guilty about having left him. For the first two years Julian had hardly missed having his often-absent father around. Gradually, it dawned he was not coming back and was not on some long tour of Australia or the Far East. He began to miss him and realise he had liked him. His father meanwhile had been meeting the folks in Japan, his relationship to Yoko was one of the East and West meeting, an encapsulation of the future. The way the globe would have to be.

Kyoko was playing in a playground on the tourist island of Majorca off the Spanish coast unaware that the people sitting watching her in a parked car were planning to kidnap her. Her mother came over to her at the swings.

'Do you want to come for a ride with Mummy?' Yoko asked her, accompanied by a tense John Lennon.

The child was delighted to see her mother, it had been an infrequent occurrence over the previous three years. Tony Cox on his return to the playground quickly put together, from the reports of the odd couple who had taken his daughter off, what had happened. He called the police.

'My daughter's been kidnapped', he explained, giving a description of the kidnappers.

Before their plane could take off, the Lennons were arrested and taken to the police station for 14 hours of questioning. The mother and her husband were told that the courts would have to decide who had custody, although no kidnapping charges would be preferred.

The magistrate had spent most of his life on the quiet, slow island although he spoke perfect English. The years had taught him their accompanying wisdom. He heard the two parents arguing their cases, then waved for the bewildered Kyoko to take his hand. Out of the courtroom he crouched down to her level and gently asked her who she wanted to live with.

'Daddy,' she answered simply.

The decision was made. Furious, the Lennons flew back to London while Tony Cox set off for the United States.

Increasingly obsessed by the loss that seemed to accompany all her loves, Yoko persuaded John to fly to New York in pursuit of her child. Tony Cox had gone to ground, private investigators were hired to track him down. The visit was recorded for posterity when John and Yoko joined Frank Zappa on stage at Fillmore East for a performance that included Yoko getting into her bag and wailing. The wickedly mischievous Zappa had the crowd chanting 'Scumbag' while Yoko writhed. But there were some blank spots in her make-up, the whole episode was faithfully put out as the fourth side of the double LP *Some Time in New York City*.

Tony Cox had to keep his wits about him as with his new wife Melinda and Kyoko he felt the full effects of being pursued by a couple with an endless supply of money – and therefore henchmen. An investigator reported to Yoko that he had been on the tail of the man and child but Cox had eluded him in a high-speed car chase.

'Man and child?' screamed Yoko. 'It's my daughter you're talking about.'

She and John had returned to the beautiful but lonely Tittenhurst Park with its thinly autographed friendship wall and its acres of rolling wooded hills. It was an island. Like the uninhabited island John had bought off the coast of Ireland in 1966 and then given to Sid Rawle, self-proclaimed hippy ruler, former shepherd and inveterate romantic who immediately proposed to any girl who would date the hoarse voiced red haired man. Lennon set to work recording in the studio at Tittenhurst with George Harrison agreeing to play on a new album that was to become *Imagine*. George riding high on the success of 'My Sweet Lord' was putting together the greatest rock'n'roll event ever, *The Concert for Bangla Desh* to raise money for the victims of that country's civil war. Madison Square Gardens was booked for August 1 for two concerts. Ringo Starr, John Lennon, Bob Dylan, Eric Clapton, Ravi Shankar, were just some of the luminaries who had agreed to appear, George seemed to have successfully combined a mystical bent with commercial popularity, a lesson not lost on John Lennon. He played around with an old theme 'Imagine this ... imagine that ...' something he had admired in Yoko's book *Grapefruit* which was now republished to scenes of pandemonium at a signing session in the large London store of Selfridges.

Lennon wrote out the ultimate utopian fantasy:–

'Imagine there's no heaven
it's easy if you try
Imagine there's no countires
it isn't hard to do
Nothing to kill or die for
and no religion too
You may say I'm a dreamer
but I'm not the only one
I hope some day you'll join us
and the world will live as one.'

It was a more sugar-coated vision than he had presented the previous year, the music had been lifted out of total relegation, it was more commercial and still saying what he thought. He felt he was getting back on course and talked about making 'Gimme some Truth' the single from the album; that was very good too, he knew, but the title song 'Imagine' had an overwhelming power to it, the power of a man who tried to spend two hours every day simply gazing out at the countryside listening to his inner voices. Klaus Voorman on bass, Nicky Hopkins on piano and Jim Keltner on drums plus the suddenly golden George Harrison put back some life into the music which had before primal therapy been Lennon's only emotional release.

Now if he felt vituperative, he would just let it come out, unsublimated, uncensored; Lennon had started to become the naked man with no masks, feeling his emotions and no longer ashamed of them. Via the medium of record he talked to McCartney, not unaware that controversy never did record sales any harm. In 'How Do You Sleep At Night?' he declaims:

'You live with straights who tell you you was king
the only thing you done was yesterday
and since you're gone you're just another day
a pretty face may last a year or two
but pretty soon we'll see what you can do
The sound you make is muzak to my ears,
you must have learned something in all those years.'

It was witty in a deadly kind of way, Lennon was rekind-ling his sense of humour, even going as far as to hold a pig by its ears in a similar fashion to the 'crofter' McCartney holding a ram on his album cover. The critics joined the condemnation of Paul's second album, though the single 'Another Day' which the barbs of Lennon had aimed at, had at last restored McCartney to the charts.

The professional conmen among the 'underground' also felt the full fury of Lennon in his dismissive 'No short-haired, yellow-bellied son of tricky dicky is gonna mother-hubbard soft-soap me with just a pocketful of hope.'

It was the most commercially successful solo album John Lennon wrote – until the rebirth that was *Double Fantasy*, but *Imagine* was the dying flicker of the once furnace fires burning inside. Yoko had ideas of bringing the talents of her husband into worthwhile consciousness-raising directions, but he had never been the man to tow the party line. He had given up the peace campaign complaining of the way Yoko had driven him ceaselessly on behalf of the cause.

A few days after the album's completion, he and Yoko flew to New York for the Bangla Desh concert, an event that was to restore people's faith in the power of the rock fraternity to be a force for good. The preparations were proceeding at a frantic pace – the event had been planned over a matter of days, so compelled did George feel to help the millions of refugees. The list of stars who wanted to appear continued to grow . . . the tickets for the two shows had sold out instantaneously. John asked the harrassed George what Yoko could do.

'Well, I've no objection to her listening in the audience,' he flippantly replied. He was king now.

John angrily demanded that Yoko appear with him or he would return to London. George – remembering the dreadful experience of the wailing Yoko emerging from a bag while he played painfully, very painfully, learned guitar to the limit of artistry – was adamant. No Yoko Ono. Even Eric Clapton wasn't getting a single spot. After half an hour John turned on his heels, ordered his car and drove to the airport leaving Yoko hysterically ranting at the quietly determined George. She followed John home the next day and tore into him for not pushing harder on her behalf. They knew the concert would be a staggering success – even without them. Indeed, George Harrison managed to eventually donate many thousands to Bangla Desh and many millions to the tax authorities.

It took several days for Yoko and John to get back onto speaking terms. Although the attempted kidnap had failed, John, Yoko and Allen Klein were absolutely confident they would outsmart Tony Cox with all the power and money at their disposal. The McCartney court case revealed that in the 18 months Klein had been managing, the group's earnings had been £9 million, more than in the previous six years. The new royalties deal had become a source of fabulous wealth. *Let it Be,* in spite of being a critical failure was a runaway commercial success, eventually selling six million copies worldwide, as many as *The White Album,* only one million short of *Sergeant Pepper.* McCartney's lawyer revealed that Klein had been convicted of tax evasion. It did not stop Lennon's support of him in the proxy war with McCartney.

The lawyers advised that Yoko should go to the Virgin Islands where she and Tony Cox had been divorced to seek custody of Kyoko in the courts. After a late night appearance on Michael Parkinson's TV chat show, the couple flew out of Britain. It was September 1971, the last time that John Lennon was to see his green and pleasant England. The doctors they had consulted about Yoko's miscarriages had told John that with his life of self-abuse and indulgence in drugs his sperm count was very low. While Yoko's two miscarriages and her age (38) also suggested it was unlikely she would be able to carry a child to full term. Getting back the child she had borne, became vital.

◀ John Lennon in 1973. An FBI surveillance team reported that his heavy
use of narcotics had even alienated his radical friends like Abbie
Hoffman and Jerry Rubin.

21 'What's Happening Man?'

The Lennon flying circus took up residence at the staid St
Regis hotel. Although they were originally simply in America to continue the battle for custody of Kyoko, the couple
found the intense excitement of New York a shot in the
arm.

Tony Cox meanwhile surfaced in Houston, Texas, where
he successfuly applied for custody of Kyoko (whose name
was changed to Rosemary) at the Houston Domestic Rela-
tions Court. Yoko was granted extensive access – 6 weeks
in the summer, 10 days at Christmas plus two weekends a
month while she was living in the United States. The move
to the United States of trunkloads of personal belongings
from Tittenhurst Park began, 18 in all soon cluttered the
rooms at the St Regis. Yoko knew New York from the days
when she was studying at Sarah Lawrence College (also
attended by Linda Eastman) a school for daughters of the
wealthy. For fifteen years she had hung out with the art
avant garde – Andy Warhol, John Cage and their numerous imitators. It had been her school and after years of
trying she had become known around the Village, at least,
as a 'name' artist. In 1966 England had seemed to be the
place. Now she returned with an ex-Beatle on her arm.
John had been giving her the 'B' side of his singles since
'Cold Turkey', but apart from the flipside of 'Power to the
People' – 'Open Your Box' – they had disappeared without
trace. 'Box' as a word for the pubic region was American
but the ever watchful EMI executives hadn't needed a
familiarity with American coloquial *lingua franca,* Yoko
had spelt out the message 'Open your legs John,' in the
lyrics.

The public image of Yoko was as a sexy siren – vividly
promoted by herself when she wasn't reassuring people by
saying she was really rather square. Certainly her upbring-

ing had been strict. Boys were not mentioned, even if they wrote out of the blue Yoko was castigated by her aristocratic mother. She must have encouraged the communication by thinking about boys. It was the imagine concept, whatever you spoke came about in Yoko's world. The wished-for sexual fulfilment (or at least an attempt) did not come until the age of 26 when she was married. Like a lot of late starters, the public Yoko was very sexually knowing, the private Yoko had a lot of problems handling sex, the image and the come-on interested her far more than the reality. She was into mind games. John thought Yoko's first big art exhibition on home turf would gain her the recognition she had been lacking and which she desperately needed in her battle with the Beatles' worldwide adulation. But no discerning critic could make much sense of her newly arranged display of an old theme – the discarded objects of a grossly consumer-orientated society.

On John's birthday, his 31st, Yoko threw a party attended by members of Apple and the Allen Klein organisation, Allen Klein himself, Klaus Voorman, Ringo and Maureen, close journalists. It became apparent that the couple had no American friends – but that was soon to change.

'Power to the People' had been written earlier in the year by Lennon fresh from an interview with the politically ultra-left Tariq Ali, a Pakistani who had made his name leading anti-Vietnam war protests in Britain. In the interview Lennon, chameleon-like as ever, spoke of his wish for everything to be shared out equally, for democracy to mean that workers took control of their lives. He was later to say he hadn't been able to solve the conflict between his professed working-class origins and his possession of so much of the world's goods. It was what made him such a source of fascination. So as he spent thousands on Tittenhurst Park he also supported the burgeoning opposition to the Conservative Heath government, sending £1,000 to some shipyard workers who had taken over their works on the Clyde when it was threatened with closure.

In the States the underground political opposition was more organised, in Britain it rarely went beyond rhetoric. The Yippie organisers of the violent demonstrations at the Democratic 1968 convention for Humphrey (which had probably helped Richard Nixon to squeeze into office) – Jerry Rubin and Abbie Hoffman – were counter-culture heroes. Lennon was eager to be courted by these leaders of dissident youth. He took part in rallies to free poet John Sinclair, jailed for 10 years when set up by an undercover policewoman to who he passed two joints. Sinclair was freed. He took part in another rally protesting the conditions at Attica State prison where many prisoners had been killed in a riot. He campaigned on behalf of the Red Indians. Yoko was back in her element and a willing Lennon got a buzz out of all the activity after lying fallow for so long in the English countryside. He saw himself as a poet, like the Yippies started to hang out at the Yippie headquarters, Max's Kansas City in Greenwich Village, he was in reality getting to know his wife's adopted home town.

The Yippie leaders paraded their new star support at press conferences, and began planning tactics for disrupting the Republican convention at San Diego early in '72. They thought they had John Lennon's agreement to play concerts there raising much needed funds, and announced it to the press. Unbeknown to them all, the dirty tricks department of the Campaign to Re-elect the President under Attorney-General John Mitchell had thoroughly infiltrated their organisation. It was quickly appreciated that Lennon could help Yippie plans for disruption, protest and strident youth rallies by providing a flood of money from concerts. Secret memos passed back and forth, the New York immigration department revoked an extension of his visa five days after originally granting it. The case passed to the lawyers and a four and a half year saga that cost Lennon $250,000 was set in train. Not that the Lennons were entirely above using the law for their own ends. During Xmas 1971 in Texas, they planned to have Kyoko/Rosemany for 10 days as stipulated by the court. First they were to spend a weekend getting used to each other again. Tony Cox refused to let Kyoko out of his sight. A tremendous row ensued. Cox, now a born-again Christian did not think the couple fit to look after the child. He took the case to court, showed a film of Lennon happily splashing in the bath when she was five, retold how Yoko had once held a broken bottle to his neck while he was in the bath for 45 minutes, how she had stabbed him in the heel. But the Lennon's laywer succeeded in putting Cox in jail three days before Christmas. He woke up screaming for his daughter in the cell. The next day the Court relented and released him on bail. The object of the battle – as is so often the case – was split in two and at one point was under a psychiatrist in California. Cox was deter-

mined to hang onto her, in spite of the Allen Klein organised lawyers who harrassed him. The Lennon's Christmas
record 'Happy Xmas, War is over' was climbing up the
charts. John Lennon had always wanted to have a Christmas evergreen hit. It came about in circumstances that
could hardly have been less full of goodwill. By March
1972 the lawyers had persuaded the Houston court to
grant Yoko custody but Tony Cox had fled again. John
Lennon dared not leave the country in pursuit, because of
his immigration problems. Kyoko passed out of Yoko's life.
The campaign for social injustices to be remedied was
intensified on a vehemently political record John Lennon
put together with Elephant's Memory, a band who had
performed two of the tracks on *Midnight Cowboy*.

1972 became a progressively nightmarish year for the
Lennons. The initial appeal of the fantastic energy of
America showed its other side, the uneasy, unceasing
struggle of powerful forces. The phone in their studio
apartment was tapped, wherever Lennon went he noticed
a burly, thoroughly unpleasant character following him. A
new single in which he adopted the stridently fought cause
of women's liberation 'Woman Is The Nigger Of The
World' was banned by practically all radio stations. He
appeared on the Dick Cavett TV show and said he was
being followed – it demonstrated to the world he had
become paranoid – but the shadowing stopped. The Mayor
of New York, John Lindsey, appealed on Lennon's behalf
to the immigration authorities. It was to no avail. *Some
Time In New York City* was released to a universal panning. It was a compendium of causes without a touch of the
lyrical musician or poet, instead came bleak slogans, Lennon had become the tool of the propagandists, but they
were causes he felt strongly about. 'The Luck Of The Irish'
bitterly said:
'Why the hell are the English there anyway
As they kill with God on their side?
Blame it all on the kids and the IRA!
As the bastards commit genocide.'

He performed songs in support of Angela Davis, John
Sinclair, the inmates of Attica State Prison. It was a reflection of what was going on. But the most interesting part of
the album was the release of two live sessions. From the
1969 Lyceum concert where George played with Yoko on
stage for positively the last time, and from the Frank Zappa

Fillmore East 1971 concert.

Derisory reviews and derisory sales convinced Lennon to start getting back to being a musician again. The FBI reported in files revealed by the Freedom of Information Act that his ultra heavy use of narcotics had even alienated his Yippie friends. His support group Elephant's Memory became just that. Allen Klein dolefully reported that in the last quarter of 1972 profits made from his 20 per cent share of the Beatles' income were only $100,000, and that was mostly from George. Lennon had committed commercial suicide. About the only good thing about the year was that Paul McCartney and he had quietly got together again for a chat. In the future he would drop in on Lennon and reminisce, once a TV producer offered them $3,400 to appear on his evening show *Saturday Night Live* while Paul was in the Dakota apartment. McCartney nearly persuaded Lennon to join him, but he declined. regretfully saying he was too tired. It was the nearest they ever came to a reunion. It had also been a strange year for Yoko, in May she had tried ringing Princess Margaret to see if a royal pardon could be obtained for the drug conviction that gave the American authorities the lever they needed to refuse Lennon permanent residence status. No royal pardon was forthcoming, instead the round of court appearances continued. In March '73 Lennon was again ordered to leave the US by the Immigration Department and again he appealed. Even though President Nixon had swept to power with an unprecedented majority of the votes, Lennon was still a marked man. But he had supporters like Mayor Lindsey for whom he had raised over £750,000 ($1½ million) with two concerts on behalf of retarded children. Allen Klein's manager's contract had come to an end and he tried to turn this to his advantage by offering to buy Apple. He united the former Beatles in opposition to his move and by the year's end John, George and Paul were suing Klein. Lennon in turn was sued by Klein for $200,000 as under the pressure of the immigration case, of trying to find a successful formula for a record, of a wife who longed for recognition in her own right yet failed to find it, he argued long and furiously. With Klein it was over a business deal. With Yoko it began to look increasingly unlikely that she would be able to conceive with her record of miscarriages and his own infertility due to ever-increasing drinking and drug use.

The summer drifted by, in September he set to work on a

new album. He and Yoko had moved from the chic radicalism of the Village to an imposing block of flats overlooking
Central Park called The Dakota Buildings. The block was
very solid, rather gloomy inside the long winding corridors,
in fact rather English. They had first looked at the block in
1971, now in 1973 they moved in to a seventh floor flat with
panoramic views across the park and city. The twelve
room apartment had formerly belonged to actor Robert
Ryan. Lennon felt more protected than in the Greenwich
Village flat. He was becoming less sensitive about having
a lot of money, slowly realising that in another century
Yoko would have been a Japanese princess instead of a
New York artist. Her family had come across to America to
represent Japan at the United Nations. She at least had no
doubts about where she truly belonged. It was persuading
John Lennon to accept his success that was the problem.

The new album was called *Mind Games,* and even when
he arrived at the Record Plant to begin recording he had
little idea what the lyrics of many of the songs would be.
That might have been no handicap if he had been at his
inspired best, but now he felt as though he was turning up
for work, it was simply time for another album. Heavy
drinking had a particularly unfortunate effect on his
inspiration. However, he could always be the competent
craftsman, the record was superbly produced by himself. It
contained some good ideas such as the mythical country of
Nutopia – which had no boundaries, no passports, no land,
only people – whose national anthem was three seconds of
silence. He was stepping back from commitment to, as he
put it, 'getting Jerry Rubin a job', the old sardonic distanc-
ing from the foibles of politicians was being re-established:

'We're playing those mind games together
pushing the barriers, planting seeds . . .
We've been playing those mind games forever
some kind of Druid do
Lifting the veil . . .
some call it magic
to search for the grail . . .
Love is the answer
and you know that for sure . . .
love is the flower
you gotta let it grow.'

The sentiments were those of the mystic, the optimist with
faith in the future, singing of love and its power of renewal.

The other noteworthy song on the album was 'You are Here', a lush love song to Yoko that wondered aloud on how two people from Liverpool and Tokyo came to be together. It was the projected great romance for which both had sacrificed everything else.

'Well now, East is East and West is West
the twain shall meet
East is West and West is East
when we complete
Wherever you are, you are here.'

That was the dream but the reality was different. At parties he went off with other women. When he looked at how the music had deteriorated, the business, the immigration problems, the animosity in the press, he started to turn on his one devoted supporter. He knew he had produced an uninspired album and now took off to see if he could redeem himself. Earlier in the year he had gone to California to help Ringo produce a solo album. John's contribution had been 'I'm the greatest.' Now he headed there to record an album of classic rock'n'roll songs with the legendary Phil Spector, only this time Lennon would simply be the performer, Spector would be allowed to produce and direct him – something he had not allowed in the past. May Pang, Yoko's personal assistant of several years, a Chinese-American of 25, went along as John's personal assistant. Yoko stayed in New York, the one place she felt at home. At the year's end she was giving a night club show, waving a pair of knickers above her head. The act didn't go down well.

22 Sinbad The Sailor

It took John Lennon a month to persuade the manic depressive, legendary record producer Phil Spector out of his heavily guarded Sunset Strip house. In California there is a palpable violence in the air, Spector it was said carried a gun in his waistband. But at first Lennon was delighted to have returned to the bachelor life on the pretext of working on another album. Yoko had checked out May Pang's horoscope and numbers – and found she offered no serious threats. Yoko's relationship was that of long-suffering understanding mother – that was Lennon's greatest need from a woman. With Yoko nearly eight years his senior it was an easy role to assign to her, while Yoko for her part tended to see men as 'doers', 'assistants', she did not really understand that they had insecurities just like women.

The non-stop closeness of the preceding five years had become claustrophobic, Lennon was, as he wrote, a jealous guy, he had even got her to write down a list of all the men she had been with. She had started it as a joke, then realised he was completely serious. It had turned into a truth session when they had both revealed the worst about themselves. Yoko wanted to carve out her own image for herself and come out of the shadow of being an ex-Beatle wife, a woman moreover who was blamed by most of the world for breaking up the Beatles. The rivalry between them had become intense, *Mind Games* had not, like the disastrous *Some Time in New York City*, given her some record time.

A jubilant John Lennon rented a huge beach house on the Pacific Coast Highway at Santa Monica, May Pang quickly adjusted to the role reversal of no longer being a servant, but mistress of the house with servants. At 25 she could provide a hotter time between the covers than her 40-year-old rival for Lennon's affections. But he had not come to California to exchange one domestic scene for another. Soon in residence at the house were Keith Moon, Harry Nilsson, and often Ringo Starr. Moon was a lengendary madman from the Who, while Nilsson was a highly successful singer with a weakness for the booze. Soon Lennon was trying cocaine and drinking a bottle of vodka plus half a bottle of brandy a day. In the studio Phil Spector had introduced the booze and before long all 28 musicians he had brought in for the recording were engaged on one long booze session. As always, Lennon just could not handle it. The recording sessions became a scene of surreal chaos, with Spector often failing to show at all, then Lennon discovered he had arranged for CBS records, to whom Spector was contracted, to pay for the studio time. Lennon was still contracted to Apple. He could see big legal battles once more ensuing on top of those with Klein and with Immigration. He asked for the tapes but Spector had gone to ground at his heavily guarded house and there he stayed. Waiting for Spector to come out of his manic phase, Lennon suggested to Harry Nilsson that he produce a record on which Nilsson would do some standards. It would be called 'Pussycats'. But it became one long round of drinking. Keith Moon reckoned he had a certain number of lives. There is the story told that while in London he had taken a dive out of a several storeys high hotel window when concerned friends wouldn't let him go out on the town because he was so drunk. On that occasion he had landed on a pile of plastic rubbish bags and scampered off into the night. Lennon decided that when your time is up you die. He didn't feel that time had come, for a dare he threw himself out of a car on the highway, like Moon he walked away from it.

Anyone who met John Lennon always described him as weird. But it was an inherited sense of the ridiculous. Once at a Los Angeles club – where he had only just arrived – he went to the gents and found an unused sanitary napkin on the seat. He remembered his mother walking down the road with an old pair of knickers on her head, he remembered one of the many Yoko pieces which had flooded into Kenwood – a box of Kotex with a broken red cup inside. The recipient should have taken the accompanying message 'Needs mending' more seriously. It was a naive, unconscious and very graphic sexual statement. John re-emerged with the Kotex stuck to his forehead, it was hilarious he thought.

'Do you know who I am?' he asked the waitress.

'Yeah, you're the asshole with the Kotex on his head,' she replied.

The world found Lennon very weird. Another night he was at the famous Troubadour club when Nilsson introduced him to Brandy Alexanders. Lennon knocked them back like milkshakes, then they hit him. He was into another dimension – the Smothers Brothers were performing. He saw how phoney the show was and began telling them so, he was back to his Cavern days, his Hamburg days, how he wanted his rock'n'roll album to be, when he had just enjoyed singing and didn't have to put over a Lennon message. Nilsson and he were summarily thrown out, a woman took a flash picture of the humiliation, the old street fighter Lennon moved in on her. She claimed he had hit her and he was forced to buy her off.

Yoko had the eerie ability to phone him wherever he was – unknown to him her tarot reader was being given six places he was likely to be and then told to decide which one Lennon was at, the tarot reader's ability began to unnerve Lennon as Yoko unerringly tracked him down. He began to talk of returning to New York, but Yoko said he wasn't ready. Forcing himself to cut down on drink and restraining Nilsson too, they managed to put out a very passable album.

Court cases (in July '74 Lennon was again ordered to leave the US) meant increasingly frequent visits to New York. With one completed song 'Nobody Loves You When You're Down And Out' and the beginnings of some others, Lennon set up house in a one-bedroom flat in New York City with May Pang and started work on a new album *Walls And Bridges* – it was to be his most successful solo album to date. Out of the long journey into night, the voyage of Sinbad the sailor where he encounters many monsters and demons only to overcome them, the artist was ready to take over and transmute this raw material into song, like 'Scared', where the advance of the years is given graphic reality.

Once in New York City at the recording studios Lennon set to work with a will. At home with May Pang he would amuse her by reciting his poetry, still *In His Own Write* in its whimsical humour. But he started some productive relationships – one with Elton John who had become a big name with his tender passionate songs. On the 'B' side of 'Philadelphia Freedom' Lennon plays. He helped out as Elton John gave his rendition of 'Lucy in the Sky with Diamonds'. In return, Elton John was asked to help out on 'Whatever Gets You Through the Night' which became the

single release from *Walls And Bridges.* The younger singer
gave Lennon back his belief in himself, he asked through
an intermediary whether John would join him in a live performance of 'Lucy in the Sky with Diamonds' if Lennon's
single got to No. 1. Since he had never had a US No. 1 after
going solo, it didn't seem much of a commitment to say
'yes'. But inexplicably it rose to the top, though never making higher than No. 36 in Britain where John Lennon had
been slowly forgotten. *Walls And Bridges* showed the artist
had reasserted his rightful position in the Lennon make-
up. The music was powerful, tuneful, the lyrics were sharp
but put across in the human tones of a man who had found
out once again that he shared the failings of the rest of the
world. Gone was the proseletysing. He spoke directly from
personal experience, none more so than on 'No One Loves
You When You're Down and Out.' There was a song for
Yoko 'Bless You', and a song for May Pang 'Surprise Sur-
prise/Bird of Paradox'. He had returned to centre, distilling
his experience and giving it a universality through words
and music. The bar room philosopher, the television bore
had been put to bed.

'Number 9 Dream' reasserted his belief that there was
magic in the air, May Pang was a breath of spring with surprise in her eyes while Allen Klein was lampooned with
lyrics every bit as biting as those previously directed at
McCartney. Klein, it seemed, left his smell like an alley cat.
Klaus Voorman on bass, Nicky Hopkins on piano and Jim
Keltner on drums were all people Lennon could
immediately get on with, and since he had a deportation
order due on September 8, the album was completed with
a sense of impending change. But another appeal was
lodged. On November 28, Lennon gave his positively last
stage performance as he fulfilled his promise to Elton John
at Madison Square Gardens. The crowd screamed ecstatic-
ally for 5 minutes as soon as he appeared. From then on he
went from strength to strength, seizing the audience just as
he had always previously managed to do. 'Whatever Gets
You Through The Night' and after 'Lucy in the Sky with
Diamonds' had the crowd in uproar, then in response to
demands for an encore he played his tribute to the man
who had helped launch the magic ship all those years ago.

'I thought we'd do a number by an old estranged fiancé
of mine called Paul.'

Then he shipped out with 'I Saw Her Standing There'.

The circle had been neatly described. Backstage Yoko and John came face to face, they said little but the eyes locked in to their very similar wavelengths. It was love all over again, they started dating.

◄ Sean Lennon, almost a miracle birth. To John Lennon all that was important was that his 'first born' should receive the love and attention he wanted and his father had missed.

23 Starting Over

In December 1974, Rolling Stone magazine came out with a story which alleged there had been an illegal conspiracy by the Nixon government – now in deep trouble over the Watergate break-in – to expel John Lennon from America. It was the breakthrough he had been waiting for in his long-fought immigration case. On January 2, 1975, a judge ruled in favour of Lennon's lawyers being allowed to look at the immigration files, he had the soon-to-be-disgraced Immigration going into reverse. Things had started to go right at the end of '74. Phil Spector, under pressure from Capitol, returned the rock'n'roll tapes that had been made in Los Angeles the previous year after keeping them under guard in his house (he had kept John and May Pang locked up in the house when they first called on him, being very weird even by Lennon standards). As though tidying up his past Lennon, who had written most of *Walls And Bridges* in a few days and then pushed his session musicians almost to breaking point by recording in 4 days, now set to work finishing the *Rock'n'Roll* album. After 5 days all the old Gene Vincent, Buddy Holly, Chuck Berry numbers he had grown up with were in the can. The album cover was a Jürgen Vollmer shot of him in a Hamburg doorway – the complete cycle had been described, the creative forces spent. Since 1960 he had been a musician and a Beatle 24 hours a day, he had given his all and then from vast reserves of that energy we only call on in an emergency he had managed to keep going through all the traumas of the Beatles break-up and then that with Yoko. He was a man travelling fast, always pushing on to the next experience, because that was where his songs came from. The wellsprings of his youth, as with any artist, held the key to his orientation on the world, but that was not the whole story, there have been plenty of abandoned children in the world who have not become musicians. But it was the overpowering blow of losing his mother for the second time at 17 that ignited an all-consuming passion for music.

He said that whenever he heard Beatles music he simply recalled the session, who sat where, who argued with who and all the mistakes that were made. But behind all this perfectionism lay the goddess of the music and that goddess, that muse, was Julia. 'Hello Little Girl' the first song he ever wrote was based on a 1930s number his mother had sung in pubs and family gatherings when she was the comedienne as well as the singer.

'You're delightful, you're delicious
isn't it a pity you're a scatterbrain?'

'Please Please Me' was written in his bedroom at Menlove Avenue, a form of release for a young man who could not grieve, music became a lifeline away from unhappiness. Both he and Paul McCartney had known death and tragedy in the family early, they sought to spread happiness, it accorded with the mood of the times. In December of '74, Julian joined May Pang and John Lennon in Florida (the 11-year-old had played drums on *Walls And Bridges'* 'Ya Ya'). Cynthia had rung to remind him that for five years he had had hardly any contact with his son. The toll of the years had been heavy, he was actually too sensitive to his environment to be able to withstand the pressures, it was his strength as a songwriter that he could so instantly tune into the mass mood but it meant he was almost a medium for the wishes of the people. His songs were personal and yet they plumbed through to the wellsprings of all common experience. Now he felt he had earned his time trying to make his own life. Yoko and he met as though for the first time. Their real problem was being unable to have a child and create their own family as his former collaborator, Paul, had done. Lennon joked in an interview 'He's got 120 kids and made 20 million records, he doesn't have time to talk,' yet the pair who were apparently so different both needed the shelter of a family after giving so much of themselves. In January 1975, John took Yoko with him to an old Chinese acumpuncturist in San Francisco. The kindly man listened patiently as John explained how a doctor had told him he had damaged himself by years of excess, sexual excess, drug excess, general excess. The acupuncturist would have none of it.

'You have a child by your wife. Give up drugs, live clean, after 18 months you get a child.'

In February on one of his visits to Dakota to see Yoko, Lennon simply stayed on. They both gave up drugs, including smoking. By spring she was writing cards to friends announcing she and John were back together and that she was pregnant. This time everything was put aside except the business of getting Yoko through her pregnancy. John spirited her away to a house in the country where no-one could find them. Still complications set in, she moved to a hospital, with John Lennon in constant attendance – one day she was given the wrong blood in a transfusion and but for him spotting the warning signals could have died. On October 9 by Caesarian section, 3 weeks before normal term delivery, Sean Lennon was born, dark haired like his mother, a healthy 8 lbs and destined like the royal line he came from, to inherit wealth beyond the dreams of men. As compensation for the 9 months of nerve wracking pregnancy, John had agreed to leave the music business alone. He would devote himself to bringing up the baby, guiding his development, he knew only too well from his own early years how critical the first five to seven years were. Yoko took over the endless business negotiations as the Beatles were finally dissolved as a partnership. Two years later all Allan Klein's claims for royalty payments were settled with a payment of $4.2 million from the four Beatles. Lawyers' fees came to nearer $10 million. Yoko invested the money that began pouring in (EMI were remarketing many old Beatle records from 1976 onwards) using the services of the resident astrologer and tarot reader. One piece of art was bought only after nearly a hundred questions had been asked of the cards. Her investments usually proved spectacularly successful. On July 27, 1976 John Lennon was given his green card No. A17-577-321, he could now travel outside the USA without fear of being debarred from returning. John, Yoko and Sean visited Japan, he was becoming fluent in the language under Yoko's guidance. It was the first of many overseas trips as he let himself be guided by Yoko and her astrologer advisers. The occasional visits of friends continued, but none of the bachelors who John had taken up with in his 15 months 'long weekend.' He had been friendly with Mick Jagger, searching out his ideas about what numbers he should put on his *Rock'n'Roll* album. Now he read Jagger in the papers while in Japan saying that he was hiding behind Sean and Yoko and had dried up musically. He had not become the recluse of popular imagination but it was true that no fresh inspiration came. He wrote 200 pages of an *In His Own Write* book but found the humour had lost its bite. he painted, played records on his juke box, watched TV interminably flitting through the channels, relying on the stimulus on the images, he read (mostly history) baked bread for a few months before tiring of this role and having anyway the services of a cook and nanny. He fed Sean, took him for walks in Central Park, found he could wander round the city mostly undisturbed. New Yorkers might say 'Hi' but they didn't gather round as they had in England. That was why he felt New York was his city. An old school friend was in New York in 1977. A man in a three piece suit recognised and greeted him, it was John Lennon walking about in the rush hour crowds. There were trips to South Africa, Spain, Egypt, Singapore, Japan again – on one occasion when protesting at being photographed a crowd of 200 gathered around the couple and Lennon's fear of the outside world, his need to insulate himself increased dramatically as Yoko and he fled for their lives. He did not become the hard working housewife he liked to project, he had – as one would expect of an extraordinarily rich man who no longer felt guilty about the fact – servants to do that. Occasionally he would be gone for days, taking off on a 'trip' somewhere, he still once or twice a year took peyote or magic mushrooms. Yoko sent him to Hong Kong where no-one would know him just so that he could learn to function by himself. He had never checked into a hotel for decades, there had always been someone to do it, he became nervous about going out, took innumerable baths as he always did when nervous, then one day he joined bleary eyed commuters on the boat ferry going to work. He was unrecognised and free – a unique experience after 17 years. The things everyone else took for granted, a family, the ability to roam at will, these had become the most precious things to him although the old Lennon who had always been sex-mad and whose only physical activity was sex could also reappear. Yoko checked out that the girls found for him would present no problems or challenges. In a distant memory of his Uncle George, Yoko and he began to buy into dairy farms, starting with one where they could disappear from view and quickly buying up more farms in the Catskill Mountains of upstate New York. Soon they had five farms and a prize herd of 250 Holstein cows. Some of these were kept in the grounds of the Long Island waterside estate where they could bathe nude and undisturbed. It was an echo of Aunt Mimi's secluded seashore home in England that he had bought her 12 years before. Every week he 'phoned her for a long hour or hour and half chat. He had become – on the surface at least – the man he had been brought up to be. He had lost the chip on his shoulder about being abandoned. In 1977, he heard his father was close to death and although Freddy was able to say little his son spent many hours on the 'phone going over his life – finally understanding what had happened to both him and his parents. They were reconciled although Lennon continued to refer in interviews to the poverty of Freddy. In fact his offer to pay for the funeral was refused by Freddy's wife. It was the ghost from which he had run all his life, and yet felt guilty about. With Freddy's death all such guilt disappeared and under the managership of the Bank of Japan director's daughter, their fortunes amassed by the day. She, with her imperial Japanese tradition to guide her, now became magnanimous, smooth talking Allen Klein into a settlement, titheing 10% of the income into the Spirit Foundation, a charity trust, running a complex business empire from a soft armchair in an office with clouds painted on the ceiling and rare Egyptian antiquities like a grey skull and golden baby's breastplate gazing at her. Paul McCartney dropped in occasionally but it was for old times sake, even then Lennon asked that he be given advance notice. His new found peace was precious. However once on a business trip to Germany with an associate, he revived the never far from the surface Beatle persona. The hotel was full they were told. John decided to admit he was a Beatle to the imperious desk clerk. He had, of course, heard of the Beatles. 'Which one of you is Paul?' he asked.

'Him, that's Paul,' said Lennon pointing to his companion, who was shown to a luxurious suite on the top floor. Lennon was given a room that was little more than a broom cupboard. Even after years of separation, the old scars from the battle for supremacy could be exposed again. 'No one could hurt John like Paul,' said Yoko.

By 1978 and 1979 Lennon had been largely forgotten. he was in the grips of passivity and depression, one of the side effects he suffered when he yielded to Yoko. But even in this most fallow period he continued to write and draw, to speak to the girls who still kept a vigil outside the Dakota reminding him that he was a Beatle as the millions of dollars in royalties from the contracts Allen Klein had renegotiated with EMI reminded his wife in the counting house downstairs. He bought up every apartment in the Dakota that became vacant, acquiring five. Several rooms were given over to a fabulous fur collection of Yoko's that had to be kept refrigerated. The flat next to theirs on the seventh floor became a store room for some of their many possessions. But now Lennon decided that the possessions that restricted were the old habits and baggage people carried around with them in their mind. At the beginning of 1976 he and Yoko had gone on a fast to cleanse themselves and bury the past. For six weeks they had existed on fruit juices and a little macrobiotic food. The former glutton was educated into the discipline of a healthy diet. Occasional stories of sadness wafted into the rarefied world he and Yoko created. Roadie Mal Evans had been shot dead by police in Los Angeles. Ringo had divorced Maureen. George had been left by Patti who then took up with Eric Clapton. George had a brief affair with Maureen, who was later set up with a £250,000 house in London by Ringo, now man about town. George went successfully into backing films starting with 'The Life of Brian' – a 'religious' comedy. In 1979 three Beatles attended a wedding celebration in Eric Clapton's Surrey mansion. A stage was erected at one end of the grounds and George, Ringo and Paul got together to sing old songs – particularly from the far off happy *Sergeant Pepper* days. Still John Lennon remained hidden away, preferring life with 'mother'. People who met them said they had the uncanny feeling they were speaking to two parts of one person. They even looked alike and would be seen walking down the streets of New York hand in hand. They had become very good friends. Sean had no idea his father had once been a Beatle until he saw 'Yellow Submarine' on a neighbour's video and was told about his father's former 'incarnation' by the neighbour. Paul, too, could proudly relate that one of his children had come across an old Beatles photograph and had successfully identified George and Ringo, but had had to ask his father who the fourth Beatle was. The ways had parted, Paul had revived his Apple concept with McCartney Productions Limited. All staff were sworn to secrecy about what went on. By buying up the rights to shows and the Buddy Holly repertoire among others, MPL's income swelled to £25 million a year by 1980. He had started it in a shabby little room, there had been no grandiose offices at 3 Saville Row second time around. John Lennon had attended the inauguration of Jimmy Carter in '76 and seemed happy to live in his era of reasonableness. In 1979 the policemen of New York received money to buy bullet proof vests, while in 1980 £25,000 was donated to buy 5,000 food baskets for the poor. John Lennon had become content to be a rich grandee in a liberal America. Hard times were over – for a while.

◀ 'Wait till I'm dead, and they'll really like me. I'll probably be knighted, sainted, God knows what when I'm dead'.

24 The Catcher In The Rye

In August 1980 John Lennon set to work on his first album for five years *Double Fantasy* – he wanted the album out in time for his 40th and Sean's fifth birthday. He had fulfilled his karma, given all the love and care a child could wish for during those years, he and Yoko had fought off every demon and fear in order to have him at all. He was laying ghosts – including the ghost that was Julian whose exist-ence Cynthia had had to remind him about. Now Julian spent half his vacation in the Dakota buildings, his father owned fifty rooms in all, they were getting to know one another again. But most of all John Lennon had killed the old demon that had sent Freddy off to sea in his early years and sent his mother off into an unwise affair, an unwished pregnancy and a desperate money situation that meant her second child was adopted and her first farmed out to a relatively prosperous aunt. He had made sure Cynthia had wanted for nothing in the first five years of Julian's life, but still he had lost him to the pressures of fame and fortune.

Yoko had received a warning from clairvoyant Deziah Holt, that they should avoid strangers with the name of Bell, Richard or Mark. Meanwhile, she had plotted a new direction on the map with astrological advice as to where John should head. The direction led to Bermuda – it might restimulate his creative juices – he was not going to return to the studio just to turn in a piece of craftsmanship.

A 63 foot yacht, Isis – Egyption goddess of life – was purchased, a five-man crew appointed and Kaptain Kun-dalini set sail for the south. Out at sea while Sean and his nanny sheltered and felt thoroughly ill along with the crew, the Kaptain took the wheel as huge storm waves crashed over the boat, forcing him to his knees. The wheel was in Lennon's hands for hours, all the rest of the crew too sick to cope, he sang out to the elements; surrounded by storm spray, great grey waves, a bleak sky, he felt himself to be a Viking, he sang and screamed into the wind, reliv-ing all the epic voyages that had ever been made, he was absolutely free. On arrival in Bermuda he felt rejuvenated by the experience of being one to one with the elemental world. He took Sean for a walk in a Bermuda park, he liked the look of a flower, peered closely through his glasses at the name. It was called 'Double Fantasy' – that was it, perfect, he had the title for an album and set to work, ringing Yoko in New York, who also got down to writing. At the end of the month, 22 songs were in the can, 14 were selected for the album.

'I say that I'm O.K., they look at me rather strange,' he said, 'tell 'em I'm doing fine just watching shadows on the wall'. It was a report back, he just had to let the merry-go-round go. It was a look inside the heavily protected household where there were no friends or enemies. He was aware of a big new departure, that was fine, let it begin he sang, he had never really been afraid of anything and the biggest adventure of them all into the unknown was about to begin. The gods were in their heavens and they had cast the perfect spell. Make a wish and let it come true for you, advised Yoko.

'There's nothing new under the sun. All the roads lead to Rome. And people cannot provide it for you. *You* can wake you up. I can't cure you. *You* can cure you.

'It's a fear of the unknown. The unknown is what it is. And to be frightened of it is what sends everybody scurrying around chasing dreams, illusions, wars, peace, love, hate, all that – it's all illusion. Accept that it's unknown and it's plain sailing.'

It was the voice of Sinbad talking in 1980, the man who had dared more, taken more and come back to tell the tale. Who had suffered and made art out of his suffering. Who had fought the most powerful government apparatus in the world and won. Who had taken a vast variety of drugs and won. Who had fed on the drug of adulation and realised the praise is never enough . . . and the criticism is always too much. Who had lost a mother's love and found the nearest replacement to it in the love of the older Eastern woman – Yoko Ono, who had not been afraid to go to hell and back, who had not been afraid to be afraid.

The album was to say that he had come through the 70s and survived, how had his contemporaries fared? It was a statement of faith in the future, he was still the idealistic dreamer he had always been, always happiest singing a love song, it was McCartney who could put down the real raving rockers. As if knowing his time was coming to its end, he started asking his Aunt Mimi to send over the trappings of his early life, his old school tie, his drawings, his early exercise books in which he would doodle, draw and write for hours. Unknown to him, four acres of Strawberry Field were sold off to build a new home for all those abandoned children. The darkness and light playing in the woods, the magic reality that dwelt alongside the everyday had become a little smaller, but he had seen it and shown it to the world. A white bulldog sniffs through the recently rained-upon woods, frisking away into the wonderful delicious world of many exciting smells. It is quiet, peaceful, the dawn of a new day, and a new world.

'If you're lonely you can talk to me', he had sung to Yoko. He had tasted that perfect freedom. He knew. 'There's a big wide wonderful world out there,' he enthused to the interviewers who flocked to see him after his five years of seclusion.

On the last day of his life, a photographer came to see him to take pictures for a major *Rolling Stone* interview. He stripped off and curled up into foetal position in Yoko's lap, that was the relationship. He might complain, asking why couldn't they be making love nice and easy, but she gave him the comfort he needed. She was 'mother'. He had cut his hair, so it looked much like it had in Hamburg. On the way to the recording studios a fan pushed forward to have the new album autographed. It was riding comfortably up the charts after two weeks but wouldn't make No. 1, he guessed. He toyed with the idea of going over to England, but Yoko was very jealous about letting him go.

It was late when they came back from the studios. They got out of the car in the street and walked into the forecourt of the Dakota Buildings. Yoko heard a voice call out 'Mr Lennon', but they were street-wise enough not to turn. She heard a car back-firing, there were five bangs almost one after another. John started faltering in his step beside her. She turned round to see the fan who had asked for the autograph earlier crouched down on one knee, two hands upon the gun. She stood rooted to the spot and screamed – but this time it was for real. John Lennon somehow staggered to the security guard's office and then rapidly losing blood he slumped to the floor.

'I'm shot', he gurgled through the blood welling up inside his mouth, pumping out through the holes in his legs and lungs. The guard called the police who arrived within minutes.

'I could see he was a goner', said the 35-year-old officer and fan who put him into the car and sped 15 blocks to Roosevelt Hospital, fifteen blocks away, 'he was gasping for breath.'

With his lungs perforated and the blood pouring out from him, John Lennon passed over in the back of the police car.

Mark Chapman calmly read his book and waited to be arrested.

'Do you know what you just did?' the policeman asked.

'Yeah. I just shot John Lennon', he nonchalently replied.

He returned to his book, The Catcher in the Rye, he was standing by the cliff edge of the rye fields ready to catch anyone in danger of falling over. The same cliff edge Lennon had walked along all his life.

Ever since the angry record burning of 1966, John Lennon had been aware that one day some fanatic was going to take a shot at him. In Texas on tour as a Beatle, someone had fired a shot at the plane. He had never expected to see 40, but he had just. His assassin had grown up in the bible belt where the fundamentalists were deeply angry at his comparing of himself to Jesus. 'Imagine John Lennon dead' they sniggered in their bible classes as they were taught rock'n'roll and the Beatles in particular were the work of the devil. Lennon said a man could make it any number of ways. They believed they had the way. He believed Sean had chosen his parents, he was more affected by the Maharishi's teachings than he cared to admit. 'Sexy Sadie' had been written while the bags were packed and he was waiting to make his exit from Rishikesh but on the course he had been the most fervent believer. He and Yoko also visited the more heavyweight Sai Baba in India. Mark Chapman was as confused as ever Lennon had been, and had mixed drug experiences with 'born again' Christianity. In his search for a self he envied the success of Lennon, he knew he could not become as rich, famous and powerful as that, so Lennon was the reason for his own lack of self-esteem. With him removed, Mark Chapman would no longer have to feel inferior. Happiness was a warm gun . . .

The Lennon will left half his estate to his wife, Yoko Ono Lennon. Sean and Julian would share the other half at the age of 25. Any person who contested the will would be disinherited. His total worth exceeded $150,000,000. Only

Ringo came to see Yoko in her distress, George and Paul made little public comment, the shock was too great. 200,000 letters of sympathy poured into the Dakota Buildings. Two million records by the Beatles and Lennon were sold in Britain alone in two months as his countrymen rediscovered their lost son. 'Imagine' was top of the charts. 'No. 9 Dream' 'Power to the People' and 'Give Peace a Chance' were his most popular singles in America.

Lennon's old friends remembered him. Micky Most, record producer, recalled how Lennon had taken an hour's break during the turgid recording session of *Let It Be* at Apple to play hopscotch with his son.

Bill Harry, founder of *Mersey Beat*, remembered how Lennon had cried when he had lost a pile of early writings and stories Lennon had given him.

John Lennon was finally revealed as just too sensitive to handle the enormous demands of being a rock star. Divorced from the Beatles and on his own he had only been able to put together one album of great songs, *Shaved Fish*, and of those 11 numbers, 3 had been recored in 1969 before the final split.

His most creative time had been between 1967 and 1969 with 'Strawberry Fields' 'All You Need Is Love' *The White Album*. But the persistence of a Japanese-American artist determined to make her book *Grapefruit* a success had resulted in one other song, an anthem for one world called *Imagine*. He had had to meet her to be able to write that, he was the chosen instrument, not in charge of his life at all. And as is the way with the totally dedicated artist, when his function was over he simply had to let it go.

'John was very very good in his last year' said Yoko.

'And so dear friends, you just have to carry on. The dream is over.'

Origins of
The Favourite Song Lyrics of John Lennon

Following are accounts of the origins and inspirations for many of John Lennon's favourite songs. However, since he always worked with Paul McCartney so closely right up until their split, all that can be said is that Lennon was the main originator of the songs, and has been recorded as saying that he liked these compositions.

The copyright in all these songs is held by Northern Songs Ltd, ATV Music and they may not be reproduced without permission.

Do You Want To Know A Secret?

Listen, do you want to know a secret
Do you promise not to tell?
Closer let me whisper in your ear,
Say the words you long to hear,
I'm in love with you.

John Lennon said that he remembered his mother singing a Walt Disney film song about a wishing well with a secret when he was very young.

The film may have been *Cinderella* or *Fantasia*, he thought, but the real inspiration for the song is a mother's love for her child. This was a treasured memory for Lennon, yet he gave the song to George to sing as his first singles vocal. It was only released in America as a single, being the 'B' side of Thank You Girl.

John Lennon was particularly angry that this was never mentioned in George Harrison's biography, *I, Me, Mine,* and he gave this as an example of George's ingratitude. Some of this typical Lennon bile can be explained by the associations the song had for him with his mother, and therefore he was looking for insults (real or imagined) to her memory.

I'll Be Back

I thought that you would realise,
that if I ran away from you,
that you would want me too,
but I've got a big surprise oh, oh.
Oh, you could find better things to do than to break
my heart again,
this time I will try to show that I'm not trying to
pretend.
I wanna go, but I hate to leave you

This song was written at the time that John Lennon met his father again after a gap of nearly 20 years.

Suddenly you realise the profound effect this visit had upon Lennon, the agonies of heartbreak it stirred up, and his reaction of trying to explain why he ran out the door of the Blackpool flat in pursuit of his mother.

Even more surprising is Lennon's view that *he* had come back again, this time as a wealthy superstar able to control and manipulate just as he had previously been manipulated.

There is more than a element of revenge and sardonic 'I told you so' in Lennon's reaction to his father. A further clue to the secret message in the lyrics is Lennon's insistence that this was one of his favourite earlier songs, although he never explained its meaning. Right up until his father died, he found it difficult to relate to him, and told many false stories about him, most derogatory.

Help!

Help me if you can, I'm feeling down,
and I do appreciate you being around,
help me get my feet back on the ground,
won't you please please help me?
And now my life has changed in oh so many ways,
my independence seems to vanish in the haze,
but ev'ry now and then I feel so insecure

Lennon claimed that it often took him two years to fully understand what his lyrics were about.

The song was quickly written for the film *Help!* during a particularly punishing schedule and at the time Lennon thought little about the song's message.

Later he came to realise that he was not writing about a brief spell in the doldrums (to which he was subject) but was depicting himself, in spite of the dizzying success, as becoming more and more insecure and unhappy with his lifestyle.

Of course, the world at large knew nothing of these private agonies, but it is easy to see the song hinting at the 'inexplicable' change in all the Beatles the following year of 1966.

Norwegian Wood

I once had a girl,
or I should say
she once had me.
She showed me her room,
isn't it good?
Norwegian wood.

I sat on a rug
biding my time,
drinking her wine.
We talked until two,
and then she said,
'It's time for bed.'
She told me she worked in the morning
and started to laugh,
I told her I didn't, and crawled off to
sleep in the bath.

One of the most lyrical songs Lennon ever wrote, this was the first song on which George's quickly developing proficiency on the sitar was put on record.

That this was a truly memorable 'one night stand' is borne out by the perfect haunting quality of the music and Lennon's voice. Yet since John did not want to tell the trusting Cynthia about his night, although he could not resist writing about it, he incorporates a line about sleeping in the bath. It is far more likely he spent the night in a bed made of Norwegian wood.

We do not know who the girl was, but it seems a certainty that in some part of the world there is a woman approaching forty with a treasured memory to match John Lennon's. He, however, could put it down on record. In fact, the perfect lyricism of which this is an example seems to be the style he most liked. Notice his final return to lyric qualities in *Double Fantasy* 14 years later.

In My Life

There are places I'll remember
all my life, though some have changed

All these places had their moments,
with lovers and friends I still can recall,
some are dead and some are living,
in my life I've loved them all.
But of all these friends and lovers,
there is no one compared to you

The song started off as a very straightforward listing of the places John Lennon used to pass on the bus journey from Menlove Avenue into Liverpool. But then he spotted that what he was really doing was reliving his life through the memory of the journey.

Inevitably, his mother's memory was closely bound up with the remembrance of times past. 'But of all these friends and lovers there is no one compared to you'. The sheer power these images of the past had over him, helps to explain the bitter sweet fascination of the song.

Especially when you remember he is writing about the time when he was getting to know his mother better during his midteens. The universal appeal of the song comes from Lennon tapping the deep wellspring within himself, which is shared by us all. He is simply more in touch with it.

Girl

*She's the kind of girl you want so much it makes
you sorry,
still you don't regret a single day.*

*When I think of all the times I tried so hard to
leave her,
she will turn to me and start to cry,
and she promises the earth to me and I believe her
after all this time, I don't know why*

*She's the kind of girl who puts you down
when friends are there, you feel a fool*

*Was she told when she was young that pain would
lead to pleasure?
Did she understand it when they said
that a man must break his back to earn his day of
leisure,
will she still believe it when he's dead?*

John Lennon claimed that the song was about a 'dream' girl. But many of the lines above read astonishingly like Cynthia. Especially the references to 'after all this time'.

What appears to be going on is that Lennon is expanding out from the particular to the general. It is certainly worth noting that in 1966 his dream girl has many of the qualities of Cynthia. Including the trait which 'puts you down when friends are there, you feel a fool'.

Although Lennon had yet to meet Yoko Ono, the song illustrates his continuing search for the dream woman, it is just that the eventual reality is far different from this list of attributes.

The last lines appear to be a protest at Cynthia driving him on to make money and ease her (and his) feelings of insecurity.

I'm Only Sleeping

When I wake up early in the morning,
Lift my head, I'm still yawning.
When I'm in the middle of a dream,
Stay in bed, float up stream.
Please don't wake me, no, don't shake me,
Leave me where I am, I'm only sleeping.
Everybody seems to think I'm lazy.
I don't mind, I think they're crazy
Running everywhere at such a speed,
Till they find there's no need
Please don't spoil my day, I'm miles away
And after all, I'm only sleeping.

Written after the frenetic touring has come to a stop, John starts to develop his exploration of the worlds inside his head.

His Aunt Mimi records that as a child he spent hours in his room happily day dreaming. He 'lived in his own world'.

Freed from the constraints of performing live before an audience, he now begins to re-explore the world of the imagination he had known as a child.

He was to take a whole generation with him as he went 'miles away'. The lyrics say it all perfectly and 15 years later in Watching the Wheels he re-echoes this archetypal theme of 'keeping an eye on the world going by my window'.

She Said She Said

She said you don't understand what I said,
I said no no no you're wrong, when I was a boy,
ev'rything was right, ev'rything was right.
I said even though you know what you know,
I know that I'm ready to leave,
'cos you're making me feel like I've never been born

Although no one realised it at the time, we are here given a graphic account of the first time John Lennon deliberately took LSD which was at a Californian party held by Peter Fonda.

Fonda was going around at the party announcing to all and sundry that he knew what it was like to be dead. This thought jumped Lennon back to his childhood and to the idea of being unborn.

While looking at his childhood he suddenly perceives it very differently from his received 'deprived child' memory which he carried round with him as a grudge.

He remembers the times he was deliriously happy and had a unique, wholly personal view of the world, a view he explores more thoroughly in Strawberry Fields Forever.

Strawberry Fields Forever

Living is easy with eyes closed
Misunderstanding all you see.
It's getting hard to be someone.
But it all works out,
it doesn't matter much to me.

No one I think is in my tree,
I mean it must be high or low.
That is you can't you know tune in.
But it's all right.
That is I think it's not too bad

Always, no sometimes, think it's me,
but you know I know when it's a dream.
I think I know I mean a 'Yes'.
But it's all wrong
that is I think I disagree.

Lennon finds his voice writing direct from experience, and giving us his own perception of life and its meaning.

His solution to the dilemmas and questions posed by life is to shrug them off as being illusionary. 'But you know I know when it's a dream'. What had previously worried him 'no one I think is in my tree' – his vision of the world as being a dream – is now turned into an advantage.

He decides that he should act on his own perceptions, whatever the cost, 'living is easy with eyes closed, misunderstanding all you see', because in the end, and this is his optimism winning out, 'there is nothing to get hungabout', 'it all works out'. When he lost his early optimism in the first part of the 70s, he also lost much of his following.

Lucy in the Sky with Diamonds

Cellophane flowers of yellow and green,
towering over your head.
Look for the girl with the sun in her eyes,
and she's gone.

Picture yourself on a train in a station,
with plasticine porters with looking glass ties,
suddenly someone is there at the turnstile,
the girl with kaleidoscope eyes.

Remembering Cavern DJ Bob Wooler's love of playing around with words, especially the first letters, Lennon writes about a dreamlike LSD trip, which had to be strenuously denied to the media if the song and record were not to be banned.

The girl with kaleidoscope eyes, cellophane flowers towering over your head, plasticine porters with looking glass ties, all look very much like dream images from a Lennon LSD trip.

These visions of a fairy tale world of extravagant beauty would be described as a 'good trip', although Lennon went on record as saying that he stopped taking LSD because 'I couldn't stand the bad trips'.

A Day In The Life

I read the news today oh boy
about a lucky man who made the grade
and though the news was rather sad
well I just had to laugh
I saw the photograph
He blew his mind out in a car
he didn't notice that the lights had changed
a crowd of people stood and stared
they'd seen his face before
nobody was really sure
if he was from the House of Lords.

Woke up, got out of bed,
dragged a comb across my head
found my way downstairs and drank a cup,
and looking up I noticed I was late.
Found my coat and grabbed my hat
made the bus in seconds flat
found my way upstairs and had a smoke,
and somebody spoke and I went into a dream.

The most memorable song of the phenomenally successful and influential *Sergeant Pepper's Lonely Hearts Club Band* LP. It is actually two songs joined, with the middle 'Woke up, got out of bed . . .' being the McCartney contribution. However, since they were still very much on the same wavelength the seams are almost invisible.

It was said that during the recording of the LP and this song in particular, the compositions took on a life of their own. For example, Mal Evans, as a joke timed an alarm clock to go off at the end of the 24 bar link passage between the Lennon and McCartney contributions. It was left on the final recording because it sounded right, as did the sound of him counting out the bars.

The whole LP is filled with such happy coincidences which led McCartney to wonder if they were all being guided by some unseen power, and if so what was the purpose of the LP. It was certainly a quantum leap forward in pop music, a catalyst for completely new lifestyles which are still being explored.

The man who blew his mind out is Tara Browne, a friend of John Lennon. The song ends on a private message from Paul to his dog Martha, inaudible to mere humans at 20,000 kHz.

All You Need Is Love

There's nothing you can do that can't be done.
Nothing you can sing that can't be sung.
Nothing you can say but you can learn how to play
the game.
It's easy.
There's nothing you can make that can't be made.
No one you can save that can't be saved.
Nothing you can do but you can learn how to be in
time.
It's easy.
All you need is love, all you need is love.

Lennon's aphoristic anthem for what became known as The Summer of Love. After *Sergeant Pepper's* ecstatic reception, the Lennon mind turned messianic. This is his first – and perhaps best – solution to the world's problems.

The vocals were recorded live during a worldwide TV link-up, and became instantaneously woven into the 'make love not war' movement's ideology. For a few short months everyone really did believe that 'our love could change the world'. What has to be remembered is that the reality was a rapidly expanding war in Vietnam, and the young were being drafted to fight it in America, while Britain was not sure if they would be sucked into a growing conflagration.

Baby You're A Rich Man

How does it feel to be one of the beautiful people
Now that you know who you are
What do you want to be and have you travelled very far
Far as the eye can see.
How does it feel to be one of the beautiful people
How often have you been there often enough to know
What did you see when you were there nothing that
doesn't show
Baby you're a rich man

Originally titled One Of The Beautiful People, a McCartney composition fragment – Baby You're A Rich Man-has been added to it. Another happy marriage, with Lennon believing he had made it, and McCartney celebrating the idea of richness.

Notice the rapid evolution of Lennon's lyrics, with superb lines like 'how often have you been there often enough to know'. In America in particular Lennon is beginning to acquire the status of youth spokesman.

He was later to tire of having to write songs with a Lennon philosophy intertwined with them. His attempts to regain a lost popularity finally took him back to writing simple words and music as McCartney has so successfully done.

But in spite of his denials Lennon was happiest writing songs with a message, he never lost his fascination with the idea of power and manipulation.

I Am The Walrus

I am he
as you are he
as you are me
and we are all together.
See how they run
like pigs from a gun
see how they fly. I'm crying.

Yellow matter custard dripping from a dead dog's eye.
Crabalocker fishwife pornographic
priestess boy you been a naughty girl,
you let your knickers down.
I am the eggman, oh they are the eggmen –
Oh I am the walrus.

Although he was later to claim the imagery he employs is sheer gobbledegook, that is untrue, it is Lennon being defensive about his most experimental work.

The first four lines were written on an LSD trip and the following three lines were written the next weekend also on LSD. Lennon batters away at the establishment shocking them out of their complacency.

The BBC found 'boy you've been a naughty girl, you let your knickers down' an alarming reference to young women's increasing interest in sex without marriage (still considered rather shocking in 1967).

'Elementary penguin' is a reference to Allan Ginsberg. Lennon claimed he had no idea that the walrus was used by C S Lewis in *The Walrus and the Carpenter* as a symbol of a capitalist, but that could be why he then tried to make Paul the walrus in Glass Onion. Lennon liked to think of himself at this stage as a nice British kind of Socialist. However, he never experienced any problems enjoying the benefits of money, and soon lost interest in 'getting Jerry Rubin a job' during his radical days in America.

Revolution

You say you want a revolution
Well, you know
we all want to change the world.
You tell me that it's evolution,
Well, you know
we all want to change the world.
But when you talk about destruction,
Don't you know that you can count me out
Don't you know it's going to be alright

Written early in 1968 while the Beatles were in Rishikesh with the Maharishi. Lennon turns his mind to the increasingly talked-about revolution which has been debated by the 'underground' in London since late the previous year.

He has to make up his mind about violence, for he feels ambivalent about the more extreme elements in Europe and America who are taking to the streets and calling for the overthrow of governments.

The phrase 'you can count me out' was also recorded as 'you can count me in' on one of the four versions of the record.

The release of Revolution was to coincide with McCartney's best song, Hey Jude, and this stole some of Revolution's thunder.

Julia

Half of what I say is meaningless
But I say it just to reach you Julia.
Julia, Julia, oceanchild, calls me
So I sing a song of love, Julia

When I cannot sing my heart
I can only sing my mind, Julia.
Julia, sleeping sand, silent cloud, touch me

John Lennon in India makes the ache inside whole as he equates his mother with mother nature and so recaptures her magic.

Yoko in Japanese means 'ocean child' and although at this stage Yoko is faraway in England, she is writing great tracts of correspondence to him; perhaps without him realising it, she is becoming part of his mother's treasured image in his mind.

Later he takes to calling Yoko 'mother' and 'mother superior' and this was the cement that bound their relationship together through all the trials.

Close listening to the voice of Lennon on this record reveals his extreme vulnerability, sensitivity and even naivety. Being a millionaire rock star is no guarantee of early maturity, Lennon liked to be the dependent, loved child in his long-term relationships with women, at the same time as he fought the role. The outside world grew to be a threatening place to him.

Yer Blues

The eagle picks my eye.
The worm he licks my bone.
I feel so suicidal
Just like Dylan's Mr Jones.
Lonely wanna die.
If I ain't dead already.
Ooh girl you know the reason why.
Black cloud crossed my mind.
Blue mist round my soul.
Feel so suicidal
Even hate my rock and roll.

Great lyrics for a great song, again written in the quietness of the Maharishi's ashram. Lennon rehearses in his mind the period of lightning change and sudden shocks that lies ahead.

He realises that his old self must die, and a new personality come in its place.

The astonishing energy and overpowering force of the song reveals just how driven a person was Lennon. And all the time he is unable to solve these clashing drives within himself, he has to make music as his escape.

After primal therapy he partially learned to release his feelings more, but this does seem to have taken some of the force and inspiration out of his music.

Happiness Is A Warm Gun

She's not a girl who misses much.
Do do do do do do do do
She's well acquainted with the touch of
the velvet hand
Like a lizard on a window pane.
The man in the crowd with
multicoloured mirrors
On his hobnail boots
Lying with his eyes while his hands are busy
Working overtime

When I hold you in my arms
And I feel my finger on your trigger
I know no one can do me no harm
because happiness is a warm gun
Yes it is.

When Yoko Ono and John Lennon first got together he said that 'when we're not in the studio, we're in bed'.

Certainly, the song is heavily laced with sexual symbolism, and there is the wry Lennon humour to give the lyrics just the right amount of bite.

The song title came from a gun magazine, but even the BBC noticed that the trigger he was talking about may have been part of a woman's anatomy.

The man in the crowd with the multicoloured mirrors, is none other than the psychedelic Marco Polo of the senses. He was never to lose his obsession with sex, and even though in love with Yoko he would take off for days on his 'explorations'.

Across The Universe

Words are flying out like endless rain into a paper
cup,
They slither while, they pass, they slip away across
the universe.
Pools of sorrow, waves of joy are drifting through my
open mind,
possessing and caressing me.
Jai Guru De Va Om
Nothing's gonna change my world

Lennon always believed that his best songs just came to him, although he could spend weeks polishing up the words as he did with Strawberry Fields Forever.

Early in 1968 he woke up with the words of the song running through his head, and was later to say that this song came nearest of anything he had done to pure poetry.

Unfortunately, the first recording which was donated to the World Wildlife Fund, never satisfied him musically. So in the filming of *Let It Be* he tried again with McCartney.

After the acrimonious break-up, a paranoid Lennon began claiming that McCartney had tried to sabotage the song. Record sales would appear to say otherwise.

Give Peace A Chance

Two one two three four
Ev'rybody's talking about
Bagism, Shagism, Dragism, Madism,
Ragism, Tagism,
This-ism, That-ism, Is-m is-m is-m.
All we are saying is give peace a chance

Written at the height of his peace campaign in 1969 it received a live premier in Toronto.

It was consciously written as the anthem for the anti-Vietnam War demonstrators and particularly in America is still one of Lennon's best-loved songs.

Lennon explained that for two million years the world had tried the solution of war, now why couldn't everyone simply 'give peace a chance'. He was never embarrassed to be totally open and vulnerable, also saying that he recognised a lot of violence within himself, which was why he cared about peace. Europe smiled mockingly, but North America took him very seriously indeed, he even got to meet Pierre Trudeau.

Paul McCartney said after Lennon's death that people would remember that Lennon had helped to speed up American withdrawal from Vietnam and that was how Lennon would like to be remembered – as a peace campaigner.

Come Together

He got O-no sideboard
He got spinal cracker
He bag production
He got walrus gumboot
Here come old flat top
He come grooving up slowly
He got joo joo eyeball
He one holy roller
He got hair down to his knee
Got to be a joker he just do what he please.

He say I know you, you know me
One thing I can tell you is you got to be free.
Come together right now over me –

Lennon was asked to write a campaign song for the Californian elections by Timothy Leary's wife. He naturally turned it into his own vision of the world.

Where Lennon asked people to come together 'over me', the never faraway *persona* of John the Baptist, the voice of one crying in the wilderness, can be heard.

His optimism for the future evaporated in the early 70s though it did reappear in *Double Fantasy*. The last LP was him talking to his generation saying 'well we survived the 70s, the 80s will be a whole lot better if we want it to be'.

Imagine

Imagine there's no heaven
it's easy if you try,
No hell below us
above us only sky.
Imagine all the people
living for today
it isn't hard to do,
nothing to kill or die for
and no religion too.
Imagine all the people
living life in peace.
You may say I'm a dreamer
but I'm not the only one
I hope some day you'll join us
and the world will live as one.

Although John Lennon had used the imagine theme in early Beatle songs – 'Imagine I'm in love with you' – it was Yoko Ono who had taken the concept futher in the book she had tirelessly promoted *Grapefruit*. Indeed it was her attempts to push the book that drove her to seek Lennon's help.

In this one song, her concern for a world of United Nations (for which her family were Japanese representatives) is brilliantly captured by Lennon. It is as if he had to meet and live with Yoko Ono in order to produce this, his most popular song.

The songs of John Lennon

Once again the proviso that Lennon and McCartney gave each other lines even when they individually were the main originator. All the songs mentioned have some Lennon contribution.

1962
Do you want to know a secret?; Love Me Do; P.S. I Love You. (unreleased studio songs)
Looking Glass; Winston's Walk; The Years Roll Along; Thinking of Linking; Keep Looking That Way; I Lost My Little Girl; I'll Be On My Way; Shout.

1963
Hello Little Girl*; Please Please Me; Misery; Ask Me Why; There's A Place; From Me To You; Thank You Girl; She Loves You; I'll Get You; It Won't Be Long; Little Child; Hold Me Tight; I Wanna Be Your Man; Not A Second Time; I want To Hold Your Hand; This Boy.

1964
Can't Buy Me Love; You Can't Do That; I Call Your Name; Hard Day's Night; I Should Have Known Better; If I Fell; I'm Happy Just To Dance With You; Tell Me Why; Any Time At All; I'll Cry Instead; When I Get Home; I'll Be Back; I Feel Fine; No Reply; I'm A Loser; Baby's In Black; Mr Moonlight; Eight Days A Week; Words of Love; Every Little Thing; I Don't Want To Spoil The Party; What You're Doing.

1965
Ticket To Ride; Yes It Is; Help; You've Got To Hide Your Love Away; You're Going To Lose That Girl; It's Only Love; Day Tripper; We Can Work It Out; Drive My Car; Norwegian Wood; Nowhere Man; The Word; Michelle; What Goes On; Girl; In My Life; Wait; Run For Your Life.
(unreleased studio songs)
Maisy Jones; Baby Jane; Rubber Soul.

1966
Paperback Writer; Rain; Eleanor Rigby; Yellow Submarine; I'm Only Sleeping; She Said She Said; And Your Bird Can Sing; Dr Robert; Tomorrow Never Knows.

1967
Penny Lane; Strawberry Fields Forever; With A Little Help From My Friends; Lucy In The Sky With Diamonds; Getting Better; She's Leaving Home; Being For the Benefit of Mr Kite; Good Morning Good Morning; A Day In The Life; All You Need Is Love; Baby You're A Rich Man; I Am The Walrus.
(unreleased studio songs)
Colliding Circles; Peace Of Mind.

1968

Revolution; Dear Prudence; Glass Onion; The Continuing Story
Of Bungalow Bill; Happiness Is A Warm Gun; I'm So Tired;
Julia; Birthday; Yer Blues; Everybody's Got Something To Hide
Except For Me And My Monkey; Sexy Sadie; Cry Baby Cry;
Revolution 9; Goodnight; Two Virgins LP.
(unreleased studio song)
Those Were The Days

1969

Hey Bulldog; Don't Let Me Down; The Ballad Of John And
Yoko; Come Together; I Want You (She's So Heavy); Because;
Sun King; Mean Mr Mustard; Across The Universe; Unfinished
Music No 2: Life With The Lions LP; Wedding Album LP; Give
Peace A Chance; Cold Turkey.
(unreleased studio songs)
When I Come To Town; Four Nights In Moscow.

1970

You Know My Name (Look Up The Number); Dig A Pony; Dig It;
I've Got A Feeling; One After 909; Instant Karma; Mother; Hold
On (John); I Found Out; Working Class Hero; Isolation;
Remember; Love; Well Well Well; Look At Me; God; My
Mummy's Dead.
(unreleased studio songs)
What Yer New Mary Jane; Have You Heard The Word; Futting
The Futz; Suzie Parker.

1971

Imagine; Crippled Inside; Jealous Guy; It's So Hard; I Don't
Want To Be A Soldier Mama, I Don't Want To Die; Give Me
Some Truth; Oh My Love; How Do You Sleep?; How?; Oh Yoko,
Power To The People; Happy Xmas (War Is Over).

1972

Woman Is The Nigger Of The World; Attica State; New York
City; Sunday Bloody Sunday; The Luck Of The Irish; John
Sinclair; Angela; Jamrag; Scumbag; Au; God Save Oz/Do The
Oz.

1973

Mind Games; Tight A$; Aisumasen (I'm Sorry); One Day (At A
Time); Bring On The Lucie (Freda People); Nutopian National
Anthem; Intuition; Out The Blue; Only People; I Know (I Know);
You Are Here; Meat City.

1974

Going Down On Love; Whatever Gets You Thru The Night; Old
Dirt Road, What You Got; Bless You; Scared; No 9 Dream;
Surprise Surprise (Sweet Bird of Paradox); Steel And Glass; Beef
Jerky; Nobody Loves You When You're Down And Out.

1980
(Just Like) Starting Over; Cleanup Time; I'm Losing You;
Beautiful Boy (Darling Boy); Watching The Wheels; Woman;
Dear Yoko.

Lennon also contributed to Elton John's, David Bowie's, Ringo
Starr's, Harry Nilsson's and Johnny Winter's recordings during
1974. For example, two tracks on *Young Americans* by Bowie
were Lennon compositions.

Six tracks from the *Double Fantasy* recording sessions were
not used. It is not known how many of these are by Lennon.

*The first song Lennon wrote, naturally enough inspired by a song his mother
sang.

Bibliography

Below are listed some of the books used in researching this
biography, with potted comments for dedicated Beatles fans.
The Beatles. Hunter Davies. Heinemann London.
The authorised version, but very spicy all the same.
Shout. Phillip Norman. Elm Tree Books. Corgi; UK.
Minutely researched. Fills in many blanks up to 1970 in the
Beatle phenomenon.
John Lennon. The Life And The Legend. Sunday Times.
One of the better instant tributes that appeared around the
world.
The Beatles A to Z. Methuen. US.
A dictionary of all the people and places connected with the
Beatles.
Strawberry Fields Forever: John Lennon Remembered.
Bantam.
A perceptive short summary plus the Newsweek interview.
The Beatles. Rolling Stone US, Star UK.
A big well-illustrated book which is short on words, what there
are, are well written.
Lennon and McCartney. Malcolm Doney. Midas. UK.
A short book that avoids anything nasty, writer wishes to prove a
point.
Lennon Remembers. Jann Wenner. Penguin. UK.
The famous Rolling Stone interview in late 1970. Lennon at his
most acid, out to demythologise the Beatles.

Paul McCartney In His Own Words. Omnibus Press.
Concentrates more on Wings than his previous incarnation.
Beatles In Their Own Words. Omnibus Press.
A short illustrated guide to the wit and wisdom of the fab four.
John Lennon In His Own Words. Omnibus Press.
The lad comes through loud and clear, but then he always did.
All You Needed was Love. The Beatles after the Beatles. John
Blake. Hamlyn.
Unusually, the writer has had some access to Paul and Ringo,
consequently good on these two Beatles.
The Playboy Interviews. David Sheff. New English Library.
The first interview after 5 years of silence, but it is less than
probing.
The Lennon Tapes. BBC. Andy Peebles.
The last interview 2 days before Lennon was shot.
One Day At A Time. Anthony Fawcett. New English Library. UK.
Times Mirror. USA.
A book by their assistant for the years 1968–70; very revealing in
parts, though some things are swept under the carpet.
Beatles for the Record. Stafford Pemberton. UK.
Good for the colour pictures, not for the commentary.
Behind the Beatles Songs. Philip Cowan. Polytantric Press UK.
Facts, figures and snippets for Beatle fans, very thin book.
The Long and Winding Road. Virgin. UK.
An exhaustive (and exhausting) compilation of UK and US
Beatle charts; plus brief details on each song recorded while the
Beatles existed.
The Beatles Apart. Bob Woffinden. Proteus. UK & USA.
A well illustrated, briefly written account of the four lads going
their own separate ways.
A Cellarful of Noise. Brian Epstein. New English Library.
A re-issue of the 1964 slender volume which is more revealing
about Epstein than the Beatles.
The Man Who Gave Away The Beatles. Allan Williams.
With the help of a Mirror journalist their first manager tells it like
it really was, or so Lennon thought.
All You Need Is Ears. George Martin. McMillan. London.
The title should tell you he knows less about writing than music.
The Beatles Lyrics. Futura. UK.
The words of all the Lennon-McCartney compositions.
A Twist Of Lennon. Cynthia Lennon. Star.
A true life confession by Cyn which gives away more than it
intends.
Lennon. A musical play. Bob Eaton.
Performed in Liverpool 1981, New York 1982. Relates the songs
to his life. Nice.

Sometime In West Palm Beach

'It's him, yeah, it's him, I can tell from the bone structure,' says the 16-year-old girl to her friends as they look down from the exterior balcony of the futuristically curved dome of West Palm Beach auditorium.

Her friends express some doubt. She checks through the viewfinder of her camera with its telephoto lens.

'Yeah, it's definitely him,' she emphatically cries, working herself and her still-doubting friend into the beginning of a frenzy that erupts into screams when the figure in the baseball hat, pulled down low over his head, with one green and one red shoe, khaki shorts and a black jacket, finally pulls his cap off as he runs into the artistes' entrance.

Just before that dramatic doffing of his hat one of the doubting girls had sneered, 'But they don't wear rough gear like that.'

'They' are stars or, in this case, sons of stars emerging into their own blaze of glory, even if it be brief. This evening we are to learn if it is all a pale reflection of a comet that has gone before.

The young Julian Lennon had spotted me with my telephoto focusing in on him as he chatted with three roadies and starts pulling very Lennonesque faces, just like his father used to do at Liverpool Art School – the clown was one of Lennon senior's more enduring personae.

But there's no mistaking who it is now. The tousled hair, waved and falling down to just below his shoulders, frames a now very recognisable Lennon face, the same shape eyes set into the similarly shaped head, the same straight angular nose, the same fine cheek bones. The primogeniture is without doubt.

As he runs into the lower depths of the auditorium, Julian Lennon gives a grin of relish to the girls, to me, a big babyish smile, God he looks so young, not a flaw on that innocent face. You realise he is savouring every second of his triumph, the half-forgotten son suddenly thrust into the limelight and in Palm Beach where he was reunited with his errant father after five long years...but that was more than a decade ago. Tonight, Julian Lennon is emphatically the star, seeking the acclamation of his followers just like his dad.

He runs onto the stage wearing a white open gown, tight black leggings, a white vest with no arms, though small he has a well-developed upper frame, only those legs look a little spindly. He goes into his first number on this the second night of his 11-city American tour.

The crowd of some 5,000 young, white, predominately female, affluent Palm Beachers erupt into a roar as he does 'It's Much Too Late For Goodbyes'.

> 'Ever since you were leaving me
> I have wanted to cry,
> Ever since you were needing me
> I've been trying to hide'

The words of the breakthrough song have an inner significance for the singer, there's no doubt about that but the crowd of girls, most in their late teens or early twenties, have started to surge forward from their neatly arranged seats in the auditorium and they are screaming some...in a distant echo of Beatlemania 20 years before.

There are some older men, three in front of me are furtively sharing a joint. But in the squeaky clean 80s there is not even cigarette smoking allowed in the auditorium, far less alcohol, many states are passing 'No Drinking' laws for the under 21s even as a tidal wave of cocaine from Colombia's poor peasants feeds their children's bellies and the American yuppy generation's egos as they crave wealth and power.

The music slows down, an usher with a torch finds his way through the crowd, followed by a young police officer. The crowd standing in the aisle are escorted obediently back to their seats. The atmosphere calms down. Julian Lennon is playing songs from his less than successful second album. By midway point the concert could start to sag but he's helped by a very powerful rhythm from his band which includes an old friend of his and a guitarist from the Rolling Stones, not to mention a frenetic drummer who knows his stuff as he keeps hammering it out.

'Alright, we're going to do some music you've got to stand up for.'

The crowd again surges forward with a cheer near the front of the auditorium. The police give up trying to usher people back to their seats now that the word has come down from the stage, from on high where a new figure of authority grows in stature by the minute.

Julian Lennon is proving himself in control of the fickle crowd just like Pop but he wants to be liked more than that sardonic figure.

'I'd like to have got a suntan,' says the pale figure on stage surveying the bronzed young Amazons before his feet, 'but it's all been inside work for me. Hey, I've got a good feeling from you!'

Yes, he's right. These well scrubbed, well behaved rich kids are with him, they want him to succeed, they will it. The lights create fluorescent colours against a changing backdrop of blue, now yellow, while the band and little Julian Lennon become irridescent blue, lights sparkle like starships through the dry ice fog…it's pure spectacle.

Two hours later Julian is finishing with 'Stand By Me', sung from the heart. Whenever he gets to the standards or even his own most popular songs he uncannily recreates John Lennon circa 1975. All that lush backing. The time Julian first helped him out on record, on 'Ya Ya' for his Rock 'n' Roll album, it's as though Julian has carried on from there.

The audience call Julian back for an encore. He does 'It Won't Be Long Now' followed by 'Day Tripper' with all the stops pulled out, an upbeat version that sounds even better than the original, an indication of how sophisticated the music business has become in the intervening years. He's glowing, feels he can relax a little, play his father's songs now that he's been called back in his own right.

Two very blonde, very tanned girls negotiate with one of the bouncers to see if they can get to see Julian. Another charge of the barrier. The guard won't let them through. Another girl, also dressed in white, also magnificently tanned and athletic as they all seem to be, pleads – to no avail.

Outside a couple of coaches wait to take the show away. The two blonde girls who had been beside the stage unsuccessfully pleading to go past now talk their way onto one of the coaches.

'We're friends,' they say.

They are forced to leave a few moments later.

'We're friends too,' they're unceremoniously told.

They watch in visible agitation as the band come out at a run and hop into the small airport bus, they are whisked away like royalty.

'Oh, he's so nice, I really wanted to meet him,' says the girl to her friend, hopping from one well-tanned statuesque leg to another.

They run for their car to pursue the disappearing bus, taking off their shoes in their race to get to the limo before it's too late.

But it's much too late for goodbyes.

John would have understood. Perhaps he does now.